Advance praise for *Adventures in Bubbles and Brine*

"What a beautiful window into the culture of fermentation in Nova Scotia! Philip Moscovitch introduces us to old timers carrying on traditions, and to leaders of the province's contemporary fermentation revival. With lots of practical how-to information and recipes, the book also explores much broader contexts, including science, food safety, history, technology, lore, and indigenous traditions. Fermentation is always a manifestation of place, and this book reflects that vividly."

— Sandor Ellix Katz, Author of *Wild Fermentation* and *The Art of Fermentation*

"As the need for new circles back to a rich, distant past, a culture of culture has been quietly blossoming in Nova Scotia. Philip Moscovitch is here to tell us the stories.

There are so many layers to enjoy in this beautifully written book — which is at once a travel memoir, a weave of lore, histories, and personal tales, and an inspiring recipe collection — chronicling the exciting fermentation revival in Nova Scotia.

Here you'll find a poetic overview of fermented foods and beverages, old and new, through visits to sausage crafters, cider meisters, cheese makers, picklers, kombucha mavens, bakers, briners (garlic scapes!) and more.

Philip encourages even the most recipe-orthodox among us to embrace the experimental nature of allowing mysterious and friendly microorganisms to find our dough, cabbage, milk, or fruit juice and work their transformations.

All the cook needs to contribute, after a few preparations, is time and trust."

— Mollie Katzen, author of *The Moosewood Cookbook* and *The Heart of the Plate*

Adventures in Bubbles and Brine

What I learned from Nova Scotia's masters of fermented foods — craft beer, cider, cheese, sauerkraut and more

Philip Moscovitch

Formac Publishing Company Limited
Halifax

Formac Publishing Company Limited recognizes the support of the Province of Nova Scotia through the Department of Communities, Culture and Heritage. We are pleased to work in partnership with the Province of Nova Scotia to develop and promote our cultural resources for all Nova Scotians. We acknowledge the support of the Canada Council for the Arts, which last year invested $153 million to bring the arts to Canadians throughout the country. This project has been made possible in part by the Government of Canada. We acknowledge the support of Arts Nova Scotia.

Cover design: Tyler Cleroux
Cover images: Philip Moscovitch

Library and Archives Canada Cataloguing in Publication

Title: Adventures in bubbles and brine : what I learned from Nova Scotia's masters of fermented foods — craft beer, cider, cheese, sauerkraut and more / Philip Moscovitch.
Names: Moscovitch, Philip, author.
Description: Includes bibliographical references and index.
Identifiers: Canadiana (print) 20190140372 | Canadiana (ebook) 20190140380 | ISBN 9781459505803 (softcover) | ISBN 9781459505810 (epub)
Subjects: LCSH: Moscovitch, Philip—Travel—Nova Scotia. | LCSH: Cooking (Fermented foods)—Nova   Scotia. | LCSH: Fermented foods—Nova Scotia. | LCSH: Fermented beverages—Nova Scotia. | LCSH: Nova Scotia—Description and travel.
Classification: LCC TX827.5 .M67 2019 | DDC 641.6/16—dc23

Formac Publishing Company Limited
5502 Atlantic Street
Halifax, Nova Scotia, Canada
B3H 1G4
www.formac.ca

Printed and bound in South Korea

Photo Credits

All images by Philip Moscovitch except for the following:
Hillary Dionne: 26
Matthew Gates – Ross Farm Museum: 28, 52
Nova Scotia Archives: 92, 96, 113, 172, 217, 253
Pete McChesney: 88, 97
Rhiannon Visser – Saltbox Brewing: 122
Shutterstock: 58, 71, 75, 77

Back cover images:
Top: Philip Moscovitch (left, centre, bottom-right); Matthew Gates – Ross Farm Museum (top-right)
Bottom: The Dutchman's Cheese Farm (left); Philip Moscovitch (centre); Pete McChesney (right)
Author photo by Nicola Davison

Contents

For Sara, and for our children,

Callum, Phoebe and Eli,

who have gamely tried all kinds of fermented

concoctions over the years.

Acknowledgements

Every year, I visit classrooms across Nova Scotia and give workshops to students on writing. One of the things I always tell them is that we tend to think of writing as a solitary pursuit — something we do alone. But the reality is that writing is collaborative. We draw on the knowledge, advice and support of so many people over the course of any project.

I am grateful to many people for helping me learn fermentation techniques, and for help in making *Adventures in Bubbles and Brine* a reality.

Thank you to Zsofi Koller for connecting me with editor Kara Turner at Formac when Kara was looking for a writer to take on a book about Nova Scotia fermentation traditions. Thanks also to Kim Pittaway, and her colleagues at the University of King's College MFA in Creative Non-fiction program and to literary consultant Sally Keefe Cohen.

Sandor Katz provided much fermentation inspiration, and Steve McCullough and Gerry Barbor walked me through the steps of winemaking (and gave me books and supplies) many years ago. Av Singh hosted workshops held by Sandor and cheesemaker David Asher, and I learned a lot from both. I am also very grateful to my mother, Angelica Vassilouni Moscovitch, and my γιαγιά (that's grandmother in Greek) for the fermentation traditions they practised and I grew up around: making yogurt and cheese, baking bread, curing olives and making wine.

I am lucky to be part of a wonderful community of supportive writers and editors. I'd like to particularly thank Sarah Sawler, Chris Benjamin, Suzanne Rent, Jodi DeLong (and the rest of the Saltscapes crew), Simon Thibault, Trevor Adams, Tim Bousquet, Kat Eschner, Vern Smith, Mark Palermo and Amanda Jess.

It would be impossible to thank all the people who I interviewed and who gave me background, but I would like to particularly recognize a few. Jay Hildybrant's enthusiastic support early in the project meant a lot to me. Jenny Gammon helped me understand the world of Nova Scotia winemaking and pointed me to stories and people I would have otherwise missed. Colin Duggan kept his eyes out for interesting fermentation stories and people and sent them my way and Hillary Dionne made my trip to Big Tancook Island a delight. John Brett's encyclopedic knowledge of cider apples and cider making was extremely helpful.

In Cape Breton, Jessica Fogarty welcomed me to the Up!Skilling Food Festival, Demmarest Haney and Joseph Parish opened the doors of their home to me to talk homesteading and cheesemaking and Andrew and Renelle Poirier went out of their way to help when my car broke down in front of their house in Beaver Cove.

My thanks to Tracy Banks for moral support and to the incredibly helpful and accommodating staff at both the Nova Scotia Archives and Halifax Public Libraries. I also appreciate the support of Arts Nova Scotia, who provided a grant to help cover travel and research costs.

A huge thank you to my editor, Kara Turner, who came up with the idea for this book, worked hard to help see it through to completion and exhibited much grace and patience. A first-time author could not ask for more.

And finally, I am ever grateful to my family for their encouragement, and especially to Sara for her love and support, her bubbly enthusiasm for so many fermentation adventures and for providing inspiration for the book's title.

— Philip Moscovitch

List of Recipes

Chapter 1

- Simple Sauerkraut

Chapter 2

- Brined Garlic Scapes
- (Almost) Instant Gratification Dill Pickles
- Spicy Fermented Nettles
- One-Jar Kimchi
- Kimchi for a Crowd
- Spicy Fall Fruit Kimchi
- (Less Than a Peck of) Pickled Peppers

Chapter 4

- Kombucha

Chapter 5

- Kitchen-Counter Cider
- Your Basic Dry Cider

Chapter 6

- Country Wine

Chapter 7

- Not Very Instagrammable Bread

Chapter 8

- Ricotta from Whole Milk
- Make-at-Home Yogurt

Introduction

It's mid-October — one of those stunning autumn Nova Scotia days when the sun is shining, the air is warm enough that winter seems a long way off and the tail end of the harvest is still coming in. Farmers' markets have an abundance of local produce, and home and community gardeners are enjoying late-season vegetables.

At the Common Roots Urban Farm near downtown Halifax, healthy-looking bunches of kale and Swiss chard continue to grow in partially harvested raised beds. The heads of sunflowers, their seeds and petals mostly gone, hang low. Piles of straw, ready to be used as winter mulch, dot the area. A few scraggly looking bean plants cling to their trellises. At the end of one of the rows of raised beds, someone has written "A life without dreams is like a garden without flowers" in marker on a sign.

Data Ram Humagai emerges from a shed near the middle of the urban farm — a two-acre piece of land on the former site of a high school. It is home to nearly two hundred community garden plots, along with beds growing food to benefit non-profits and other local groups. Data Ram, who came to Halifax after spending two decades in refugee camps in Bhutan, works here as the head gardener.

He hands me two pint-size Mason jars filled with traditional Bhutanese-style fermented vegetables. One contains daikon — a moderately spicy Asian radish — and the other green beans. They were grown and harvested here at Common Roots.

I open the jar of daikon, smell the powerful, musty aroma, then dip my fingers into the oily brine and pull out one of the pieces of radish. The bitter tang of raw daikon is gone, replaced by more complex flavours. It tastes both sweet and tart.

In Bhutan, Data Ram tells me, making these pickles would involve burying them underground for a month or so, then packing them into jars and leaving them out in the hot sun to ferment for two or three days. After that, they could be stored in a cool place and enjoyed for up to a year. Here he dries them on racks for a couple of days before adding spices and jarring them — and because Nova Scotia is nowhere near as hot as Bhutan, he leaves them in the jars for longer, until their fermentation gives them the right balance of flavours. Then he moves them into a cool place for storage.

I twist the cap off the jar of green beans. Despite having been fermented in warm weather, they retain a crunch. I'm overwhelmed by the flavour of the beans, combined with ground spices in the jar. They are like nothing I have ever eaten before: crunchy, spicy, with a taste that seems to evoke the soil they grew in. Earthy.

They are wonderful.

Flavours like these are one of the reasons I started experimenting with fermenting foods and drinks. There is something seemingly magical about fermentation, about microscopic organisms acting on fruits, vegetables and grains and completely transforming their properties. Think of the difference between a cucumber and a crunchy, salty, kosher pickle. Or the bite of sauerkraut versus sliced fresh cabbage. Or, more dramatically, the heady feel of a delicious sparkling wine compared to the flavour of a grape picked straight off the vine.

These dramatic changes are caused by the process of fermentation: bacteria and yeasts guided by humans so we get the results we want.

Sandor Katz is the author of *Wild Fermentation* — one of the books that helped kick-start the rekindled popular interest in fermented foods — and the encyclopedic *The Art of Fermentation*. Go to any fermentation workshop and you are likely to not only hear his name, but also see a couple of his books on display as essential guides.

He has described fermentation as "manipulating the environment to promote the growth of certain organisms and discourage the growth of other organisms."

For instance, in lacto-fermentation (also called lactic acid fermentation) we encourage the growth of lactic acid bacteria, which preserve and change the taste of food. This is the process that turns cabbage into sauerkraut. It's also used for many of the other kinds of fermented foods in this book.

Fermented foods are all around us, and so are the yeasts and bacteria that produce them. Coffee, chocolate, bread, wine, beer, brined pickles, spirits, cured meats — these are all, at least in part, results of the process of fermentation.

Humans first harnessed the power of fermentation at least 10,000 years ago. Some techniques have remained essentially unchanged for centuries, if not millennia, while others are aided by new technologies.

In 2013, I got a message from my oldest son, Callum, a Grade 12 student on an overseas exchange. He sent me a link to an article about *Wild Fermentation*, saying he thought I would be interested in it.

Some fermented foods were already part of my repertoire. With the encouragement of a friend who liked experimenting with strange homemade wines (green tea and jasmine was probably the oddest of his combinations), I had tried my hand at making wine with whatever was on hand. I made dandelion wine, with dandelions from our lawn. Because I bottled it too soon, it continued to ferment in the bottles and several of them shot out their corks while aging in the basement. I stood in the kitchen as the corks boomed out of the bottles one at a time, listening to what sounded like gunshots and trying to figure out what was going on. The bottles that survived held a tasty, slightly sweet wine that packed a real kick. I made elderflower wine (delicious), and wine from the crabapple tree in our backyard (colourful and tasty, in a boozy kind of way). I picked apples from the old orchard trees near the house and turned them into a very dry, alcoholic cider. When my daughter, Phoebe, was in junior high, she asked if you could make wine from anything, I said more or less, yes. As long as it had sugar the yeast could ferment into alcohol, you could make wine from it.

"Can you make wine from kiwis?" she asked.

"I don't see why not."

"Can we do it?"

So we did. I bought a three-pound basket of kiwis at the supermarket, and we turned it into half a dozen or so bottles of a surprisingly refreshing white wine.

I'd also been making bread for decades. One or two loaves at a time early on, when my wife, Sara, and I were students, and up to five or six (which would disappear alarmingly quickly) when our three children were all living at home. At one point I was using a sourdough starter sent to me by one of my Greek cousins. It was a descendant of the sourdough culture my grandmother had used in her mountain home. Baking with it made me feel

Homemade kosher dills.
A bit of a gateway drug for
fermentation.

a visceral connection to her and the generations of bakers who came before her, making wonderful crusty breads in their wood-fired brick ovens.

But my interest in fermentation really blossomed after Callum sent me that link. In Sara's words, I was soon "fermenting everything in sight."

I bought cabbage and a large ceramic crock and fermented enough sauerkraut to last a year. I started experimenting with kimchi recipes, turning nappa cabbage and a mix of spices and hot peppers into an addictive condiment that not only went well with Korean food, but was also an ideal complement to hot dogs or a simple meal of rice topped with a fried egg. We had made vinegar-based, canned dill pickles for years, but now I tried my hand at traditional kosher dills, fermented in a food-grade plastic bucket, with a delicious, salty crunch. "Oh my God," Sara said the first time she tasted one. "I feel like I'm at Schwartz's." (That's the classic Montreal smoked meat restaurant, where a kosher pickle on the side is *de rigueur*.) I snipped garlic scapes — the flowery part of the garlic plant that you remove in order to encourage the bulbs to grow — and fermented them in brine, with local smoked peppers. I plucked stinging nettles out of the garden and fermented them with garlic and hot peppers — an acquired taste, I'll admit, but an interesting one.

What made me fall so hard for making and consuming fermented foods and drinks? And why are we seeing such a boom in interest in these products — whether made at home, or purchased?

I think there are a few reasons.

Let's start with the foods themselves. The bite of those green beans Data Ram gave me. The joy in a glass of locally produced sparkling wine. The complicated, unique flavours we can't get from any other methods.

Sitting in a North End Halifax café — drinking iced tea while snacking on lightly fermented carrot sticks — Sandor Katz talks to me about the fermented food revival. He is in Nova Scotia to teach a series of workshops, sharing the knowledge he's honed during a couple of decades of practice on a farm in rural Tennessee, and in his travels around the world.

Sandor grew up on the Upper West Side in New York, and was bitten by the fermented food bug early. He fondly remembers sour garlic kosher pickles as "a special favourite food as a kid in New York" — whether they came from the legendary Guss's pickle stall or "this amazing appetizing Jewish emporium called Zabar's."

He thinks the pull of these unique flavours is what makes people so passionate about fermented foods.

"If you walk into any gourmet food store anywhere in the world, the foods that people get excited about — the foods that people are willing to pay exorbitant prices for, the things that people crave, and think about, and dream about, are the products of fermentation: cheeses and cured meats and breads and coffee and chocolate, not to mention beer and wine.

Sauerkraut in a cast-iron pan at Ross Farm Museum.

People get excited about the foods and beverages themselves."

His mission is to not only promote these foods, but also share knowledge about how to make them.

Sandor says, "You are taking some of the most exciting foods, with some of the edgiest and most compelling flavours, and there's just this air of mystery to them. And then you figure out many of them are actually incredibly simple to make and you can do them usually at home in your kitchen. You can overcome whatever fear you might have about it, and feel empowered to make these things yourself — and that makes you want to experiment and share your excitement with a lot of other people."

My research for this book bears that out. People come to fermenting foods for a variety of reasons, but they often seem to quickly get hooked and expand their repertoires.

Some people are drawn to fermentation because they've heard that the probiotics are good for their health and they want to try making foods with them at home.

Or maybe they are trying to recapture some of the flavours they remember from childhood. I watched a woman in her thirties taste a traditionally aged sauerkraut made on-site at the Ross Farm Museum, on the South Shore. She took a bite and her eyes lit up. "It's delicious. My family's from the South Shore. Oh, this brings back memories."

Or maybe, in a world in which so much food is commercially processed and standardized, and where consistency is prized above taste, many of us are beginning to value experimentation and the unexpected. Not every batch of kimchi will be the same. No two vintages of grapes will produce identical wines. Every batch of cider fermented with indigenous yeast growing on the fruit will be one-of-a-kind.

In addition to providing unique flavours, the products of fermentation are among the oldest human foods. In summer 2018, archaeologists found a stone fireplace with the burnt remains of bread baked from grains including barley and oats. It was 14,500 years old. That predates the development of agriculture. We don't know whether the bread was fermented or not, but I would be surprised if the dough hadn't been left out in the sun for at least a short period of time — enough for the wild yeasts to begin working on it.

Archaeologist Patrick McGovern — an expert on ancient fermented beverages — says humans were brewing alcoholic beverages in China by about 7,000 BCE, and making grape wine and barley beer in the mountains of present-day Iran by 5,400 BCE and 3,400 BCE, respectively. And in a *Smithsonian Magazine* story on him, McGovern says he believes a limestone vat for treading on grapes — dating back to 400 BCE — is the earliest French wine press.

Eating, drinking and making these foods connects us to our history. Their persistence is a tribute to human ingenuity, and the live bacterial cultures many of them contain are of benefit to our health.

Plus, experimenting in the kitchen with products that are not all that complicated to make, and that lend themselves to endless variations, is just plain fun.

Every year, *Saltscapes* holds Expos celebrating Atlantic Canadian food and drink. When I stopped in for the spring 2018 edition held in a cavernous former hardware store, I was struck by how, increasingly, those products have the distinctly tangy and rich flavours that come from fermentation.

A family business run by immigrants from Iran (one of them an engineer) handed out free samples of lively fermented spiced vegetables, including a traditional Iranian pickle called torshee. At the Sober Island Brewing Company camping-trailer-turned-beer-stand, people lined up for glasses of beer including an oyster-infused stout — a product marrying two different Nova Scotian traditions. One of the owners of Solas Kombucha was busy explaining the various flavours of the fizzy drink on offer, and two brothers dressed in rough-spun tunics evoking the Middle Ages talked to visitors about their brand-new meadery on the South Shore.

In Nova Scotia, as in many other places, fermented foods and drinks are enjoying renewed popularity among consumers, while at the same time there is a renaissance in their production — with the rise of many new companies specializing in these products.

As of 2019, Nova Scotia has more craft breweries per capita than any other province in Canada. The craft cider revival that washed across North America has arrived too, leading to the growth of small cideries and renewed interest in planting centuries-old apple varieties that may not make good eating, but sure make for tasty cider. The wine industry is maturing, with talented vineyard managers growing classic varieties like Chardonnay and Pinot Noir — once thought impossible here — alongside hybrid grapes designed for cool climates, and unusual varieties that winemakers are using to produce unique flavours. The number of sourdough bread makers has grown, and so have the varieties of breads they produce: from deliciously sour ryes with a sunflower seed accent, to classic French baguettes and loaves

Ingredients for making kimchi.

made in the Acadian tradition. Some are maintaining a particularly local focus, using grains grown here or even milling them into flour themselves, at their bakeries. We have a dozen different kombucha makers. And while classic sauerkraut remains a staple on supermarket shelves, a new generation of fermenters is creating sauerkrauts with a twist and selling kimchi at farmers' markets and local shops.

"People start fermenting things because they can, because they're growing crops like cabbage, and because they have discovered alcohol," says Dr. Ruth Holmes Whitehead, a curator emeritus at the Nova Scotia Museum.

Many of the fermented products I discuss have roots going back to the earliest European settlers in Nova Scotia, and were a part of daily life here.

There is little evidence that prior to European contact, the Indigenous Mi'kmaw population practised fermentation, though Dr. Whitehead, the author of several books on Mi'kmaw history and culture, says that pre-contact, the Mi'kmaw "had a truly magnificent diet" that was much healthier than that of Europeans five hundred years ago.

Many of the ferments in this book became possible in North America because of colonists who grew wheat and other crops, farmed animals for meat and milk and produced alcoholic beverages, which were unknown to Indigenous people. The French who tried to make a go of it at Port Royal brought hard cider with them, and almost immediately planted apple trees so they could make more. Some claim the first grapes for winemaking were planted on a south-facing slope in Bear River by Louis Hébert in 1611. On farmsteads across the province, cured meats were one of the sources of protein that helped families get through the winter. Acadians developed their own distinctive style of outdoor ovens for baking bread, and German settlers who arrived in Nova Scotia in the 1750s brought the tradition of making sauerkraut with them. The fermented cabbage dish not only provided some access to vegetables through the winter, it also helped sailors keep healthy while at sea. The Nova Scotia Fisheries Museum displays a typical early twentieth-century weekly meal plan for fishermen aboard Lunenburg-based saltbankers, or fishing schooners. Sauerkraut (both raw and cooked) is a staple of the week's meals.

Apples, cabbage and other vegetables, grapes and berries are all plentiful in Nova Scotia, and are commonly used in fermented foods. Some regions of the province also have micro-climates where hops — a staple in many craft beers — thrive.

When we make these foods today, many of which use live yeasts found in the atmosphere, we are in a very tangible sense connecting with the past.

Talk about fermentation and you hear the word "terroir" a lot. In simplest terms, "terroir" means the particular flavour of a place. It's what makes cider made from Nova Scotia-grown apples fermented with indigenous yeasts taste different from, say, ciders made in Somerset, Brittany or Washington State. Rachel Lightfoot, of the Lightfoot & Wolfville winery, calls it "the sense of the place where something came from." Location, climate, soil, effects of the sea and the wind, even local traditions: these can all be considered part of a food's terroir. Rachel adds, "It's a sense of 'somewhereness' — what makes that particular place unique" expressed through food or drink. A unique sense of place encoded in a local product. Cider maker and fermentation consultant Alexandra Beaulieu Boivin talks about "the deepness of terroir" in wild apples. Wine expert Sean Wood says when it comes to wine, the particular Nova Scotia terroir is expressed as "aromatic, crisp, and light" with a distinctive mineral character. You can really taste terroir in cheese too. I remember driving to a cheesemaker's in the Magdalen Islands and having to stop the car just before the shop to let their herd of cows cross the road. The cheese we bought was infused with the salty flavour of the sea beside the field where they grazed. Gouda maker Jeff McCourt told me that visitors from Holland often express surprise at the taste of his cheese. "We have Dutch people who come over and say it's not like the gouda they have at home. Well, no it isn't. Our milk is that much better, we have salt air, the grass is different here, and the cows eat a different diet. It really is a true representation of terroir."

Fermentation produces wonderful flavours, connects us to local producers, is good for our health and is a direct link with local cultures — both the culture embodied in history and tradition, and the microscopic live cultures embedded in our fermented foods.

If you want to try your hand at expressing terroir in your kitchen, this book does offer you some recipes. Some have been generously provided by people I've interviewed, who want to share their love of fermented products. Others come from my kitchen. You don't have to make any fermented foods to enjoy this book, but I do hope you will consider giving some of them a try. In Chapter 10, I discuss fermentation tips and techniques and give you an overview of the basic equipment you will need. I encourage you to read the chapter before trying the recipes. It will help you choose the right equipment and understand the basic methods for fermenting many different foods and drinks.

This book is an overview of fermented foods and drinks that have a history in Nova Scotia and that are currently being made — many of them undergoing revivals. Even in a small province like Nova Scotia, the wealth of products is astounding, and I am not able to cover all of them. You'll notice, for instance, that I don't get into mead production or the boom in craft distilleries. It would be impossible to write about all the fermented foods and drinks being produced here, so I've had to make some difficult choices. It's also a personal book, not an encyclopedic overview of the fermentation scene. You'll come along with me as I travel the province, meet producers, dig into archival materials and try my hand at fermenting a variety of foods and drinks. Each of these chapters could probably be the subject of a book on its own. I encourage you to take *Adventures in Bubbles and Brine* as a starting point for your own explorations of Nova Scotia ferments.

1

Sauerkraut
The Classic Nova Scotia Ferment

Sauerkraut is bully
Sauerkraut is fine;
We ought to know it
For we eat it all the time.
Put the cabbage in the "barl",
Stamp it with your feet,

When the juice begins to rise
The kraut is fit to eat.
Put it in a pot.
Set it on to "bile,"
Be sure to keep the cover on,
Or you'll smell it half a mile.

— A traditional sauerkraut song, reproduced in the 1953 handwritten cookbook *Dutch Oven*, by the Ladies Auxiliary of the Lunenburg Hospital Society. The song dates back to at least the late nineteenth century.

It's a stunningly beautiful October day on Big Tancook Island in Mahone Bay — Nova Scotia's sauerkraut capital for a couple of centuries. As the ferry from Chester pulls in at the end of the fifty-minute crossing, I spot Hillary Dionne waiting for me on the dock. Hillary's family moved here from Wakefield, a suburb of Boston, when she was eight years old. Her father had been involved with the Apollo 11 mission that landed Neil Armstrong and Buzz Aldrin on the Moon. But by the late 1970s, he was looking for a change of pace. "He and my mum thought they would probably buy a

Sheila Rodenhiser with buckets full of her homemade sauerkraut.

place somewhere else in New England," Hillary says drily as she navigates her minivan around an array of potholes in the packed dirt road.

Talk about fermented foods in Nova Scotia and the conversation will quickly turn to sauerkraut — the province's best-known ferment.

Hillary is taking me to meet Sheila Rodenhiser, who, at seventy-five, is one of the last sauerkraut makers on the island.

In the living room of the home where she has lived for fifty-five years, surrounded by more photos of Elvis Presley than I've ever seen in one place, Sheila looks across the road at the trees, shrubs and wild raspberries growing where there were once seemingly endless rows of cabbage.

"Oh, there was cabbage fields everywheres on the island. Oh yes. I mean the island, if you were to see it back then towards now, you'd never believe it

. . . This island don't look nothing like it did back in them years," she tells me.

Although Sheila has lived her whole life on Big Tancook, she didn't start making sauerkraut until the 1980s, when she learned the art from her then-neighbour Evelyn, wife of the late master kraut maker Percy Langille.

Some years, Sheila would have "cut in" by now — cutting in being the local term for making sauerkraut. But this year, it's still too warm. She'd like the temperature to be a bit cooler when she's fermenting the cabbage in her unheated outbuilding, but not so cool that it slows the process down too much.

Once the temperature is right, Sheila will head to the mainland and buy her annual ton of cabbage.

"Ton" here, by the way, is not a euphemism for "lots." She literally buys a ton, making 2,000 to 3,000 pounds of sauerkraut a year. A lot, but considerably less than the 7,000 pounds of cabbage she used to cut in.

Sheila makes sauerkraut using only the three classic ingredients: cabbage, salt and water, and she prefers to go by instinct instead of using a recipe. Traditionally, Tancook sauerkraut was made in puncheons — wooden barrels or half-barrels, but Sheila uses plastic barrels.

She explains the process: "First you sprinkle a layer, just a tiny little bit, of salt in the bottom of the barrel, then I add cabbage on top, then more salt and push it down . . . I just use my hands and push. Then I start another layer and add more salt, and when we get it full to the top then I pour a bucket of water on top. Just plain water. I don't measure nothing."

Once Sheila has covered her kraut, she leaves it while "it froths up. Froths, I call it." She pauses. "There's another word," she says, trying to remember.

"Fermenting?" Hillary asks.

"Yes. Ferments. It just comes all up. The water will come up the next day after you got it cut in. And then, three or four days later you'll see it bubbling and bubbling and it comes right up — sometimes all over the floor, because the barrel was too full to start with. And then all of a sudden one day you go by and it's just gone down. It goes down. And that's just about when it's done and ready to pack up."

Moon, Tides and Kraut

Traditionally, Nova Scotia sauerkraut makers cut in their kraut in October or November, when the Moon is new or waxing.

The Ross Farm Museum in New Ross is dedicated to showing what farm life in the area was like in the late 1800s. Staff dress in period costumes, work out of buildings dating back to 1817 and practise traditional arts including blacksmithing, working fields with oxen — and making sauerkraut.

Site manager Barry Hiltz grew up on a nearby farm himself and follows the old tradition of making sauerkraut in accordance with the cycles of the Moon. "We wait for the waxing Moon, cut it in, add sea salt and let it work for twenty-one days. That's the old German tradition," Barry says.

At Ross Farm they make about half a barrel of sauerkraut a year, cutting the cabbage with a kraut knife Barry built in the 1980s, based on a traditional design.

"We use wooden barrels — which was traditional. You put down a layer an inch or two thick of coarse salt, add the cabbage and stomp it down with the stomper [an implement featuring a large round piece of wood at the end of a sturdy handle], which compacts it and breaks down the cabbage. That's where your liquid comes from," Barry explains.

Then, you wait for the Moon to work its magic.

Cabbages and kraut cutter at Ross Farm Museum.

Traditional kraut knife and stomper at Ross Farm Museum. The cabbage goes in the box, which slides back and forth across the knife blade.

"The Moon works on sauerkraut like it does on the tide. When you fill a half-barrel, you don't fill it more than five inches from the top. Then you put a wooden board and a big rock on top . . . The pickle will rise over a period of twenty-one days and at the end of it the top of your sauerkraut will be dry," Barry says.

In his memoir *The Rooster Crows at Dawn,* Lee Zinck of Blandford (born in 1907) recalls the powerful effect of the Moon on his father's sauerkraut. After using "brute force" on the kraut knife to cut the cabbage, it was then salted and weighed down. And that's when the fun started. "In about six hours, fermentation would take place," Zinck writes. "Patches of foam, or white froth, would appear on top of the drum . . . The full Moon had a tremendous effect on the fermentation of the sauerkraut. The gases went wild at that time and, if confined to an area that was airtight, would blow the top completely off."

Some hold that it's the tides, not the Moon, that play a critical role. A 1973 profile of Tancook Island sauerkraut maker Calvin Hutt doesn't talk about the Moon at all — but it does point to the effects of the tide on the fermentation process. The story, from the Hants Journal, says "An interesting sidelight of 'kraut' production is to be found in the fact that the brine, or the broth, or the juice or the pickle — it goes by many names — rises and falls in the puncheon with the rise and fall of the ocean tide in the nearby Atlantic . . . At high tide, it is said, the puncheon frequently overflows, while at low tide, the level of the pickle drops. No one seeks to explain this phenomenon. It just happens — and is accepted as fact."

Sheila Rodenhiser's kraut cutter.

The fermentation usually takes about two weeks. Sheila then packages it up into pails (ten, twenty or thirty pounds) and calls her customers on the mainland to tell them it's ready. "I pack it in tight and I put juice all over the top. All my customers always say, 'Make sure you have juice on my kraut,' so that's what I do."

Sheila's next-door neighbour, Verta Rodenhiser, also makes kraut — about fifty pounds a year, for her own use. The two women show me their kraut knives, set up in outbuildings beside their homes. The word "knife" doesn't capture the spirit of these homemade cabbage power-shredders. Imagine a bucket reminiscent of a washbasin mounted on top of a large rectangular box. Fitted into the bucket is a round piece of wood with two blades — formed by cutting a scythe blade in half — set into it. Unlike the traditional kraut knife, these machines are electric. Both Sheila's and Verta's kraut knives are painted white. Sheila got hers from Backalong, the other side of the island, maybe thirty years ago. Verta's originally belonged to Percy Langille. Using these machines, they can cut a thousand pounds of cabbage a day without too much trouble.

The traditional kraut knife, used both on the island and the mainland, is a simple and effective contraption built with one purpose only: to slice up cabbage. It looks like a giant mandoline, up to four or five feet long, and consists of a wooden box fitted into tracks and gliding back and forth along a board with two or three knife blades built into it.

I've used one of these old kraut knives and it's not easy going.

At a sauerkraut-making workshop in Halifax, workshop co-leader Elizabeth Peirce cautions those of us taking a turn with the kraut knife: "Be careful. We don't want any human blood in our sauerkraut." The open pattern of the cabbage leaves makes it hard to shred, the cabbage catching on the blades each time I slide the box forward. I find myself muscling it over the sharp edges before pulling it back, then repeating the action again. And again. And again.

It's slow, hard, frustrating work. And I'm cutting an embarrassingly small amount of cabbage: about two pounds. Enough to make one modest Mason jar of sauerkraut.

Simple Sauerkraut

This is a dead-easy recipe for making sauerkraut. You don't need any special equipment, and you can enjoy your sauerkraut a week or so after you make it. Sauerkraut can be very flexible. Ferment this for a week or two, and it should be tasty and have a fresh flavour with a bit of crunch to it. If you prefer your sauerkraut softer and with a more pungent flavour, just leave it to ferment longer. You can make sauerkraut using only cabbage, salt and a touch of water, but there are endless variations possible. Try experimenting with the flavourings below, or make a classic kraut.

You can measure your salt by volume (as in the recipe) or by weight. If you choose weight, weigh your cabbage and calculate what 2 per cent or 3 per cent of that weight is. The result is the amount of salt you should use. So a 1 kg (2.2 lb) cabbage would take 20–30 g (0.7–1 oz) of salt. The variation in the amount of salt gives you some flexibility for how salty you make your kraut.

Materials
- Knife
- Mason jar (ideally a narrow-mouth jar with rounded shoulders)

Ingredients
- 1 kg (2.2 lb) green cabbage (between a quarter and a half of a medium cabbage)
- 1 tbsp plus 1 tsp (20 mL) fine sea salt
- A bit of extra water to cover the cabbage, if necessary

Optional flavourings
If you'd like to add a bit more oomph to your sauerkraut, consider adding these — either on their own, or in combination.

Whole peppercorns, dried dill, caraway seeds (a classic, and a staple in Bavarian-style sauerkraut), sliced apple, hot peppers, ginger or garlic

Method
Cut the tough core out of the cabbage and discard. Remove and keep one of the thick outer leaves of cabbage.

Thinly slice or chop the rest of the cabbage and put it in a bowl. You can use a mandoline, but for a small amount of sauerkraut a knife works just fine.

Sprinkle the sea salt over the shredded cabbage and let it sit for ten minutes or so.

Squeeze and massage the cabbage. I like to grab it, then squeeze and twist. Do this for a good five minutes. Your shredded cabbage will decrease in size dramatically as the liquid comes out. If you prefer, you can use a drink muddler or a wooden spoon to mash it down.

Add the optional flavourings, if using, and mix in with your hands, squeezing the cabbage a bit more while you do.

Taste the mixture. It should have a nice salty bite, but not be overwhelmingly salty. If you find it too salty, add a bit more cabbage.

Pack the cabbage tightly into a Mason jar. Squeeze it down hard, so the liquid rises to the surface. (Add the liquid from the bowl that came out of your cabbage if needed. You can also add a bit of water if the liquid doesn't quite cover.)

Take the cabbage leaf you set aside and cut or tear it so you can jam it into the jar under the shoulders. You want your sauerkraut to remain submerged, and the leaf can help keep it down below the surface of the brine. If you have fermentation weights, use those instead of the cabbage.

Put a lid on the jar. Metal can rust because of the salt in the brine, so use a plastic lid or place plastic wrap under the metal ring of the jar. Place the jar in a cupboard or on the kitchen counter in an area with relatively warm room temperature.

Check your sauerkraut daily. Make sure it's submerged, and if not, press it down. If you see a bit of white mold at the surface, remove it. It's harmless and the cabbage underneath will be safe in its brine. If the cabbage leaf covering the kraut develops mold, replace it.

When the sauerkraut reaches the flavour you like (after at least a week) place it in the fridge to stop the fermentation process. Enjoy at your leisure. Depending on how you like your sauerkraut, this amount could last you anywhere from a couple of meals to several months.

How long should you ferment your sauerkraut?

This is really a question of taste. Traditionally, Nova Scotians seem to enjoy their sauerkraut crunchy. This requires a shorter ferment — usually a couple of weeks. If, like me, you prefer a richer and more complex flavour, let your kraut age longer — up to a year or more.

Sauerkraut (which literally means "sour cabbage" in German) has a history dating back millennia. The ancient Romans ate fermented cabbage, and surviving records show that so did workers building the Great Wall of China. During the thirteenth century, Genghis Khan's people are said to have brought their version of fermented cabbage west to Europe, where it eventually caught on in eastern Europe and Germany.

In the mid-eighteenth century — when Tancook Island was being settled, mostly by Germans — sauerkraut helped save the age of sail. As ships undertook longer and longer journeys, their crews began to fall victim to scurvy, a potentially fatal illness brought about by a lack of vitamins. On a BBC website called "Captain Cook and the Scourge of Scurvy," historian Jonathan Lamb summarizes the symptoms of scurvy as noted by ship's chaplain Richard Walter: "Skin black as ink, ulcers, difficult respiration, rictus of the limbs, teeth falling out and, perhaps most revolting of all, a strange plethora of gum tissue sprouting out of the mouth, which immediately rotted and lent the victim's breath an abominable odour." Charming.

Determined to discover the cause of scurvy, the British conducted an experiment in the 1760s by sending out a different set of food stores with each of the voyages to the Pacific undertaken during the decade. Famously, Lamb says, Captain James Cook's ships carried "proper quantities of sauer Kraut." Only five men on Cook's expedition came down with scurvy and none died.

Cabbage is a very hardy vegetable — I've left green cabbage out on the kitchen counter for weeks and it has still been fine to eat. But it isn't hardy enough to last a whole winter at room temperature, or through the duration and heat of Pacific voyages like Cook's. In addition to preserving the cabbage so that it's palatable and doesn't putrefy, the process of fermenting it into sauerkraut actually increases the available B vitamins for us to metabolize.

Fermented foods seem to attract a lot of wild health claims, and sauerkraut is no exception. I was fascinated to learn these claims go back a century or so. In 1929, the *Journal of Agricultural Research* published a paper by two home economists, an agricultural chemist and an agricultural bacteriologist about some of these supposed health benefits of sauerkraut. They write, "There is a considerable amount of advertising before the public proclaiming the value of sauerkraut and sauerkraut juice as sources of the vitamins . . . but these seem to be based upon general observations rather than upon experimental evidence."

The four of them conclude that in fact there are indeed significant levels of Vitamin C in sauerkraut, though they caution that those results may not hold for industrially produced (e.g., canned) product.

Interestingly, a 2014 paper in the journal *Global Advances in Health and Medicine* found the amount of Vitamin C in sauerkraut varies, depending on whether the cabbage was grown in summer or winter, and that the amount of salt also affects the amount of Vitamin C we get when we eat sauerkraut.

In theory, sauerkraut sounds simple. As Sheila Rodenhiser says, cabbage, water, salt. Figure out the right proportions, let it ferment for a few weeks, and enjoy. That's one of the reasons so many fermentation workshops for beginners focus on sauerkraut: it's hard to mess up. As Sandor Katz says, "It's easy, there's no potential danger, you don't need special equipment, you don't need special starter cultures, you can enjoy your results relatively quickly, and it's incredibly delicious and healthy. It has so much going for it."

At the sauerkraut workshop I went to, we all experimented with different combinations of ingredients. By the end of the evening, the contents of the dozen Mason jars all looked wildly different: a jar with delicately cut green cabbage, an ethereal light pink kraut containing cabbage and shredded beets, a mostly purple one with flecks of green — and mine, a mix of red and green cabbage, with the red dominating, giving it a pleasant purple hue.

But even though the basics are the same, there are plenty of decisions that will affect the taste, texture and quality of your kraut.

Let's start with salt. Traditionally, Tancook Islanders swore by coarse sea salt from the Turks and Caicos Islands (also known as "Turks salt" or "Turks Island salt") for sauerkraut making. How much salt? The minimum is 2 per cent (compared to the weight of the cabbage), and 3 per cent is generally considered the maximum. It may not seem like a big difference, but even within this range the amount of salt will affect flavour and crunch.

Some sauerkraut makers discard the core of the cabbage because it is tougher and doesn't shred as well. Others think that's where much of the vegetable's sweetness and flavour reside and are horrified that anyone would throw it away.

In a 1973 profile of the late Tancook sauerkraut maker Calvin Hutt, then fifty-seven, an unnamed writer from the *Hants County Journal* summed up the choices this way:

> *[Making sauerkraut] sounds like a simple proposition — an easy exercise anyone might be able to follow but the secret, if such it is, is not that simple for it involves what kind of cabbage to grow, which cabbage to 'cut' and which to discard, what quantity of salt to use, how tightly the barrels should be packed, and what temperature should be maintained in order to effect the desired 'Cure.' Herein lies the answer to the quality of the Hutt product — an answer gained over a lifetime of experience and known to few.*

While you can add other flavourings to sauerkraut — apples, cumin, ginger, for example — a 1959 article on Tancook sauerkraut by Elma Wright

My homemade red-and-green cabbage sauerkraut (clearly the red colour dominates).

in the *Dartmouth Free Press* says island residents "find that the traditional methods work very well. They regard some of the methods used elsewhere with mingled incredulity and disapproval. One lady remarked, with eyebrows raised, that somewhere in Ontario they made sauerkraut with vinegar, and another contributed with mild horror that she had even heard of carroway being added."

What remains of the last cabbage house (where cabbages were stored over winter) on Big Tancook Island. These buildings once dotted the island.

Although it had been around for more than a century, Tancook sauerkraut's popularity took off during the First World War.

In *Tancook Schooners: An Island and Its Boats,* Wayne O'Leary writes that until the early twentieth century, most people who farmed on the island might have produced "a little kraut on the side" but that most production was for their own use. But during the war "Tancook cabbage sold for twice as much . . . as it had previously, and sauerkraut reached record wholesale prices."

Sheila Rodenhiser's father used to go to Halifax, sometimes by boat, and peddle cabbage in fifty-pound bags.

Schooner captains took cabbage and sauerkraut into the city too. O'Leary says that about 80 per cent of the cabbage sold in Halifax during the 1930s arrived on Tancook schooners.

The fields of Big Tancook were once awash in cabbage. "Dotted here and there in fields and behind barns are the storage dugouts where the crop is kept during the winter. These look like the rooftops of buried houses sticking up out of the ground, and within the substantial walls the cabbage keep perfectly till required, with a stove moved in sometimes in exceptionally cold weather to keep them from freezing," wrote reporter Elma Wright in 1959.

Fifteen years later, Calvin Hutt was growing 6,500 cabbages a year for sauerkraut.

Twenty years after that, in 1995, Percy Langille told photographer George Bellerose that only a handful of people planted cabbage on the island anymore.

And in 2019, it's all gone.

Those dozens of cabbage houses that once dotted the island? They are all gone too. Hillary Dionne takes me to see what's left of the last remaining cabbage house. She parks her van on the dirt road leading to Tancook Elementary (2018–2019 enrollment: six students) and we walk across to the building. The roof has caved in and lies sadly buckled over collapsed window frames. Through an opening I can see debris in the basement, including an old wooden barrel lying on its side. Hillary says the main truss supporting the roof collapsed about fifteen years ago. This, along with a few rock foundations scattered in overgrown fields, is all that's left of the Tancook cabbage houses.

Serious attempts at growing cabbage on the island ended for a couple of reasons, but the main one is an infestation of deer, beginning in the 1990s. Hillary tells me a hunter she knows estimates there are now three hundred deer on the island. That's one hundred per square mile. Around the same time, Sheila says, cabbages grown on the island began suffering from unprecedented infestations of grubs.

Tancook Island cabbage is a particular variety. A descendant of the cabbages Germans brought here, and bred for sauerkraut making. It was grown continuously for nearly two hundred years. If the variety does survive, it will be thanks to the efforts of people like Barry Hiltz of the Ross Farm Museum and farmer Chris Sanford.

Chris lives in Laconia, on the South Shore, where she grows 150 varieties of vegetables for seed.

Chris doesn't particularly like green cabbage, and when she started her business had no plans to grow it for seed. Then, in the summer of 2015, she heard about the endangered Tancook Island cabbage. Soon after, a friend who had been to Big Tancook gave her some seeds saved by a resident. Eventually, Chris went out to the island and collected a few more. And as she grew the cabbage it began to grow on her.

"It struck me that this one was unique," Chris says. She describes the Tancook cabbage as "very stout and sturdy, with a taller stem and very broad leaves . . . I was told that it should have only two leaves that overlap at the top. I think that has to do with when you're cutting it for sauerkraut and processing it: If you cut it in half you're not losing much on the top. So that's something we breed for. I really hadn't seen any other cabbage like it. It's a really nice cabbage. Really nice flavour. Mild and crunchy."

They're growing the cabbage at the Ross Farm Museum, too. In his diary for June 29, 1841, Edward Ross — whose family owned the farm where the museum is today — wrote: "I took a basket of Cabbage plants from Mrs. Gray (as she had them there from Tancook and in a fair way to perish) and took the trouble of carrying them all the way home. I arrived home early. We finished planting to day." A hundred and seventy years later, Barry Hiltz and two other staff from the Ross Farm Museum made Mrs. Gray's trip in reverse, going out to the island to see if they could bring home some seeds. "We spent the day chatting with three old fellows who used to work in the cabbage fields. I thought they'd be reluctant to give up their information, but it was the complete opposite," Barry recalls. "They realized if the cabbage was going to survive, they would have to help it. One fellow came out with a little bag of seeds and he said, 'Here, take these. They're the last of the cabbage seeds I have.' It was quite moving."

The micro-climate in New Ross is different from Tancook Island — about 5 degrees cooler, Barry says — so instead of broadcasting seed in April he waits until June. Since Ross Farm doesn't have cabbage houses, Barry studied other methods of overwintering cabbage, and adopted an Acadian technique of covering root crops with hay. He pulls out the cabbages, builds boxes with a wire mesh on top to place over them, then covers the cabbage plants with sawdust and three feet of hay.

Ross Farm grows about 150 heads of cabbage a year and uses ninety pounds or so of the crop to make sauerkraut.

Chris Sanford says the story of Tancook Island cabbage is not unusual — "something like 75 per cent of the varieties of vegetables that were being grown 100 years ago are extinct now." It's a fate she's hoping the cabbage can avoid — and, as more people start to grow it, making more seeds available, the chances of its survival increase.

Even though she didn't set out to grow green cabbage, Chris says now she feels a bit like Frodo — the character from *The Lord of the Rings* who reluctantly finds himself caught up in a quest. "You don't want to do it, but you have to. I feel a sense of responsibility."

They may not be growing cabbage on Big Tancook Island anymore, but Nova Scotia's two commercial sauerkraut makers are not far away. In fact, they are less than a five-minute drive from each other, near Lunenburg.

Both M.A. Hatt and Son ("Manufacturers of Tancook Brand Sauerkraut") and Krispi Kraut ("Home of Krispi Kraut Sauerkraut") operate out of low-slung, shed-like buildings and keep their product lines simple. And both are family businesses: Tancook is owned by Cory Hatt, who says he learned the secrets of sauerkraut making from his father, and Krispi Kraut by the Rhodenizer family, who have used their own traditional sauerkraut recipe for more than forty years.

Although you'll find either Tancook or Krispi Kraut sauerkraut in many Nova Scotia grocery stores, Sheila Rodenhiser has never tasted either of them. "I've never tried neither of their krauts, so I can't say a bad thing about any of them . . . I don't know nothing about them," she says when I ask her.

But for many other Nova Scotians and ex-Nova Scotians returning for a visit, these sauerkrauts represent the taste of home.

On the day I stop in at Krispi Kraut, Lorna Eisan and Jessica Rhodenizer wear bright yellow gloves as they scoop sauerkraut out of large rectangular bins and pack it by hand, one package at a time, into the company's signature blue-and-white cartons. Jessica is a member of the family who owns the business. The Rhodenizers grow 90,000 heads of cabbage a year, starting the plants in a greenhouse, then growing them out on their own farm and nearby properties. Although the scale of production is different, the process remains much like the one Sheila and Verta use in their outbuildings on Big Tancook.

The cabbages are stored in a large room behind the production area. The staff make sauerkraut once a week, usually on Friday mornings, but sometimes on Saturday. They start by trimming any blemishes off the cabbages using a large knife reminiscent of a machete. Then the plants are cored in a wall-mounted machine that looks a bit like a giant pencil sharpener.

After the cabbage is shredded by machine, it's time to salt and layer and leave it for two weeks to ferment in one of the seven tanks in the back room.

When demand is high, it can be a challenge to keep up — there is only so much space in the small plant, and the cabbage needs time to ferment, the batches rotating through the different tanks. "But I've never had anyone come in and we say sorry, there's no kraut," Jessica says. "So it works out."

Although she's only twenty-one, Jessica seems like an old hand here, manually filling each carton quickly, checking its weight and making sure each one has the right ratio of juice to kraut.

A woman named Heather Hyson walks in. "How much sauerkraut do I need for 150 people, do you know?" she asks. She's organizing a fundraiser for a local firehall. "We're doing a sauerkraut and sausage supper. We've got ninety pounds of sausage, about a half-pound per person." Jessica puzzles over the amount, and I interject, suggesting maybe 150 grams per person. "Don't give me grams!" Heather says. A quick call to plant manager Kevin Rhodenizer — who has managed the Krispi Kraut plant for forty-two years — settles the question. Forty pounds, he says. No more than a third of a pound per person.

Cooking and Baking with Sauerkraut

The classic way to eat sauerkraut in Nova Scotia is warmed. Heat the sauerkraut and serve it with a mess of sausages or pork chops and mashed potatoes.

Of course, there are all kinds of other ways to eat it too — in a sandwich, as a side-dish or even on its own. I have a friend who likes to settle in and watch baseball with a fork and a carton of sauerkraut. Sheila Rodenhiser likes making sauerkraut soup.

You can even bake with it — for example, by replacing the zucchini in a zucchini cake recipe with sauerkraut. Marie Nightingale, author of the classic *Out of Old Nova Scotia Kitchens* cookbook, has a recipe for sauerkraut chocolate cake. And in an undated community cookbook published by the Ladies Auxiliary of the FPW Firehall (it serves the communities of Fox River, Port Greville and Wards Brook in Cumberland County), I found a recipe for sauerkraut gingerbread.

Sauerkraut and traditional Lunenburg sausage at Ross Farm Museum.

The kraut in the bins is almost all gone now. Jessica fires up the plant's old steam sealer, puts on ear protection and rolls a bin filled with about one hundred cartons up to the machine. She lines them up, one at a time. The sealer moves each carton down the line, letting it sit a few seconds under a heater that activates the adhesive. At the next stop on the conveyor, the machine presses two sides of the carton together briefly — long enough to seal it. Now the kraut will go off to a grocery store or stay here for direct-to-customer sales.

Every year, in early spring, Ross Farm celebrates traditional farm foods cooked over an open hearth — including sauerkraut made here on the farm, heated in a cast-iron pan on a spider grate over an open flame. Inside the farm's Rosebank Cottage, built in 1817, Gail Larder and Helen Jarvis are busy cooking sausages, prepping pie and tending the sauerkraut.

Gail grew up on a farm close by and says many of the traditional late-1800s activities at Ross Farm are similar to those her family practised daily. Her father made sauerkraut, and — following a Lunenburg County tradition — would put a whole apple or two in the barrel with it. "When dad made it, it was probably saltier, because it had to keep all winter. We didn't have a refrigerator," she says.

Once the sauerkraut is warm, I tuck into a bowlful. The sauerkraut is delicious.

"When this generation is gone from the farm, the next generation will have to learn the skills that are second-nature to us. People are far removed now from what we do here," she says.

A young family walks in, and Gail serves them each a bowl of sauerkraut and some traditional Lunenburg sausage — also made on the farm. She talks about how her father grew just about everything she needed as a child, then asks, "How's the sauerkraut?"

"Delicious," the woman says. "My family's from the South Shore, so I grew up on this stuff. I'm a Keddy. That's a German name. My father made sauerkraut and we always had it for the winter. Buckets and buckets."

2

Fermenting the Harvest

Enjoy Vegetables Year-round

Mercedes Brian is packing fermented pickles — she calls them "Montreal Garlic Dills" — into jars and remembering how she first fell in love with pickles like these as a teenager.

"We moved to Montreal when I was fourteen, and I grew up eating these," she says. "The flavour certainly is evocative for me. I remember going to the Atwater Market — and we didn't go that often, but I remember those pickles and wanted to make them again. Those childhood memories are really powerful."

Mercedes started Pickled Pink, her fermented veggie and kombucha business, back in 2012, and still runs it out of her home in Wolfville. It's late fall and she's working in her clean and bright 7 x 12-foot cold room, filling jar after jar to sell at her market stand in Halifax. Typically, you start fermented veggies at room temperature, then put them in a cool place for storage. To make sure her ferments stay at their optimal state, Mercedes keeps the temperature down here low using a fan and a device called a CoolBot — an electronic temperature controller that allows air conditioning units to run cooler than they normally would. Ideal for keeping those veggies right where you want them.

Fermented vegetables — brined dill pickles (also called kosher pickles), kimchi, sauerkraut, fermented carrots — have become a staple across the province. I've seen jars of brined veggies for sale not only at farmers' markets, but also in wineries, at bakeries and at small groceries in villages like Earltown. It's not uncommon for restaurants to offer side dishes of home-fermented carrots, beans or other vegetables. And it's not just a Halifax thing. I've had them served as side dishes in Advocate Harbour, Lunenburg, Summerville and North Sydney.

It wasn't always this way. Back in 2012, when Mercedes started her business, she wasn't aware of anyone else selling fermented vegetables. "At that point, if you Google-searched 'fermented vegetables Nova Scotia' mine was the only name that came up. And I was the only one I know of who was selling." After selling at the Wolfville Farmers' Market, she moved to the historic Brewery Market in Halifax. "The first question the first customer asked me was 'Are these lacto-fermented?' and I kind of knew I had found my place. I liked that I was the only person doing it locally — but I knew I wasn't going to be the only one for long."

She was right. On a busy Saturday at the Brewery Market, Mercedes answers questions about her veggies and hands customers tastes of kombucha in small cups. Nearby, Zoe Beale's table is filled with jars of sauerkraut, kimchi and spicy fermented kale. Across the harbour, at the Alderney Landing Market, Jamie Tingley and Sarah Fisher (who also double as a mental health nurse and graphic designer, respectively) do a brisk business selling fermented vegetables made at their farm in Cow Bay, under the name Sour Beast Ferments. Like most fermenters I've met, they're happy to talk with customers, explaining how fermentation works and what goes into their jars. And then there are fermented hot sauces — including Steve Hatcher's hyper-local Revenge de l'Acadie, featuring hot peppers that ferment and age for several months before Steve combines them with other ingredients, including vinegar from local Acadie Blanc wine.

Like many people, Mercedes first tried fermented foods for health reasons — in her case, a persistent candida problem. She says more and more people seem to understand the health effects of fermented foods, but, as she points out, health benefits alone aren't enough to explain the booming popularity of these products. Even if you start eating something for your health, you won't stick with it if you don't like the taste.

"More and more people understand that we have a microbiome [more on this in Chapter 9], that our gut is really important, that as healthy as our gut is — that's how healthy we will be," Mercedes says. "But they wouldn't come back if they didn't add delight to meals, as I say. Some people don't like them at first, and then they come back and say, 'Woah, I didn't like this when I started and now I have to have some on every plate.' That's a pretty good business model — to have something people want to come back for. And they also feel it's good for them."

People first turned to fermenting produce for a very simple reason: pickling vegetables in brine was a way to preserve the harvest long before the invention of refrigeration. Vegetables don't conveniently ripen at a uniform rate throughout the year. When late summer and early fall hit Nova Scotia, suddenly everything ripens at once. Markets are filled with pickling cucumbers for a few weeks — and then they're gone.

Some crops can be safely and easily preserved using other techniques: braid your garlic, hang it in the basement and it should last until your next crop is ready the following summer. Root vegetables like carrots, beets and parsnips, and tubers such as potatoes will also store well for extended periods. But even some of these crops can also be preserved (and maybe even improved) through fermentation. And others, green beans for instance, will only last fresh for a very short time. If you want to enjoy their crunch for months after the harvest, fermenting them is the way to go.

We have come to think of boiling-water-bath canning — what we usually refer to when we say "pickling" — as a traditional way to preserve food. But the reality is that this kind of pickling is a relatively recent industrial innovation, made possible by advances in sealing technology.

Heating foods and preserving them in sealed glass vessels goes back to the early nineteenth-century, when French chef Nicolas Appert developed the technique after experimenting for fourteen years to get it right. With the money he made, he set up a cannery that ran for over a century until it shut down in 1933.

The Mason jar, patented in 1858, was an improvement to Appert's method, as it offered an easy airtight seal. During the 1960s, as the post-Second World War infatuation with highly processed and industrialized food began to wane (in some quarters anyway), canning enjoyed a resurgence, as back-to-the-landers and those inspired by the homesteading movement took to pickling as a way of preserving their own vegetables at home.

Eventually, that home preservation movement led to a resurgence in preserving vegetables in a more truly traditional way — through fermentation.

During the early eighteenth century, Acadians used advanced farming techniques to grow the same range of vegetables they would have been accustomed to eating in France. But as they were forced onto colder, rockier and swampier land, their vegetable production declined. In *A Taste of Acadie*, their book on traditional Acadian cooking, Marielle Cormier-Boudreau and Melvin Gallant say, "Acadians used very few kinds of vegetables in their cooking. In fact, there were no more than six or seven varieties central to the traditional diet which included turnips, cabbage, beans, corn, peas and onions." They also harvested and preserved wild plants. Most vegetables were eaten fresh seasonally, with some stored in cool rooms for the winter. Later, as the Acadian vegetable garden repertoire expanded to include produce such as carrots and cucumbers, preserving with salt became more common too.

Cabbage can be turned into sauerkraut, as we've seen, but another common practice was pickling whole small cabbage heads as well as the whole cores that had been removed from cabbages destined for sauerkraut.

Carrots, green beans, cucumbers, onions and beets all lend themselves well to being preserved in brine. Several years ago, my friend Av Singh, an agronomist and small-farms consultant, vividly described visiting a small organic Nova Scotia farm, going down the stairs to a refreshingly cool root cellar, plunging a hand into a bin filled with brine and pulling out a handful of green beans. They were a year old, and he said they were as crunchy as if they had just been picked, and deliciously salty and flavourful.

Barry Hiltz of the Ross Farm Museum on Nova Scotia's South Shore has slightly less fond memories of old pickling traditions. "They used to ferment and pickle just about everything," he says. "Something that was very common around here was called pickled heads — and when you tell people that, they look at you like you have three heads. After you cut your cabbage, several heads will start to grow off the stump — and what you want for pickled heads are cabbage heads about the size of a softball. They just fit in your hand — maybe four or five inches across or smaller. And they would pickle those as a head; occasionally they would cut them in half and then pickle them. I can remember going down to get them out of a barrel and it was one of the grossest things that ever was. You'd reach down into this slimy barrel and then take them up to the house and rinse them off."

Some old Nova Scotia recipes refer to fermented pickles as German-style. Ted Eaton's book *Waste Not, Want Not: Some Interesting Recipes of Old Acadia* offers two early 1800s recipes for pickling cucumbers. While we tend to think of preserving vegetables with either water-based or vinegar-based brine, many older recipes combine fermentation with vinegar preservation.

Eaton has a simple recipe for pickled cucumbers that involves cutting them into thick slices, salting them, leaving them to stand for twenty-four hours and then covering them with boiling vinegar. They sit "in a warm place for a time" before adding peppers and ginger. The pickles are ready in just a few days. Eaton also has an old recipe called "German Method of Keeping Cucumbers for Winter." Again, it starts with slicing and salting cucumbers. But after letting them stand for twenty-four hours these pickles are layered in a jar or crock,

Cutting up vegetables for pickles at Ross Farm Museum.

with alternating layers of fruit and salt between them. "Take out as many as needed for use at any one time, wash well in cold water and dress with vinegar, salt and pepper to taste."

Nellie Lyle Pattinson uses a similar technique for preserving onions in her classic 1923 *Canadian Cook Book*. The recipe produces onions ideal for the classic ploughman's lunch. You peel small onions, mix them with salt, then cover them with boiling water and leave them overnight. The next day, drain and dry the onions and pack them into a crock with vinegar and spices, adding a bit of sugar every day for about two weeks. (I'm not sure why boiling water. I assume the purpose is to kill unwanted bacteria, but the lactic acid fermentation would take care of that anyway.)

As tastes change, so, too, do preservation techniques. Some older recipes used a lot of salt. Most contemporary recipes call for using a 2 per cent salt concentration. In other words, if you are preserving a kilogram (or 1,000 grams) of vegetables, use twenty grams of salt. Many older recipes go much heavier on the salt. The advantage is that vegetables can be preserved longer and retain more crunch this way. The disadvantage is they need to be soaked — or at least rinsed — before eating to make them palatable.

At its simplest, the process of fermenting vegetables works like this: Choose the vegetables you want to preserve, mix up a simple brine of salt and water, submerge the vegetables in brine and leave them to ferment.

When we ferment, we don't just let bacteria take over and alter our food. Instead, we control the environment and create optimal circumstances for the bacteria we want to promote — in this case *Lactobacilli*.

The salt in the brine helps keep unwanted bacteria — those that can cause the veggies to rot — at bay as the *Lactobacilli* develop. Once they start multiplying, the *Lactobacilli* become quite exuberant. As they reproduce, the brine will bubble and probably overflow your jar (so keep it on a plate or tray for the first week or so). They also start to dramatically lower the pH of the vegetables and brine, which has a two-fold effect: putrefying bacteria can't survive in a more acidic environment, and the acidity contributes to vegetable preservation. That acidity is also the reason people tasting ferments like kosher pickles may think they have had vinegar added to them. There is no one moment at which fermented vegetables are ready to eat. It's up to you to decide when you like their flavour and texture. At that point, refrigerate them. The drop in temperature will slow down bacterial activity to a near-stop, so your vegetables will not ferment any more. Even though, unrefrigerated ferments may be safe to eat for months, for the most part, their texture will likely deteriorate. It's best to refrigerate them when they are ready.

On a brisk spring day, I sit in a group of about a dozen people in a re-purposed school gym — now part of a centre for social innovation — as Laura Rutherford explains this process. We are at the Island Food Network's Up!Skilling Food Festival, a day-long event held in Sydney, where participants learn all kinds of food skills, including several involving fermentation: breadbaking, cheesemaking, kombucha brewing and making fermented vegetables. Laura is teaching one of the first sessions of the day.

After spending twenty-five years in Toronto, where her jobs included working as a bartender in an after-hours jazz club, Laura left the West End of Toronto with her teenage daughter and moved to a rural property she calls Alchemy Acres, near Baddeck, in central Cape Breton — where she plans to farm, preserve and hold house concerts.

"My goal is for people to feel comfortable experimenting and recognizing that fermenting vegetables is something they can do, because often they are scared and think it's unsafe," Laura says.

As she packs carrots into a jar, she explains, "What's going to happen is when the bacteria start having a party in there, there's going to be some expansion. Just check every couple of days to see what's going on in there. Once the party's settled down a little bit, if the liquid has gone down below the veg, get your brine and top it up . . . When the party's over, I usually use a really clean cloth and wipe around the edge of the jar. Close it up tight now, because you're done. And put it somewhere cool."

One of the things I find interesting about vegetable ferments is how we can apply this simple technique to produce a pretty wide range of flavours by altering just a few variables. What veggies do you choose? How long do you leave them to ferment? How salty do you want to make your brine? What spices will you add?

And all of this is possible without any special equipment. "I love the idea that I can do this all by hand. You don't need to use any power. Slow food and low-tech — that excites me," Laura says.

Over time, you develop your own favourite tips and techniques. I went through a few years of making garlic dill pickles that were just okay — too salty, not salty enough, a bit yeasty — until I hit on a recipe that produces delicious dills every time. (Try it yourself — the recipe is on page 64.)

Laura has her own signature techniques. She likes to put a whole or half onion in every jar of vegetable ferments and adds a spoonful of rejuvelac to each jar to kick-start the fermentation. Rejuvelac is a lightly fermented cabbage concoction: Laura blends two cups cabbage with two and a half cups water in a food processor until it reaches the consistency of coleslaw, then leaves the mixture to ferment in a jar for forty-eight hours before adding some of the liquid to her jars of veggies.

At the workshop, Laura finishes layering onions and carrots in a jar, adds some garlic, then pushes down with a blender tamper to make sure the vegetables stay below the brine, and to force any air bubbles up out of the jar. Now it's time to ferment — and then enjoy the veggies. And once they're all gone? "We fight over the garlic," Laura says, "and my daughter likes to drink the pickle juice at the bottom of the jar. She usually drinks it with a shot glass. Apparently, I need to make more pickles."

As Nova Scotians have rediscovered traditional fermented vegetables, we have also started expanding our palates and enjoying other traditional vegetable ferments from around the world. When engineer Zhila Russell moved to Canada and couldn't find the traditional Persian pickles she craved — known as torshee — she started a company making them in Bedford. And in a province where sauerkraut has been popular for centuries, the traditional Salvadoran equivalent, curtido, is showing up at market stands. Made with ingredients including cabbage, carrots, onion, garlic, hot chilies and sometimes cilantro, curtido is a refreshing condiment or slaw. It is a classic accompaniment to Salvadoran pupusas, but is also one of those wonderful, flexible side dishes you can eat with just about anything.

But the import that has caught on most dramatically is kimchi, a typically cabbage-based Korean pickle.

The first time my family tasted kimchi it was in a decidedly non-traditional dish. We were in Sackville, New Brunswick, for the annual Sappyfest music festival, and one of the vendors was the Food Wolf, a food truck from Halifax known for its odd fusions of flavours. The cheapest item on the menu, and hence the one we ate most often, was the K-Dog: a hot dog dressed with Sriracha mayonnaise and topped with kimchi.

The whole family was sold, right from the first bite. The kimchi was spicy without being overwhelming, packed with complex flavours alongside the heat and loaded with umami — a satisfying, savoury taste often associated with rich foods like broths, soy sauce, cured pork, shiitake mushrooms and some cheeses.

After that, we started to eat kimchi at breakfast with brown rice and eggs, at lunch on homemade K-Dogs or in tuna or grilled-cheese sandwiches and at supper with stir-fried veggies, miso soups or Thai-style fried rice.

I showed a neighbour how to make it, and soon she was serving up penne with kimchi for her family and putting it on pizza too.

Trying to explain its appeal, Lim JaeHae of Andong University in South Korea writes, "Kimchi is an example of harmony between salty, spicy, sour, and sweet tastes. It is harmonious as well in terms of ingredients and color." Waxing philosophical, he also argues that it embodies values including complementariness, diversity, independence and harmony among ingredients.

I knew kimchi had truly arrived when I went to a local professional wrestling show, and saw the burly, bearded guy sitting beside me pull a Mason jar full of kimchi out of his backpack and hand it to a friend. Later, during breaks in the faux-violence of body slams and headlocks the two of us swapped favourite kimchi recipes and ingredients. I told him about fruit kimchi (see recipe on page 79), and he introduced me to Korean food writer and YouTuber Maangchi and the "emergency kimchi" she made while on holiday in Mexico.

Why do people get so passionate about kimchi? And how has it gone from being an obscure Korean condiment to an ubiquitous one, even in Nova Scotia?

Kimchi is like sauerkraut on steroids. It may be an acquired taste, but once you have acquired it, it's hard to imagine living without it. Koreans make many different types of kimchi, depending on the seasons and other factors (see recipes for two different types on pages 73 and 76). In North America, the best-known kimchi is made with shredded cabbage (usually nappa, but sometimes regular green cabbage) and a mix of other vegetables, including radishes and carrots. It is flavoured with a paste of onions, garlic, ginger and dried hot peppers or pepper flakes. Mix it all up with salt, leave to ferment for a few days, weeks or months and then enjoy.

I have spoken with many Nova Scotians who were first introduced to kimchi by international students from Korea: a clear benefit of internationalizing the province's student population! It's not surprising that kimchi would provide the taste of home for Koreans. We're talking about a country whose electronics industry survived a financial crisis in the late

Kimchi ingredients before adding dried chilies.

1990s solely because of the strong sales of kimchi fridges — small appliances specially designed for fermenting and preserving the national condiment.

You know how they say it can take decades to become an overnight sensation? That applies to kimchi too.

Of course it's wonderful and delicious, but it didn't become popular on its own. Its success is the result of a long-running campaign by South Korea to promote its culinary traditions as one of the world's top five cuisines. Koreans supplied kimchi to Olympic athletes as far back as 1984 and made it an official food of the Seoul games in 1988. At the 2008 Korea Food Expo, they launched a campaign called "Global Promotion of Korean Cuisine." One of the ways the campaign promoted kimchi was through somewhat dubious-sounding health claims, saying it promoted weight loss as well as increased sperm counts for men.

I find making kimchi incredibly satisfying. I think it's the combination of simple ingredients, most or all of which can be grown or harvested locally, along with the mix of salty, sweet, hot and sour flavours. And kimchi is so flexible. You can use it the traditional way — as an accompaniment to Korean food — or with hot dogs or on pizza. It's also easy to make (I

Kimchi, before being bottled.

recently did up a batch with a thirteen-year-old who had never made it before; she texted me updates on its progress as it fermented), stores well for months and is easily adaptable to local circumstances. Don't have nappa cabbage? Use green cabbage. Can't find daikon or other spicy radishes? Use carrots or other veggies instead, and increase the hot peppers. Don't have access to Korean dried chilies? Local ones will do just fine, and if you really want that classic red colour, grate a little beet into it.

Some Koreans would say this kind of adaptation is completely in keeping with the spirit of kimchi. In the book *The Humanistic Understanding of Kimchi,* Lim JaeHae argues that to become truly global, kimchi must adapt to local foods and traditions. "When kimchi goes to Japan, it needs to become Japanese kimchi, to accompany Japanese sushi. If it went to China, it needs to be Chinese kimchi that is harmonious with Chinese dumpling. In America it should make a happy combination with a hamburger [note: it does!] . . . The globalization of kimchi should be based on the principles of balance and independence and diversity. Monopolistic globalization that is blindly pushing traditional Korean kimchi is not different from the imperialistic globalization of Coca-Cola . . . Multiple small-quantity productions and sharing the diversity of Korean kimchi culture with the people of the world will be the true globalization of kimchi."

And that brings us to people like Zoe Beale.

Zoe is a fixture at local markets, selling jars of her homemade kimchi and other products, under the name Zoe's Ferments. And even though she is in the kimchi business, she is happy to share her recipe (ingredients: green cabbage, radish, carrot, ginger, garlic, chili and salt) and teach others how to make their own.

Over the course of a summer, Zoe spreads the gospel of kimchi through a series of workshops. On an early May evening, I go to one of them — sitting around bright purple tables at Dee Dee's Ice Cream in North End Halifax (the business is run by Zoe's mother, Ditta Kasdan) along with a pair of women here to learn the art of kimchi making. Neither of the women has done any fermenting before. "Not on purpose," one of them says.

Zoe learned to ferment from her Russian grandmother. Her first introduction to kimchi came from Korean students staying with her uncle. When she started her business, she was fermenting buckets of kimchi in her apartment — until someone complained to her landlord about the smell. Before kimchi became widely known in the West, Korean students abroad also faced this problem in university dorms, where North Americans objected to the aroma of kimchi. Now, she uses the properly equipped commercial kitchen here at Dee Dee's.

Over the next couple of hours, Zoe explains the principles of lactic-acid fermentation and we chop and pack kimchi ingredients into Mason jars — prudently wearing bright yellow rubber gloves, which slowly turn a dusky red colour from the chilies.

Zoe names the individual farms her ingredients come from and explains why she uses green cabbage instead of the more traditional nappa: "It's accessible year-round, it's more familiar to people, it's native to here — or at least commonly grown — and I like the crunch and heartiness."

We also taste some ferments Zoe has brought with her, including cabbage hearts left over from kimchi making, and kimchi at different stages of aging. The jar that's been fermented for two weeks is tasty but doesn't compare with a four-week-old batch. Its flavours have blended more fully, offering a much more satisfying taste.

Although fermenting vegetables is probably one of the safest activities you can carry out in a kitchen — far safer, for instance, than cooking hamburgers without a meat thermometer, or wiping your counter with a cloth that's been sitting on the edge of your sink — Zoe says fear of danger is one of the reasons people tell her they hesitate to make their own kimchi — that and the fact that many recipes don't bother with precise instructions or amounts. Read a canned dill pickle recipe, and you'll get exact amounts and processing times for the jars. Read a kimchi recipe, and the instructions will probably be a lot looser. "People can be intimidated," Zoe says. "It's not an exact science. You play around with different temperatures and different amounts of salt, and that can make a huge difference . . . But there is very little that can go really wrong."

Even though I make my own and usually have several jars on hand, I still enjoy buying kimchi made by others. Each fermenter brings their own signature style. Some use fish sauce, some go heavier on the spice, some add seaweed. One of Zoe's signatures is the large chunks of carrot she adds in with the shredded cabbage. If the women at her workshop stick with it, they may develop their own styles too. At the end of the evening, they both seem much more confident about their ability to do this at home. One of them says she has a book on fermentation but has never read it. "I feel comfortable doing this now," she says. "I'm going to try it."

Among people I've talked to, the main impediment to trying home fermentation of vegetables is fear of botulism. I don't hear the same fear when it comes to other ferments, but that may be because it's pretty obvious if your yogurt has gone bad or your bread is moldy. The danger with botulism is that it is deadly, and you can't tell if it is present since it is odourless, tasteless and impossible to see.

But the good news is that fermenting vegetables presents no risk of botulism.

Three jars of ferments made by Zoe Beale.

Fear of what's going on in that brine and whether or not it can do us harm is natural enough. We hear a lot of emphasis on food safety — which, don't get me wrong, is extremely important. But many people confuse fermenting with boiling-water-bath canning, despite the processes being completely different.

In canning, we heat vegetables in an acidic environment to a temperature that will kill botulism spores. Then, a tight seal on the jar prevents any putrefaction. In fermentation, we encourage the presence of specific bacteria to acidify and preserve food without heating.

Canning does have some advantages. For one thing, it can preserve food for a long time — but at a cost. The live cultures that preserve fermented vegetables are absent, killed by the acidity and high temperature. I have a wonderful Mennonite recipe for making dill pickles. Once they have been processed, the jars can sit on my basement shelf for a year or more, and when I open them up the pickles remain tasty and crispy. My fermented kosher pickles don't last as long (typically we finish them within four or five months), but they remain salty, crunchy, tasty and filled with friendly bacteria. And once they are gone, there are other ferments — beets, carrots, sauerkraut — that hold up well through the rest of the winter months. And unlike meat preserved in brine (which was sometimes known as "salt junk"), fermented vegetables are generally delicious.

Canning can be dangerous if it's not done properly. As any decent cookbook or guide will tell you, avoid rusty or dented lids, process jars in boiling water for the amount of time listed in the recipe, make sure you use vinegar of the proper strength in your pickles and ensure your lids are properly sealed. I was on the verge of making mustard pickles using homemade vinegar a few years ago, when I realized I had no way of measuring its level of acidity (and I wasn't about to rush out and buy pH testing strips while the water was heating in the canning pot). You can't fool around when you are canning: it is the most common cause of botulism outbreaks in the United States. Nearly a third of the 145 recorded outbreaks from homemade foods are linked to home-canned vegetables. By contrast, the US Centers for Disease Control (CDC) points to only two sources of botulism linked to fermentation. The first comes from Indigenous Alaskans fermenting meat, fish and eggs. Traditionally, these are aged in grass-lined holes in the ground. Botulism can make an appearance when they are instead fermented in glass or plastic jars, which don't allow air to circulate. The only vegetable-based case of botulism that the CDC lists comes from 2012 in New York City, where one person was confirmed to have gotten sick after eating home-fermented tofu. The store that sold the tofu failed to practise basic food safety — storing it in water that was unrefrigerated and uncovered. The patient got sick after fermenting the tofu and eating it raw.

So don't be scared to try fermenting your own veggies. It's not dangerous.

The process can go wrong, of course, but it should be obvious if something is off. A bit of surface mold on top of your brine? Skim it off. If your vegetables are submerged in brine they will be fine. Foul smell, discolouration or brightly coloured molds? Throw it out. Over years of fermentation, I have had the occasional batch go sideways, but that's usually because I've neglected it — for example, leaving kimchi to ferment without checking every day or two to ensure that all of it is submerged in brine. The terrifying thing about botulism is that you can't see, smell or taste the toxins, so you have no sensory feedback to let you know the foods you're eating could be dangerous. That's not the case with fermented vegetables. If they've gone bad, you'll know it. And, as the saying goes, when in doubt, throw it out. You still need to practise common-sense food safety, of course: use clean jars, wash your hands and make sure your veggies are not contaminated.

And if you don't want to take my word for it, here is what *Food Safety News* — hardly a bunch of radical fermenters — has to say about the safety of making and eating fermented vegetables:

> *For those who have apprehensions about food safety, [US Department of Agriculture Microbiologist Fred] Breidt said that fermented vegetables can be safer than raw vegetables, thanks to the ability of lactic acid, which forms during fermentation, to hunt down and kill any harmful bacteria that might be present. 'It's almost bulletproof,' he said, referring to fermentation of vegetables . . . Humans probably adopted fermentation about 12,000 years ago — at the dawn of civilization — and Breidt said the technology rapidly spread from region to region. 'We still do it the same way today,' he said. 'Why? Because it works. It's hard to mess it up. Things can go wrong, but it's rare.'*

Here are some recipes for fermented veggies (and one with fruit) to get you started. Before you try them though, one quick word about water. Chlorine kills bacteria. That's why municipalities put it in their water. But we don't want to kill our friendly lactic acid bacteria when we are fermenting. So if the only water you have available is chlorinated, let it sit out overnight before using it to make brine, or run it through a Brita or similar filter to remove the chlorine. I have never used distilled water myself, but you certainly can use it if you like.

Brined Garlic Scapes

Garlic scapes are delightful. The top part of the garlic plant, the scapes are cut off mid-summer to encourage growth of the garlic bulb.

Scapes used to be a rarity at markets, but now I see heaps of them every summer, as people realize they are delicious in their own right.

Garlic scapes are only around for a couple of weeks, so if you want to enjoy them the rest of the year, you'll have to preserve them. As I write this it's the dead of winter, and I have a jar of garlic scapes in the fridge that I fermented in July. I recently took some to a party as an antipasto and they were a hit.

Garlic scapes can be bulky, so this recipe is designed for a one-gallon jar. You can scale it up or down if you like. The recipe also calls for optional vine leaves. I use these for just about any vegetables I ferment because they release tannins that help keep the veggies crunchy. If you have a friend with a vine, ask for a few leaves. They are also readily available for purchase at many supermarkets and at Mediterranean and Middle Eastern specialty shops.

Materials

- 1-gallon glass jar (If you can't find a large jar, use 4 1-quart/L Mason jars or a bucket as described in Chapter 10)
- Large bowl
- Large spoon for stirring

Ingredients

- 3/4 lb (340 g) garlic scapes
- 1 to 2 vine leaves (optional, to help keep the scapes crunchy)
- 1 tbsp (15 mL) whole black peppercorns OR 2 double-smoked dried peppers or other chilies

Brine

- 7 1/2 tbsp (115 mL) salt
- 6 cups (1.5 L) of water

Method

If you are trimming your own garlic scapes, cut off the blossom end (that's the thin end with the flower) and cut off the tough woody part at the other end of the scape. Be ruthless. In the past, I've trimmed too conservatively in order to eat more of the scapes, but the truth is the chewy fibrous bits are not going to get any better by sitting in brine. Just compost them. Keep only the most tender parts of the garlic scapes.

In a large bowl, mix the salt into the water and stir to dissolve fully. This is slightly saltier than your standard brine, but I find it works better for garlic scapes. Stirring vigorously should dissolve the salt. If you like, you could heat the water slightly to dissolve the salt more easily, but let the brine cool completely before proceeding.

Add vine leaf (or leaves) and peppercorns or chilies to your jar(s) or bucket.

Pack in the garlic scapes.

Pour the brine over the garlic scapes. If you don't have enough to submerge them, mix up a bit more, with a ratio of 1 tbsp (15 mL) salt to 1 cup (250 mL) of water.

Weigh them down and cover the container. If you are using jars, seal with a plastic lid or use a cloth or plastic wrap underneath a metal lid. (Direct contact between the brine and the metal lid may cause the metal to rust.) If you are using a bucket, cover with a tea-towel or tight-weaved cloth held on with an elastic band to prevent dirt or flies from contaminating the contents.

Leave sitting at room temperature for the fermentation process to take place. I like to leave them on the kitchen counter, out of direct sunlight, or on a shelf in the basement if the temperature is not cool. After a week, taste every couple of days. Refrigerate when they reach the flavour and texture you like.

Yield: One gallon (4 quart-sized / 1 L jars)

(Almost) Instant Gratification Dill Pickles

I'm writing this the day after my wife Sara and I finished the last of a batch of these half-sour pickles. "These are the best fermented pickles you've made so far," she said.

I hope you'll be as enthusiastic.

Kosher pickles are brined, or fermented, instead of canned in vinegar. Full-on kosher dills are made in a saltier brine. That allows them to stay crunchy for a long time, and provides that salty, sour, flavourful kick that we love.

This recipe uses a lighter brine. Less salt means the pickles will ferment faster, so you can enjoy them in the space of a few days or a week. Who wants to wait? The downside is they will not keep as long. So you'll have to gobble them all up with friends within a few days of making them. Or store them in the fridge, where they will keep for several months.

I like a little spice to my pickles, so I have included hot peppers, but you could substitute whole black peppercorns or omit them altogether. Lately, I've fallen in love with dried, double-smoked chilies. If you can get these, they provide a bit of a satisfying, smoky flavour.

This recipe makes a 1-quart jar of pickles — just the right amount to eat quickly, or to put in the fridge without taking up too much space. If you want to make a larger amount, just scale up the recipe accordingly.

Materials

- Large bowl
- 1-quart (1 L) Mason Jar

Ingredients

- 1 lb (450 g) of small pickling cucumbers or larger cukes cut into spears
- 1 vine leaf (to help keep pickles crispy)
- 2 large or 3 to 4 small cloves of garlic
- 2 smoked chili peppers, or other hot peppers of your choice
- 1 sprig fresh flowering dill (substitute dry dill or a few stems fresh non-flowering dill if flowering is not available)

Brine

- 1 tbsp (15 mL) salt and 2 cups (1/2 L) of water

Garlic scapes packed into a jar.

Method

Use cucumbers that are as fresh as possible. Carefully wash and scrub them to remove any dirt. If you come across any that are bruised or scored, discard them.

Cut off the blossom end of the cucumber. That's the end that was attached to the plant. It's important to remove the blossom end because it contains an enzyme that can cause the cucumber to soften or rot. Place the cucumbers in a bowl.

Stir the salt into the water, mixing well so that it all dissolves. Set this brine aside.

Wash a 1-quart Mason jar, and place the vine leaf, garlic, hot peppers (if using) and dill in the jar.

Add the cucumbers, packing in as many as possible. I like to save a couple of large ones for last and put them at the top, wedged against the shoulders of the jar. This prevents the cukes from floating up in the brine, keeping them completely submerged, which is where we want them.

Pour the brine over the cucumbers, making sure they are fully covered. None of the cucumbers should be exposed. If any are exposed, either pack them in more tightly or remove them from the jar.

Seal with a plastic lid or use a cloth or plastic wrap underneath a metal lid. (Direct contact between the brine and the lid may cause the metal to rust.)

Leave on the counter for three to five days, checking the pickles every day to make sure the cucumbers remain submerged, and skimming off any scum that may form on the surface. Don't worry, it's harmless.

Once the pickles have achieved the taste you like, refrigerate them to prevent spoilage.

If your brine becomes cloudy, your pickles are still fine to eat. The cloudiness comes from yeasts. If you like, dump out the brine in the jar, mix up a fresh batch and pour that over the pickles before continuing to store.

Yield: 1 quart (1 L)

Spicy Fermented Nettles

This recipe may be an acquired taste. But if you acquire it, I think you will love it.

Many people see nettles as a weed — and sure, you can try to eradicate them. But a more fun (and tasty) solution is to eat them. Over the last few years, people have been re-discovering them, and using them in preparations including nettle pesto and steamed nettle greens.

Stinging nettles grow wild in some parts of Nova Scotia, and now some Nova Scotia farms are growing them. We have a patch of nettles growing at the bottom of our front yard, and I get out there and harvest them a couple of times a year. I dry most of them for tea, but I also enjoy making these as a condiment to accompany dishes like fish curry or Thai fried rice.

Before we get to the recipe though, a few words of caution on how to handle nettles.

These greens are called "stinging nettles" for a reason. If you touch their leaves, you will feel a distinct sharp sting that may persist as a tingly or slightly itchy sensation. I confess that I don't mind this feeling. After the first couple of stings, I get used to it, and even start to slightly enjoy it. Then again, I had a grandmother who lived in the mountains of Greece and would strike her back with nettles, because she said it got her circulation going and helped with her arthritis.

If you want to avoid being stung, wear gloves and long sleeves while handling nettles.

And don't worry about stinging your tongue. Cooking or fermenting the plants will get rid of the sting, and you'll be left with tasty greens.

Materials

- Large bowl
- Medium bowl or large measuring cup for brine
- 1 pint (500 mL) Mason Jar
- Weight or cabbage leaf to cover

Ingredients

Brine

- 1/4 cup (60 mL) salt and 1 qt (1 L) water

Veggies

- 8 oz (250 g) fresh nettle (thick stalks removed)
- 3 to 4 large cloves of garlic
- 1 to 2 in (2.5 to 5 cm) ginger
- 1 habanero pepper, or other hot pepper of your choice, or chili flakes

Optional ingredients

- A few splashes of fish sauce (look for a kind without potassium sorbate, because it is a preservative that can inhibit the bacterial growth we want)

Method

Add the salt to the water and stir well to dissolve. Set brine aside.

Wash the nettle, and if it has any thick stalks remove and discard them.

Put the nettle in the brine and submerge it. Use a plate to cover it and a weight to press it down so the nettle remains underwater (a glass measuring cup filled with water makes a good weight). Leave overnight or for up to twenty-four hours.

Drain the nettle in a colander, but don't squeeze out any excess water. (If you like, at this point you can snack on a couple of the crunchy stalks too.)

Once the nettle has drained, taste a leaf. It should be quite salty, with a good bite, but still pleasant to taste. If it seems too salty, soak it in plain water for a few minutes. If it is not salty enough, sprinkle a bit more salt directly onto the nettle.

Put your pile of wet nettle on a cutting board and slice it crosswise, then place it in a bowl.

Crush or dice the garlic, grate the ginger and finely dice the hot peppers. (Wear gloves while dicing the peppers.) Adjust the amounts of each of these ingredients to your tastes. As written, the recipe should be deliciously spicy and garlicky, but not overwhelmingly so.

Add the spices to the nettle and mix thoroughly in the bowl. Mash or squeeze the nettle well. This may cause some dark green liquid to come out of the nettle-spice mixture.

Squish the nettle and spice mixture into a 1-pint Mason jar, preferably one with a standard, narrow neck. As you squeeze the nettle down, some liquid will come out of it. The nettle should be completely covered by the liquid. If it's not, add a bit of the juice from the bowl.

Use a fermentation weight or a cabbage leaf mushed under the shoulders of the jar to keep your nettle submerged in brine. (See Chapter 10 for information on fermentation weights.)

Cover the jar with a standard or plastic Mason jar lid. If you use a metal lid, place plastic wrap or parchment paper under the ring so the salty brine does not corrode the metal.

Now the magic happens. Leave the jar in a warmish place, or at room temperature. Over the next week or two, the nettles will start to ferment. You may see bubbles forming, and the liquid could spill out, so it's a good idea to place the jar on a dish.

Open the lid of the jar every day to release pressure and to check that the nettles are submerged. If any have risen to the surface, push it down using clean fingers.

You are unlikely to see any whitish surface mold, but if you do, skim it off. The submerged contents will still be good to eat.

After a week or so, taste the nettle. The flavours should be deepening and becoming more complex. When the nettle has reached a flavour you like, put it in the fridge. This will stop the fermentation.

Serve as a condiment with dishes such as fried rice, tofu scramble, stir fries or miso soup.

Yield: 1 pint (500 mL)

One-Jar Kimchi

I love making kimchi. It seems like one of the most satisfying ferments. This is a great starter recipe. It's easy and it only makes one jar. I have used this recipe to introduce friends, relatives and neighbours to kimchi for years — and most recently made it with a friend's thirteen-year-old daughter, who was very enthusiastic about the whole process.

Materials

- Large bowl for cabbage mixture
- Small-to-medium bowl for spice paste
- Bowl/measuring cup for brine
- 1-quart (1 L) Mason Jar
- Weight or cabbage leaf to cover
- Large spoon or spatula for stirring

Ingredients

Brine

- 2 tbsp (30 mL) of fine (not coarse) sea salt and 2 cups (1/2 L) of water

Veggies

- 16 oz (450 g) nappa cabbage
- 1 small-to-medium carrot (optional)
- 4 oz (125 g) spicy radish (or not spicy, if you prefer)
- 1 tbsp (15 mL) chopped sliced dried seaweed of your choice (optional)

Spice paste

- 1 medium onion, finely chopped or grated
- 2 oz (50 g) ginger, grated
- 3 cloves garlic (or more, to taste)
- 2 tbsp (30 mL) fish sauce*
- Hot peppers to taste (either crush your own dried peppers or use 1 to 2 tbsp (15 to 30 mL) of dried Korean chilis for kimchi; you can find crushed dried Korean chilis at specialty shops)

* Optional, but if you use it — and I recommend you do, unless

you want a vegan kimchi — go for a kind that does not have preservatives, because they can hinder the fermentation.

Method

Brine

Add salt to the water and stir until dissolved. Set this brine aside.

Veggies

Slice the cabbage thinly. Grate the carrots and slice or grate the radish. (Some people like a variety of shapes for the vegetables.)

Put the vegetables, including the seaweed, in a large bowl.

Pour the brine over the vegetables. If it doesn't cover them, add more brine.

Let the vegetables sit all day or overnight.

Drain the vegetables, reserving 1/2 cup (125 mL) of the brine.

Taste the vegetables. They should have a pleasantly salty taste with a bit of bite. If they are not salty enough, add more salt. If they are too salty, cover them with water, let sit for a bit and then drain. Kimchi maker Zoe Beale says, "It should taste like a really salty salad — like if you were at a pot luck and tasted it, you might think, 'This salad is really salty, but I would still eat it.'"

Spice paste

Mix chopped onions, grated ginger, finely chopped garlic, fish sauce (if using) and peppers in a bowl. Stir well. (You can use a spoon or spatula to do this if you don't want to cover your hands in hot chilies.)

Add the spice paste to the chopped vegetables. Mix thoroughly.

Now use your hands to squeeze and massage the contents of the bowl. Get right in there, squeeze, twist and wring them out. You want to soften the vegetables and release their juices.

Pack tightly into a clean quart-size Mason jar or other similar container. As you press the kimchi down into the jar, it should release more juice. Fill the jar most of the way to the top. If the vegetables on top are not covered in liquid, add the reserved brine.

If you have extra kimchi, pack it into a second jar.

Seal with a plastic Mason jar lid. If you don't have a plastic lid, cover with a tea towel (that you don't mind getting wet and pungent) or a paper towel, and attach with an elastic.

Leave to ferment for 1 to 4 weeks, or longer.

If your jar has a lid on it, untwist it once a day to release pressure, especially in the first week to ten days. It may bubble over anyway, so keep it on a tray with some cloth or newspaper underneath it. Make sure the veggies are submerged. If they are above the level of the brine, use clean fingers to push them down. Add more brine if necessary. If you see some discolouration at the surface, remove it. The submerged kimchi will be fine.

The taste will develop over time, and once it reaches a point you like, refrigerate it. I have successfully kept kimchi for up to a year, and there is no reason it can't keep longer.

Yield: 1 quart (1 L)

Kimchi for a Crowd

If you're like me and you develop a kimchi addiction, you may want to make larger amounts than the one-jar recipe.

The one-jar kimchi recipe (see page 73) goes into more detail on techniques, so I encourage you to read it before making this recipe.

Materials

- Very large bowl for cabbage mixture
- Large bowl for brine
- Medium bowl for spice paste
- Mandoline (optional)
- Large (gallon-sized) jar or bucket for fermentation
- Weight to cover
- Large spoon or spatula for stirring
- 5 to 6 1-quart (1 L) Mason jars

Ingredients

Brine

- 20 tbsp (300 mL) salt and 20 cups (5 L) of water

Veggies

- 5 lb (2.25 kg) nappa cabbage (about 2 large or 3 medium cabbages)
- 2.5 lbs (1.15 kg) radishes (I like to use a mix of spicy and less spicy varieties)
- 1 large leek
- 1/2 cup (125 mL) dried seaweed (optional, use dulse if you want to keep things really local)

Spice paste

- 5 large onions (about 5 oz or 150 g)
- 5 oz (200 g) ginger
- 12 medium-to-large garlic cloves
- 4 oz (100 g) dried Korean chilies
- 1/4 cup (65 mL) fish sauce (use a brand that does not contain preservatives, because they can inhibit the growth of bacteria). Omit for a vegan version

Method

Brine

Dissolve the salt in water to make the brine. I have a large measuring cup and do 4 cups of water at a time, and I use a very large metal bowl. Set the brine aside.

Veggies

Slice the cabbage. I like to slice it in half lengthwise, then slice thinly across. You may find it helpful to use a mandoline.

Grate or slice the radishes.

Chop the leek.

Add all the vegetables to a large bowl, mix and, if using, sprinkle the seaweed over them.

Cover the vegetables with brine and let stand several hours or overnight.

Spice paste

Slice the onion, grate the ginger and chop the garlic.

Mix and stir with a wooden spoon or a spatula.

Stir in the chilies and fish sauce (if using).

Drain the brine off the vegetables. Taste them. They should be pleasantly salty. If you would like them saltier, sprinkle a bit more salt on.

Add the spice mix to the bowl, then vigorously massage and squeeze the kimchi for several minutes to break down the vegetables and release liquid.

Pack into one or more 1-gallon jars or buckets.

Ensure the kimchi is covered with brine (add more if necessary), cover and leave to ferment 5 to 7 days. The fermentation can be quite vigorous, causing liquid to spill over the top, so place your bucket(s) or jars on newspaper or a cloth.

Check every day to ensure the veggies are submerged in brine (after a few days they will have a tendency to rise).

Once the kimchi has reached the flavour you want (this could take longer than a week, depending on your taste) pack into Mason jars. The number of jars will depend on what size you use. Yield varies, but I generally find this recipe fills about 5 quart-sized Mason jars. Refrigerate or place in a cool room. The kimchi will last for at least six months. I have kept some large batches for up to a year.

Yield: Approximately 5 quarts (5 L)

Spicy Fall Fruit Kimchi

Late summer and early fall in Nova Scotia bring an abundance of fresh fruit. While jams and preserves are a great way to enjoy fruit through the fall and winter, this kimchi is a savoury alternative with bite.

As with most of the recipes in this chapter, treat the proportions as a guideline. You may want it more or less spicy and garlicky. You may love ginger or hate it. Adjust accordingly.

Gravenstein apples and Clapp pears provide a nice tartness and crunch, which contrasts beautifully with the softer and sweeter Burbank plums.

I've used piri-piri peppers, which are very small, but pack a big punch. On the Scoville scale (which measures the heat of chili peppers) they come in at about the same heat concentration as bird's eye chilies or Scotch bonnet peppers. I like piri-piri peppers for their pleasant citrusy flavour. You could substitute other dried or freshly grown local hot peppers instead if you prefer.

Because you are fermenting the fruit, you don't need to buy top-quality produce. Bruised apples or mushy plums are fine.

Materials

- Medium-to-large bowl
- Mortar and pestle or spice grinder (can use a coffee grinder)
- 1-quart (1 L) Mason jar

Ingredients

- 1 lb (450 g) plums
- 1 large or 1 1/2 small Gravenstein apples
- 1 tart pear
- 1 small onion
- 4 medium garlic cloves
- 2-in (5-cm) length of ginger
- 1 tbsp (15 mL) plus 1/2 tsp (2 1/2 mL) salt
- 1 1/2 tsp (7 1/2 mL) fish sauce (use a brand without preservatives; omit for a vegan version)
- 1 1/2 tsp (7 1/2 mL) fresh lemon juice
- 3 to 4 piri-piri peppers (or other hot peppers)

Method

Dice the plums into 1-in (2.5 cm) pieces.

Dice the apples and pear into 1/2-in (1.25 cm) pieces (because the fruit is harder it will hold its shape better at a smaller size).

Finely chop the onion and garlic. Peel and coarsely grate the ginger.

Put all the fruit and vegetables in a medium or large bowl. Add the salt, fish sauce and lemon juice.

You can toss this mixture with implements like salad forks, but your results will be better if you get right in there with your (clean!) hands. Stir and lightly squeeze the fruits and vegetables so they

Chopped fruit for fruit kimchi.

release their juice. Some of the plums will wind up getting mushy, and that's fine.

Crush the piri-piri peppers with a mortar and pestle or spice grinder. Stir them into the mix. If you choose to keep mixing with your hands after adding the peppers, make sure you wash them carefully afterward, and be careful to not touch your eyes or other sensitive body parts.

Pack the ingredients tightly into two 1-pint (500 mL) jars or one 1-quart (1 L) jar so the liquid rises until it has covered the fruit mixture. Place a weight in the jar so it covers the fruit and keeps it under the surface of the liquid. A fermentation weight (see Chapter 10) works best here. Run your finger or a piece of cloth or paper towel around the inside top of the jar to remove any pieces of fruit stuck to it.

Cover tightly with cheesecloth or lid and ferment 7 to 10 days or longer, until flavours are well blended. Check the kimchi every day and push it down with your fingers to avoid discolouration at the surface. If the kimchi does discolour, simply skim off the top layer and compost it. When the flavour has developed to a point where you like it, refrigerate the kimchi to stop the fermentation. This fruit kimchi does not last as long as vegetable kimchi. Enjoy within a month of making it.

Enjoy as a condiment with fish, stir-fried veggies or a tofu scramble. It's also dynamite on hot dogs!

Yield: 1 quart (1 L)

(Less Than a Peck of) Pickled Peppers

Can you say, "dead easy and delicious"? This is probably the simplest recipe in the book. These peppers work on quesadillas, in tuna salad, on burgers, in grilled cheese sandwiches — you'll find yourself coming up with more and more uses for them.

I like to use a mix of jalapenos and more fiery, long, thin peppers. But I've also made these with whatever my favourite market stand is carrying, or even with peppers marked down at the supermarket.

Hot peppers ready for brining.

Materials
- Medium bowl/measuring cup for brine
- 1 pint (500 mL jar)

Ingredients

Brine
- 1 tbsp (15 mL) plus 1/2 tsp (2.5 mL) salt
- 1 cup (250 mL) water

Veggies
- 1 vine leaf (available at Mediterranean and Middle Eastern specialty shops)
- Mixed hot peppers (if you don't like too much heat, use jalapenos)

Method

Dissolve the salt in the water, stirring well. Set this brine aside.

Place the vine leaf in the bottom of a 1-pint (500 mL) jar.

Cut the tops off the hot peppers and slice the peppers into thick or thin rounds (depending on your taste)

Pack all the peppers in a jar.

Pour the brine over the vegetables. If you have too much, just use what you need to cover the vegetables.

Use a weight, piece of cabbage or something else to weigh down the veggies and keep them submerged. Cover the jar with a lid or cloth. Ferment at room temperature for 5 to 7 days or longer, if you like, then refrigerate when they have reached the desired taste. I tend to not like my peppers overly fermented, so I keep the fermentation period relatively short for these. The peppers are at their best for 3–4 months but will easily be good for up to a year or more.

Yield: 1 pint (500 mL) jar

3
Preserving Meat
Searching for a Cure

Pete McChesney keeps looking at his phone.

But he's not checking Facebook or Twitter, keeping up to date on sports scores, or obsessively playing a game. No, he's using an app to monitor the temperature and humidity in the meat curing chamber downstairs — one he built himself using mostly scraps he picked up for free.

Right now, it's showing a temperature of 17 and 8/10 degrees Celsius.

We walk down the stairs to Pete's basement and he opens the door of the curing chamber. It's a small, unheated room, the floor a concrete slab. An air conditioner kicks in if the temperature gets too high. Pete only cures meat during summer and early fall, when the slab retains enough heat to keep the room at its ideal minimum temperature of 15 degrees Celsius (the ideal maximum is 17). A dehumidifier in the room rumbles to life when the humidity hits 74 per cent. "If it's too humid you can get weird molds and stuff. And if it's too dry, the outside will dry too fast and form a hard shell

— and the meat will rot from the inside out," Pete explains.

In addition to his app, Pete monitors the temperature through a hard-wired digital temperature and humidity display he bought on eBay years ago. It's connected to sensors inside the curing chamber. Having two different systems ensures a fail-safe in case one of them malfunctions.

When you're curing meat, you've got to pay attention to temperature and humidity. Not only can they affect the taste and texture of your meat — they can be a matter of life and death.

Pete is a man who likes to talk about meat, a walking encyclopedia of cured flesh who can reel off fat percentages and specialized ingredients, tell you how long a prosciutto needs to hang, refer to arcane techniques like encasing aging muscle-meats in beeswax and casually refer to things like "the Tuscan fennel salami everyone knows." Listening to him, I find myself saying "That sounds fantastic!" a lot.

Pete grew up on a farm near Antigonish and now lives in Boutiliers Point, near the head of St. Margaret's Bay. To get to his house, you climb a steep road, then an even steeper driveway. Books on wine (his partner, Jenny Gammon, is a sommelier) and cured meats abound.

He is an exploration geologist by training who used to work in Quebec, Ontario, the Arctic, the American Southwest, part of South America and South Africa — in search of deposits of valuable minerals. His specialties? Platinum, copper and nickel.

While he was in South Africa, Pete fell in love with boerewors — a farmers' sausage he describes as "vinegared and coriander-heavy." But at age thirty, he got smashed up in a bad car crash in South Africa that left him unable to work for months. Back home in Nova Scotia, during his recovery, Pete found himself missing boerewors. With nowhere to buy it, he started making it himself. "It was a natural step to go from there to curing stuff," he says. Now, it's gone from activity to passion to near-obsession.

I ask him to give me a quick tour of what's hanging in the chamber.

He points to a whole eye of round, then reaches for a salami made with

Pete McChesney making sausages.

local Dragon's Breath Blue cheese. "Boy, this one is going to be stinky," he says with delight. "I made one of these earlier in the year and replaced all the fat with blue cheese, but it was too rich. This time I replaced half the fat with blue cheese — you can see the veins running through it." He squeezes the salami gently, moving his hand up and down the casing. "This one is getting pretty close. You could eat it right now, but I want to leave it to dry a bit more. It's a matter of personal preference."

Hanging next to it is an espresso salami — made with ground coffee and port. Then a Swiss-style bündnerfleisch with white wine. "It's supposed to have mountain herbs, but I couldn't find any information on what they are. I even contacted two Swiss butchers and they just said, 'It's mountain herbs!'" The bündnerfleisch is covered in mold from the penicillium family — similar to the micro-organisms in blue cheese.

ABOVE: Pete McChesney's award-winning espresso salami.
LEFT: His homemade curing chamber.

Then he's got two kinds of salami made with highland beef and, in the back of the room, what he calls his experiments, including a spreadable salami that's 85 per cent fat, flavoured with five-spice powder and Szechuan peppercorns. Sadly, not everything works out. Bake a bad loaf of bread and you may be able to salvage it. But if meat is not curing properly there is only one thing you can do with it. "This is Corsican liver salami, but it's an experiment that's just not working," Pete says. "I might have to toss it. It's been in here for months and it's just not doing anything. It's not drying right."

Pete is an amateur, but a talented one. He has done some charcuterie consulting for local businesses, and in early 2018 placed third overall in a New York–based North American charcuterie competition for his espresso salami. (He plans to enter his Dragon's Breath Blue salami in a future edition of the contest.) He is not allowed to sell his products though, because they are not made in an approved, inspected kitchen. So they mostly go to family and friends.

We head up to the kitchen, where Pete is going to put together some ginger salami. After a few minutes, he checks his phone. The temperature in the curing chamber — which had gone up from our body heat when we were in the room — is dropping again.

"How often do you check it?" I ask him.

"Uh, too often," he says. "Sometimes I just lie in bed and check it. It's got a 350-foot range. It's awesome. But too much data is not always a good thing."

In the days before widespread refrigeration, your options for storing meat were very limited. Chickens were easy. You could slaughter a chicken, pluck it, cook it and eat it the same day. But when it came to larger homestead or game animals — pigs, cows, deer, moose — the only way to not waste the meat was to find a way to preserve it, usually with smoke, salt or brine.

Dr. Ruth Holmes Whitehead, formerly of the Nova Scotia Museum, says that, traditionally, Mi'kmaw families would have smoked and dried meats, including sausages. Eels were a mainstay of the traditional diet. " They ate a lot of eel, which was easy to prepare, as opposed to butchering 1,000 pounds of moose meat and leaving it out to dry. You'd let the eels smoke from the brace poles in your wigwam," Holmes Whitehead says. "It's so easy to do. They ate raw meat, roasted meat, smoked dried meat, sausages with berries added in and lots of fat in intestinal casings, and they ate boiled stews — that sort of thing. They smoked the sausages, hanging them from — I guess you could call it the ceiling. The fire was always going."

Ramona Himmelman lives in a house on the west bank of the LaHave River. From her living room you can watch the ferry crossing twice per hour each way. She is used to looking out over the river. Her husband, Brady, was the ferry captain for over forty years. Ramona, who is nearly ninety when I visit her, grew up on one of the nearby LaHave Islands, in a home with no electricity. Her father was at one time the oldest resident in Lunenburg County and lived in the family home until he was a hundred. Ramona looks out at the old apple tree in her backyard and remembers how her family would put away lots of different kinds of food, including meat, which would be salted and eaten over the course of the winter. "They say you shouldn't have salt — shouldn't have this or that — and, I mean, Dad grew up on salt fish and salt meat. Everything was salted. We didn't have refrigeration when I was growing up."

I've read about storing meat in a bucket in the bottom of a well, where the icy water would keep it cool during the winter, and about keeping it in a heavily salted brine. Not the most appetizing, perhaps, but it was a way to not waste cuts that might be relatively inedible otherwise.

Barry Hiltz of the Ross Farm Museum remembers many of those traditional practices from his own childhood, including preserving meat in brine. He says, "Quite often what they would pickle would be an old cow or ox they had to slaughter. They would corn some of it to give it flavour." Barry says while you might get a good roast out of a bull, oxen are different. "An ox — he's probably ten or twelve years old, worked all his life, gristly. But they would pickle it and corn it and give some to their neighbours."

In his memoir, Lee Zinck of Blandford provides a vivid description of "pig-killing day" in his household growing up, and all the ways various parts of the animal were preserved — through pickling, drying and other techniques. Sausages need casings, made from the pig's intestines — so making them was one of the first tasks. Casings were scraped, cleaned with hot water and baking soda and then brined to preserve them.

The next day, he recalls, "was a busy one for my mother" — starting with making two kinds of sausages. The first included organs, head and other less palatable meats cooked for an hour before being turned into sausages combining meat, spices, summer savoury (a local favourite on the South Shore, and still widely grown on Big Tancook Island), onions, salt and pepper, mixed by hand and stuffed into casings stretched over a hollow ox horn. "When the casings were tightly filled, their ends were tied together and they again were put in a hot-water bath for a few minutes. The pig's puddings as they were called, had to be eaten within ten days, as no cold-storage facilities were available in those times."

As we've seen in earlier chapters, *Lactobacilli* — the star bacteria of many kinds of ferments — convert sugars to lactic acid, making foods more acidic, crowding out other bacteria and, through this fermentation process, keeping foods edible for longer.

Meat is not a source of sugar, but other products that can be added to sausages are (say, the onions and savoury in the recipe above). The hot-water bath kick-starts fermentation, with the actions of the *Lactobacilli* keeping the sausages from going bad quickly. But, unless you have carefully monitored conditions, there is a limit to how long these sausages will keep. (This is also why, not surprisingly, early studies of botulism focused on the consumption of sausages.)

Zinck's mother would prepare another set of sausages, these made from pork and/or beef with a different spice mix. They were either pickled or dried to preserve them.

And while mother made sausages, father cut the carcass up, and smoked ham and bacon. "Only a limited amount could be kept fresh due to lack of refrigeration. The rest of the animal was cut into small portions about three pounds in weight, placed in a watertight barrel and pickled with salt from Turks Island. When required, this cured pork was soaked in fresh water overnight and cooked with cabbage or sauerkraut. The amount of salted meat from a full-grown pig would supply a family for a good many months."

Recipe for pork pickled in brine, from Lunenburg County, 1809.

An 1809 recipe at the Nova Scotia Archives explains how to pickle pork in brine. It's a relatively simple process:

"Take an ounce & half of Salt Petre, rub that well in, then rub the pork with common Salt, put some Salt at the bottom of the Tub, or Pan, & fill all the Corners with Salt . . . In a few days after it is put into the Pickling-Tub, make some strong Brine, and when cold the next day, pour it on sufficient to cover it, the Pork must be put in as close as possible and covered entirely with the Brine."

The same page has a recipe for sausage flavoured with salt, pepper, onion, lemon thyme, sage and parsley.

If a large amount of pickled beef is more to your taste, the Archives have a nineteenth-century recipe for you too: "To 4 gallons of water add 1 1/2 lbs of brown sugar or molasses, 2 ounces of Saltpetre, 8 lbs of salt, put them into a pot and let them boil, carefully taking off the scum as it rises; when no more comes, take it off and let it stand till cold. It is a great improvement to add 1/2 an ounce of allspice, the same of black pepper, and 18 or 20 cloves. When your meat is cut up let it stand an hour in water . . . dry it & put it into the vessel it is to remain in and cover it quite over with pickle." The writer of the recipe (we know only that it was written between 1816 and 1886, but not by whom) extols its tenderness after three months in brine.

Fortunately, today we have far more options when it comes to enjoying dried and otherwise cured meats in Nova Scotia. The last decade has seen a new interest in these traditional foods. At the Nova Scotia Community College, culinary arts programs are investing in equipment and teaching dry-curing skills to a new generation of students. And it's not unusual to visit a farmers' market and find traditional German or French dried sausages in a variety of flavours.

Salting, curing, drying, brining: What role does fermentation play in all this?

Many sausages do include a discrete fermentation stage. After the meat and other ingredients are mixed together, they are left for up to a couple of days, allowing lactic acid bacteria to develop and start fermenting the food. This stage needs to be carefully managed to ensure you've got the right kinds of bacteria developing. Some sausage makers will wild-ferment, allowing the microbes present in the sausage to do their thing, while others may inject them with a starter culture to get them going, and to have more control over the process.

Then the sausages are hung to dry in a coolish but humid environment. You might think a drier environment would be better for, well, drying, but that turns out not to be true. If you dry sausages (I'm using the word here to include all kinds of stuffed, aged meats, like salamis) too fast, they can form a hard casing on the outside. When that happens, moisture can't escape, so instead of drying nicely at a slow, uniform rate, the sausage will stay moist on the inside — and the trapped moisture will make it rot from the inside out. Typically, a sausage is dried and ready to eat when it has lost 30 to 40 per cent of its mass, which is why it's important to weigh each one at the start of the process. Salamis are made with a mix of fat and meat. While the meat will get lighter through drying, that's much less true for fat. Pete McChesney's spreadable salamis are 80 per cent fat (instead of the typical 50 per cent or so). The high fat content means the sausage will never harden no matter how long it dries.

For other forms of meat preservation, the role of fermentation is much smaller. There is some microbial action involved in smoking, drying and salting, but it is not the key process in preserving or flavouring the meat. Meats that are hung up to dry also benefit from microbial action on their outside. Remember the penicillium colonies on the outside of Pete McChesney's bündnerfleisch? It plays a couple of different and important roles. Pete explains that these dry microbial colonies "impart flavour but also regulate the speed of dehydration."

I've seen photos of Frédéric Tandy, but I don't recognize him when I arrive at his shop, Ratinaud, in North End Halifax. It's before opening time, and I walk past the two men smoking and chatting in front of the shop, on my way to knock on the front door.

"I am Frédéric," he tells me, disposable coffee cup in one hand and cigarette in the other, before unlocking the door and leading me inside.

Although Nova Scotia has a long history of sausage making and meat curing, Frédéric was one of the first to bring French-style charcuterie and saucisson sec (dried sausage) to the province.

Frédéric did not have a master plan to bring French sausages to an under-served market. No, he just replied to a job ad for a chef in Canada back in 2001. He says, "I didn't even know where I was going at the time. They didn't tell me until I had gotten the job, and when they said the position was for the Keltic Lodge in Cape Breton, I was like, 'What the fuck is that?' We had just gotten Internet at my house, so I went to look it up and was like, 'oh wow.' I packed up my stuff, and that's how I wound up in Nova Scotia."

When he opened Ratinaud (the business is named for his grandfather), Frédéric found that although Nova Scotia has long traditions of Acadian- and German-influenced sausages, classic French charcuterie was not well known — either by consumers or by the baffled regulators and inspectors

Pete McChesney hanging the freshly made sausages.

who he says didn't know what to make of his meat-curing techniques.

"A lot of countries make charcuterie in different ways. The Germans smoke a lot of things. When you move down to France, or Spain or Italy it's mostly dry cure. I make traditional products like we do in France — like saucisson sec, which is a huge classic in France . . . We did a lot of dry curing in the first restaurant where I worked, and like everything else, once you have a good foundation you can start experimenting on your own."

Frédéric is known for products that aren't loaded with too many extraneous flavours or a lot of smoke, even though he knows "people really like strong flavours here: really spicy, very smoky." He prefers to let the taste of the meat take centre stage. "What comes with it, the spices, or the garlic, or the herbs — it should be complementary."

We sit at the large stainless-steel counter in the restaurant behind the shop, an hour before opening. Wooden shelves hold a variety of preserved

Captain Bennett Comeau, left, and his brother-in-law Louis Burridge fill bait bags with pickled herring, Cape St. Mary, December, 1950.

ingredients, including carrots, beans, celery and a brilliant orange vinegar with marigold flowers. "We preserve as much as we can for the shop. We work with the seasons, and summer is only so long," Frédéric says. During the fall, he's out mushroom-picking most weekends, later dehydrating the mushrooms — including boletes, chanterelles, hedgehogs and black trumpets — to use as flavouring in dry-cured sausage.

Hams that have been curing two years hang in the window overlooking the street, where they'll stay for three more months. ("This is a product made with three ingredients: pork, salt and time," Frédéric says.) When you're in a business making products that take a long time to develop — like cured meats and cheeses — you need to plan ahead. Frédéric shows me his curing room, saying there is "a lot of money hanging in here." If you run out of cured hams, you can't conjure up another one on short notice.

Frédéric says he is not trying to create a new trend. "I'm just carrying on the tradition of my country. I'm just doing what I love." But at the same time, he is also adopting the flavours of his adopted province, incorporating local ingredients: "what nature has to offer," including sea parsley, juniper berries and pine tips.

Traditionally, the Mi'kmaw people of what is now Nova Scotia preserved fish and meat by drying and smoking. For people who travel, this is a far more practical approach than, say, brining. The weight of most foods

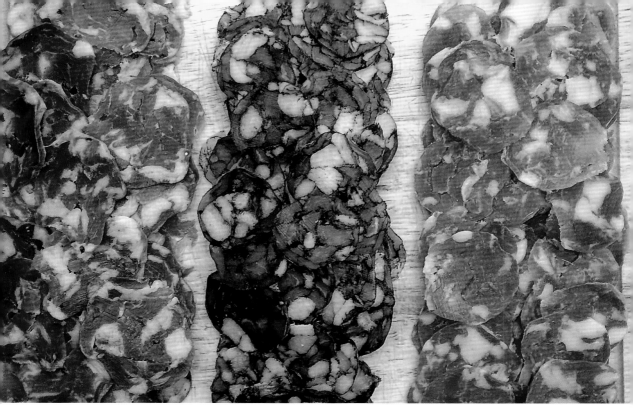

LEFT TO RIGHT: Ginger, espresso and preserved lime salami, made by Pete McChesney.

comes from moisture. If you are harvesting meat or fish seasonally and want to be able to transport it when you move, smoking and drying are ideal.

Although these are not, strictly speaking, processes of fermentation, there is still some minimal fermentation activity going on. In *The Art of Fermentation*, Sandor Katz writes, "Of course, flesh does not dry instantly, so there is always some level of incidental microbial activity along the way. In dried meats, such as jerky, biltong, and pemmican, and dried fish, such as stockfish and salt cod, microbial growth and enzyme activity that occurs during drying may indeed even contribute to the flavor and texture of the resulting product." Even though there may be some minimal fermentation in this process, it's not what preserves the meat. The drying or smoking does that.

Pete McChesney washes his hands, puts on a pair of gloves, and then starts hand-mixing the ingredients for his ginger salami. Pete — remember, he's a scientist — is a big believer in precision. When he creates a recipe, he works in weight and percentages, not volume. It's more accurate that way. He weighs 646 grams of fat on his digital scale and adds them to the 1,562 grams of hand-diced pork waiting in a large roasting pan on the counter. Then he adds his other ingredients: salt, finely rasped candied ginger, ginger powder, black pepper (7.1 grams, coarsely crushed in a mortar and pestle) and Prague Powder 2 (a combination of sodium nitrate, sodium nitrite and table salt). He considers adding a few cocoa nibs too, but then thinks better of it.

"So, it's three-fold preservation," he explains. "The salt right away kills something like 90 per cent of the microbes. And the secondary step is the fermentation. Some of those microbes that survive, *Lactobacillus,* produce lactic acid — the same as in kimchi or sauerkraut. They consume the sugar, turn it into acid, and that drops the pH down and kills a bunch more of the microbes. Then the longest-term preservation is the dehydration. You just remove the moisture and bacteria can't grow."

The doors on the kitchen cupboards are covered in post-it notes with hand-written recipes for seemingly endless combinations of meat, fat, spices and other flavourings. Cumin seed salami, lemon-poppy sausage, coconut milk and allspice bacon, a vegetarian fruit "salami" made with dates, almonds and Grand Marnier — all with amounts carefully measured down to the gram. There are also notes on a Nutella salami he hopes to make. "That's going to be a weird one if I get around to it."

Once he's packed the ingredients into casings (using a piece of equipment called a vertical stuffer — no hollow ox horn here), it's time to leave the sausage to ferment.

He says, "Depending on what temperature you ferment at, it's usually only twelve hours to maybe seventy-two hours. I typically ferment at 25 degrees Celsius. For fermentation, you want warm and humid, so I usually just use the oven turned off. Some people adapt a cooler. They put warm water in it. And some will put a light in to warm it up a bit. But I've figured out that my oven will get up to 50 degrees with just the light on. So I'll turn the light on for an hour beforehand and then put my thermometer in there to see when I get it to the exact temperature I want."

While the oven warms up and the sausages hang over the kitchen sink, Pete goes to the small wine fridge in a back room and returns with cured meats for us to try: his award-winning espresso salami, which looks luminous, like stained glass, when you hold it up to the light; an odd salami that resulted from a misguided attempt at using hops from his garden for flavour; a subtle rose-flavoured dry sausage.

Since he only cures during the summer months, I ask Pete what he does the rest of the year: "Obsess, think, plan. Organize n y notes."

You've probably noticed that one of the aims of this book is to demystify home fermentation. I encourage you to experiment, to play around with recipes and find what works for you. To alter things like the concentration of salt in brine, for instance, if you are making fermented vegetables. Don't worry, I've told you, it's safe. You can't harm yourself by doing this.

None of that applies to this chapter.

"You can kill someone," Andrew Stevens says bluntly. Andrew is academic chair of the School of Business at the Nova Scotia Community College's (NSCC) Akerley Campus. He's responsible for overseeing (among other things) the cooking and baking programs at the school. We walk through the various kitchens — past students cutting up meat, tasting a white kimchi made with Asian pears, slicing delicious local cheeses, kneading and preparing various breads — and stop in front of the school's latest acquisition. It's a shiny new stainless-steel Italian-made "Maturmeat" brand curing fridge. Through fine-tuned controls, its marketing pamphlet says, it "reproduces a series of microclimates ideal for the traditional maturation of meat" while a touch-screen controller "automatically manages the temperature, humidity, air speed, pH monitoring [as meats ferment, the pH drops] . . . for the duration of the recipe."

The machine will set you back about $25,000. Not something for the home cook.

Want to cure meats traditionally made in mountainous regions? They may not do so well at sea level — but with a bit of technological help from a fridge like the Maturmeat, you can simulate that mountainous environment.

Nobody at NSCC is using the device yet though, because first they have to put together what's known as a HACCP plan. That stands for "hazard analysis and critical control points." It's an approach that requires

Curing Salts

The simplest way to add sodium nitrate to meat being cured is to use curing salts.

But be careful, because curing salt terminology can be confusing.

Traditionally, many recipes called for potassium nitrate — aka saltpetre — for curing meat. But it is trickier to work with and doesn't produce as consistent results as sodium nitrate.

Enter curing salts, also known as Prague Powder. Prague Powder #1, also called Insta Cure #1, is made up of a mix of table salt and sodium nitrite. It's used for quick-cured meats.

Prague Powder #2 combines table salt, sodium nitrite and sodium nitrate. Over time, the nitrate breaks down into nitrite, helping to preserve the meat.

Prague Powders include regular salt because typically the amount of nitrate or nitrite used in a recipe is so tiny that it's hard to considering all potential hazards in a process and coming up with a plan to test for them at key points in the process. Was the truck the meat came in on properly refrigerated? Is the pH in those sausages low enough as they cure? Are we properly monitoring the temperature in the curing chamber?

Until the school has systems in place to anticipate and manage hazards, the machine will stay empty.

When it comes to curing meats, botulism is the big hazard.

Botulism comes from the *Clostridium botulinum* bacteria. The bacteria are extremely common. You can find them in soils and on the leaves of vegetables, for instance. Slice up some cabbage, and there's a decent chance you're consuming botulism bacteria as you eat them. But they aren't toxic. The trouble comes when spores germinate — and that can only take place in an anaerobic environment. Say, among the contents of a sausage that's curing under improper conditions.

We've known about the connection between cured meats and botulism for nearly two centuries. Back in the 1820s, a German doctor named Justinus

measure properly on its own. It takes less than 10 grams of curing salts to preserve nearly 4 kilograms of salami. Trying to measure out the less than half a gram of sodium nitrate you need for a smaller recipe is nearly impossible. "If you took pure sodium nitrate and tried to add the right amount, you're going to overdo it every single time," Pete McChesney says. "So for safety it's diluted with table salt."

It's important to understand that curing salts are not the same as regular salt. (Generously salting food at your dinner table with Prague Powder is dangerous.) To avoid confusion between regular salt and curing salts, the latter are typically dyed pink. As a result, they are sometimes referred to in recipes as "pink salt."

But the newfound popularity of Himalayan pink salt has added another potential layer of confusion. If you see a recipe calling for pink salt, that means curing salts, including sodium nitrate. Make sure you don't use Himalayan salt, which does not include nitrate or nitrite, and which won't help prevent botulism.

Kerner fed sausages linked to two hundred cases of poisoning to animals and noted the results. (He also, rather rashly, tried some himself and experienced symptoms of botulism. Anything for science, I guess.) In 1895, three Belgian musicians died after eating an infected salted ham. Analysis of what remained of the meat showed the presence of bacteria forming spores, confirming Kerner's work.

The most recently discovered strain of botulinum (the toxin produced by *Clostridium botulinum*) is believed to be the deadliest substance in the

What's the Deal with Nitrates and Nitrites?

Nitrates and nitrites have gotten a lot of bad press. Spend a few seconds searching online and you will come up with plenty of natural food and wellness websites offering a range of warnings on the dangers of processed meats like bacon and salami. Some are carefully worded and mild, urging you, for instance, to avoid cured meats because they may increase the risk of certain illnesses.

Others take a much more dramatic approach, featuring dire language about how cured meats can damage your body and claiming they are unsafe in even the smallest amounts.

Often, concerns about the safety of cured meats revolve around the use of nitrates and nitrites in preserving them.

So what are they? And how do they work?

Nitrates and nitrites are shorthand for sodium nitrate and sodium nitrite. (Many old recipes call for saltpetre — potassium nitrate — as a curing agent. Fun fact: it's also a component in gunpowder.) While salt kills many of the bacteria found in meat, it won't do in the bacteria that cause botulism. Hence the use of nitrite, which "completely inhibits *Clostridium botulinum* growth, almost completely inhibits *Clostridium perfringens*, and slows the growth of many other pathogenic bacteria such as *Listeria monocytogenes*," according to a publication from the University of Wisconsin's Meat Science and Muscle Biology Lab.

Nitrites are used in quick-cured meats such as bacon. Nitrates are essentially nitrites in time-release form. For meats that cure a world. As little as two billionths of a gram (that's right — two billionths) can be fatal.

The reason we process canned vegetables at high heat for a specific amount of time is to kill the spores. (Since canned vegetables are anaerobic, they provide a perfect environment for the spores to multiply if they are not heated properly.)

Meat is trickier though, because there are more variables involved, and because you can't lean on a relatively simple solution like high heat.

long time — hams hanging for two years, or salamis aging for weeks or months — sodium nitrate is used. Over time, it breaks down into sodium nitrite, providing anti-microbial action over a long period.

I won't get into the debate over whether nitrates are harmful or harmless — you can find plenty of people arguing each side. But I do want to say a few words about cured meats that claim to be nitrate-or nitrite-free, or that say they use all-natural ingredients. Nitrate (which gets converted into nitrite in our bodies) is found in most vegetables. In fact, 95 per cent of all nitrite we consume comes from nitrates in vegetables.

Celery contains high concentrations of nitrate, so some processors use nitrate derived from celery to cure their meat, and then label the results "nitrite-free." Trouble is, if the nitrite-free meat is cured using celery seed extract — guess what? It's not nitrite-free. CBC News quotes physician and University of Ottawa professor Yoni Freedhoff as saying, "For all intents and purposes, it is bio-chemically identical."

In some ways, meats preserved with nitrate derived from celery may be a worse choice, because it is harder to monitor the precise amount of nitrate being added. As a story from McGill University's Office of Science and Society says, "So what does all of this mean? Basically, that buying 'organic' hot dogs or bacon with a view toward living longer by avoiding nitrites makes no sense . . . It is possible to avoid cured meats completely and still have a terrible diet while one can have a healthy diet by occasionally indulging in these tasty morsels. Emphasize a mostly plant-based diet? By all means. But dogmatic tirades against hot dogs? That's ideology, not science."

Writing in *The Atlantic*, Dr. Bradley Wertheim says the behaviour of the botulism bacteria is predictable — so the ways to prevent illness remain consistent. "The basics of botulism control — careful attention to salt and water balance, moisture, acidity, temperature, and oxygen content — stay the same. *C. botulinum* is no feral beast: it is a creature of habit, though fortunately, a rare one. Adherence to time-vetted recipes and practices can prevent a trip to the intensive care unit."

"If you know what you're doing it's safe. If you don't know what you're doing it's very dangerous. There are cocky people who think they know what they're doing and refuse to listen to any warnings," Pete McChesney says. Sometimes people resist using curing salts because they have an old family recipe that omits them. "It's all anecdotal stuff. 'Oh, my grandmother never did this. The old guys never did it this way before.' Those people can get botulism if they don't watch out."

Pete is active in online charcuterie forums and on Instagram, sharing knowledge and letting people know if their practices are unsafe. "The consequences could be lethal. Be afraid of botulism, but recognize that the amount of people who get botulism from cured meats is insanely low. When in doubt, throw it out. Tossing $10 or $20 worth of meat is way better than getting yourself sick or making someone else sick."

Pete says sometimes people will post photos of their cured meats on Instagram and ask him if they are safe to eat. "I'm not going to look at a picture and tell you if you can eat it," he says, before repeating, "When in doubt, throw it out."

While all this may seem terrifying, fear of botulism shouldn't prevent people interested in curing their own meats from trying it at home. It just means you need to exercise caution, be attentive and precise in your measurements and processes and not cut any corners.

Frédéric Tandy of Ratinaud encourages people to explore making their own charcuterie, if that interests them. "There is a lot of fear because it requires a certain amount of knowledge, technique and equipment. And you need to do it carefully, because you can nearly kill yourself if you don't," he says. "Like everything, it's a craft. I've seen more and more people on social media experimenting at home and I think that's great — even if it is competing with me! Like any craft, people have fun with it and experiment with different flavours."

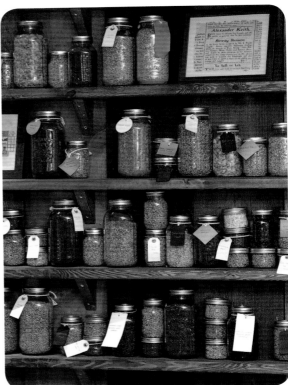

4

Sudsy Stuff

Beer and Other Brews

On the way to Meander River Farm and Brewery, Sara and I stop several times to check our route — turning around more than once on small country roads when we realize we are heading in the wrong direction. Finally, there it is, in the rural community of Ashdale, in Hants County. A modest sign on a sawhorse points to the small parking lot behind a wooden building with a bright red roof.

It's a sunny fall day at Meander River,a family farm, winery and cidery run by the Bailey family. We each order a drink, greet the dogs who lie languidly on the cool floor and chat with Alan Bailey.

A group of four arrives, gets drinks, then asks if they can have a tour of the brewery, to which Alan says sure. The word "tour" may be overselling it. The brewery is small, and we cram into it as Alan starts a batch of Meander River's Homegrown — a beer he makes only once a year, using fresh hops grown here.

He pours three twenty-five kilogram bags of locally malted grain into a tank, and another bag of malt from out of province. "I'd like to say we use all local grain, but we don't yet," he says. "But we do our best."

As he stirs the grain into the tank, several bags of hops — eighty pounds total — sit on the brewery floor. The bags hold two varieties: the bitter Galena and the more aromatic Newport, all harvested here on the farm.

The resinous cones of the hop plant help impart bitterness and aromatic flavours to beer. Most hops are kiln-dried, then turned into pellets for long-lasting storage. Meander's Homegrown only comes around once a year because it is wet-hopped — meaning it uses these fresh hops, which are only available at harvest time.

Alan says Meander River doesn't grow enough hops to justify the cost of a mechanical harvester. Instead, they turn to the community, inviting friends, family and neighbours to come and help in exchange for plenty of food, beer and cider.

Alan looks at the clock. "Ten to one," he says.

At ten to two, he'll move the liquid into a boiling tank, where it will boil for another hour. While that's happening, he'll clean the original tank, add hops, pour the liquid back in and let it sit on the hops for fifteen to twenty minutes.

The Craft Brewers Association of Nova Scotia lists nearly forty member breweries on its website, and that doesn't include breweries who choose not to belong. Meander River — which started brewing in 2014 — is just one of a wave of dozens of small breweries that have opened across Nova Scotia in the last decade, many of them in small rural communities like this one. As I write this, Nova Scotia has more craft breweries per capita than any other province — a distinction it has held for several years.

That doesn't mean we produce the most craft beer by volume though — because some of these breweries are truly tiny. As Craft Brewers Association president Emily Tipton says of Boxing Rock, the brewery she co-owns, "We have been the third-largest craft brewery in Nova Scotia for years. And we're not very big."

There is no one defining characteristic of the craft beer movement. Some breweries are urban, others are rural. Some stick to specific styles, others experiment with an array of styles and flavours. Some are traditionalist while others make beers with unusual ingredients like oysters, lobster or beets.

Beer is one of humanity's oldest beverages. Patrick McGovern, aka "the beer archaeologist," has devoted his career to studying and helping re-create ancient alcoholic beverages. He's confirmed that pottery jars from China held a fermented drink made from rice, honey and fruit about 9,000 years ago and discovered the oldest known barley beer, from the mountains of Iran. (It dates from 3,400 BCE.)

And McGovern's work shows people have been adding all kinds of flavourings to beer for a long time. A *Smithsonian Magazine* story about him by Abigail Tucker says "ancients were liable to spike their drinks with all sorts of unpredictable stuff — olive oil, bog myrtle, cheese, meadowsweet, mugwort, carrot, not to mention hallucinogens like hemp and poppy . . . [In] the tomb of the Pharaoh Scorpion I . . . a curious combination of savory, thyme and coriander showed up in the residues of libations interred with the monarch in 3150 BC." You may have heard real beer is only made with four ingredients: malt, water, yeast and hops. Time to re-think that.

Drinking beer — or beer-like drinks — has a long history in Nova Scotia too.

Indigenous people in North America made a spruce-based drink and likely shared the recipe to help European settlers. In 1535, Jacques Cartier and his men became stuck in the ice of the St. Lawrence River, unable to return to France until the thaw. As a result, most of the crew came down with scurvy. They were saved by a brew made from a coniferous tree, which provided essential Vitamin C. And while we may not know its exact identity, fir, spruce or cedar are considered likely candidates.

Fermented spruce beer, a likely descendant of spruce tea, caught on among settlers in New France. Botanist Pehr Kalm described its production as he saw it in 1749, on a visit to New France. A decade later, British General Jeffery Amherst recorded his own spruce beer recipe in his journal:

> *Take 7 pounds of good spruce & boil it well till the bark peels off, then take the spruce out & put three gallons of molasses to the Liquor & and boil it again, scum it well as it boils, then take it out the kettle & put it into a cooler, boil the remainder of the water sufficient for a barrel of thirty gallons. If the kettle is not large enough to boil it together, when milk-warm in the cooler put a pint of yeast into it and mix well. Then put it into a Barrel and let it work for two or three days, keep filling it up as it works out. When done working, bung it up with a Tent Peg in the barrel to give it vent every now and then. It may be used in up to two or three days after. If wanted to be bottled it should stand a fortnight in the cask. It will keep a great while.*

British officer and diarist John Knox wrote that the British troops who took the Fortress of Louisbourg from the French received an allotment of spruce beer — largely to fend off scurvy. Knox describes a very minimalist recipe: "It is made from the tops and branches of the Spruce-tree, boiled for three hours, then strained into casks, with a certain quantity of molasses, and, as soon as cold, it is fit for use."

Not much aging going on there.

The Nova Scotia Archives also have a recipe on file from the Uniacke family papers, which cover recipes from four generations, up to the late nineteenth century. This one calls for ground juniper, tea berry leaves, prince's pine, black spruce branches and needles and "a handful of hops and one of barley" along with treacle. It also calls for a cup of "good yeast" for every two gallons of liquid, and notes that one should use "more of black spruce than any other herb."

Dr. Trudy Sable, director of the Office of Aboriginal and Northern Research at the Gorsebrook Research Institute of Saint Mary's University, says she knows of interviews with Mi'kmaw elders dating back to the 1940s in which they talk about making a green alcoholic drink but one that was more akin to tea or a beer than to liquor. In an email, Trudy tells me producing this drink "in the face of alcohol restrictions by the government is an intriguing story to me of adaptation and resistance."

If you are curious about spruce beer and don't want to go out to the woods to harvest tips of branches from local coniferous trees, spruce beer continues to be made today — as a very niche, specialty item, mind you. For several years, Garrison Brewery has made a seasonal strong spruce beer, using spruce and fir tips from Meander River, and blackstrap molasses from Saint John.

Of course, spruce beer wasn't the only brew early settlers were drinking. In a book of recollections of his life in New France in the mid-1600s, Pierre Boucher said those who could not afford wine drank beer. (Below beer came a wretched-sounding fermented drink called bouillon — and, for the truly desperate, there was always water.) Beer was a safer bet than water, because the process involved boiling, which would kill off nasty micro-organisms. And then there were hops, which also provided protective qualities. They took off in popularity in the late Middle Ages, providing an anti-bacterial component to beer and allowing it to keep and travel better.

Halifax has been in many ways a navy town for centuries, so it's no surprise that within a month of its founding in 1749 the town had issued its first liquor licence, with sixteen more to follow by the end of the year. Not bad for a place with only 3,000 residents. Starting in 1759, members of the Royal Highland Regiment stationed in Halifax received an allotment of two quarts of beer a day.

"Taxation drives a lot of the history of beer," University of King's College professor Ian Stewart tells me. And that's certainly true of British

North America. "Beer was more than a staple beverage of the colony, it also provided the government with one of the earliest sources of taxable revenue," writes Allen Winn Sneath in *Brewed in Canada*, his comprehensive history of the Canadian brewing industry.

For generations, brewing in Nova Scotia was dominated by one family: the Olands. Members of the family founded the two dominant breweries in the region more than a century ago: Moosehead Breweries and the Oland Brewery, though both have undergone several name changes over the decades. The other big name in brewing in Halifax was Alexander Keith, later elected mayor twice. Keith's Brewery, the second-oldest in Canada, was sold to the Olands in 1928.

As of 2019, Moosehead, headquartered in New Brunswick, is the last major Canadian-owned brewery in the country. And Oland is now part of multinational behemoth Anheuser-Busch (AB) InBev.

Alexander Keith, a Scotsman who arrived in Nova Scotia in 1817, opened his brewery in 1820, by the harbour in Halifax. It's the second-oldest continually operating brewery in the country after Molson, founded in 1786 in Montreal. Keith originally made ginger and spruce beers, along with a strong ale and porter. The current small-batch brewmaster at Alexander Keith's, Stefan Gagliardi, says Keith's India Pale Ale is the oldest continuously brewed beer in North America — although you could consider the claim a bit dubious, given how much the recipe has changed since Alexander Keith first brewed the beer.

Four decades after Keith founded his brewery, across the harbour in Dartmouth Susannah Oland was making a homebrew she called "Brown October Ale" in a shed behind the home she shared with her husband, John, and their nine children. Thinking that the beer might have commercial potential, the Olands founded their company, John Oland and Son, in

Ruins of the Army & Navy Brewery (owned by the Oland family) in Turtle Grove, after the Halifax Explosion, 1917 or 1918.

October 1867. After John's death the name was changed to S. Oland, Sons and Co., with Susannah using her first initial rather than her full name to hide the fact that the company was owned by a woman.

The growth pattern of breweries in Nova Scotia pretty much followed the same pattern as the rest of North America. After decades of consolidation and cheap (and largely tasteless) beer, a backlash began against the stranglehold of the big breweries. In 1971, the Campaign for Real Ale (CAMRA) began in Britain. Within a few years, craft breweries began appearing in Canada. One here, one there. Then, the floodgates opened. The United States was home to all of two craft breweries in 1977. Over twenty years later that number had increased to more than 1,700.

For a long time, Kevin Keefe was the voice in the wilderness when it came to Nova Scotia microbrews. His Granite Brewery, founded in 1985, was only the second brewpub and third craft brewery in the whole country, according to Christopher Reynolds and Whitney Moran in *East Coast Crafted*, their guide to Atlantic Canada's craft breweries. Keefe, they write, "has inspired countless brewers."

It took more than a decade before another pair of microbreweries hit the scene — Garrison and Propeller, both of which opened in 1997. A smattering of other breweries and brewpubs opened in the early 2000s, and then, in the years after 2010, brewery after brewery opened up. And these weren't just in the province's urban areas. No matter where you are in the province, you should be able to find a local brew within a short drive. Yarmouth, Wolfville, Tusket, Tatamagouche, Nyanza, Liverpool, Mahone Bay, Shelburne, Guysborough, Antigonish, Sheet Harbour, Parrsboro, Amherst — all these towns, and many more, have their own craft breweries.

Wearing a black leather jacket and looking a bit haggard, Ian Stewart flops down beside me in an alcove at the Wardroom — the pub at the University of King's College in Halifax, where he has taught a course on brewing and civilization. I would offer him a beer, but it's late afternoon and the bar hasn't opened yet.

Stewart walks me through some of the history of brewing — how it went from being a domestic activity mostly carried out by women to a more centralized process. (Much as cheesemaking did, as we'll see in Chapter 8). The shift began in earnest all the way back in the 1600s, with technological innovations like the copper brewing kettle. Industrialization intensified with the arrival of the steam engine, which could drive many brewery tasks, including hoisting bags of malt, stirring and mashing and heating more efficiently with steam pipes instead of fire. (At least one UK brewery, Hook Norton, has a still-functioning nineteenth-century steam engine that it occasionally fires up for visitors.)

As cities grew, breweries moved to urban centres and industrialization allowed them to scale up production to feed their markets.

Between 1950 and 2000, the four largest breweries in the US went from a collective market share of 20 per cent to more than 90 per cent. Canada — and Nova Scotia — faced the same trends. As Harvey Sawler writes in his history of Moosehead, *Last Canadian Beer*, Canadian breweries consolidated in the decades following the Second World War, with one company — the not-very-imaginatively-named Canadian Breweries — buying up nearly thirty breweries in Canada and reducing the number of brands they brewed from 150 to eight over a thirty-year period.

And in Nova Scotia? At the turn of the twentieth century, the British-based Halifax Breweries Ltd. bought five Maritime breweries, making an early start on consolidation. In 1971, Oland would be bought by Labatt (itself later purchased by a multinational conglomerate), marking the end of independent brewing in Nova Scotia — until the craft beer revival came along.

Stewart points out that this consolidation happened in large part because of technologies of scale and quality control. But it also had to do with what beer writer Stephen Beaumont called "median taste." For whatever reason, mid-twentieth-century North America seemed to prize standardization and consistency (think fast food). The craft beer movement pushes back against that — not only in making flavourful beers that don't necessarily appeal to all — but in celebrating the fact that different batches may not all taste the same.

Interestingly, one of the factors that drove the consolidation of breweries across North America — technology — has also fuelled the craft boom now that once expensive equipment has come down in price and size. "The capacity to control fermentation, the capacity to control bacterial infection, CO_2 content, oxygen content and the fine measuring technologies of alcohol content — all these things were the result of long historical and technological developments in order to increase the quality of how beer is made, but also how beer is managed and how it's shipped and sold," Ian says. "Now the point is that if you go into a small microbrewery, they're using technologies that are in a sense the result of the industrialization of brewing. But they're using them in order to resist some of the implications of the industrialization of brewing. Technologies are always like that. They change how things happen, and then they get implemented in ways that can actually belong to social movements that are an alternative to the dominant."

Chemical engineer and brewery owner Emily Tipton is one of the people who have brought brewing back to rural and small-town Nova Scotia.

On an October evening, the co-owner of the Boxing Rock Brewing Company walks up to the front of the room at the T-Room pub on Dalhousie University's Sexton Campus. She is a guest of the Ladies Beer League, and tonight she's speaking to an audience made up largely of engineers about why craft brewing is a great career choice for them.

After working in the oil industry and as a consultant ("pimping out my brain to other people") in Canada, the US, the UK and Indonesia, she and her then-husband Guy wound up moving from England to Shelburne, on the South Shore of Nova Scotia in 2007. Why Shelburne? They had visited on their honeymoon a few years earlier and fallen in love with the place — in large part because of the great sailing.

But that left Emily with a problem. She needed work.

"Beer was totally not on my radar as a career option," Emily tells the room. "Shelburne is probably one of the only places in the world there are no jobs for engineers . . . Boxing Rock was my problem-solving solution and my engineered solution to rural economic development and creating a job for myself in rural Nova Scotia. And as a result, I think it's proof that engineers make great entrepreneurs. As well as pretty decent brewers." Once she hit on the idea of making beer, she invited her friend and fellow chemical engineer Henry Pedro to join her, and he moved with his family from Toronto to Shelburne. Together they founded Boxing Rock

In less than a decade, Boxing Rock became one of the province's largest craft breweries, and when I meet her, Emily is president of the Craft Brewers Association of Nova Scotia.

"Beer itself is not an innovation. But in 2011 making craft beer in Shelburne was," Emily says.

She likes to tell a story about how there were no interesting beers on tap anywhere in Shelburne. When her father-in-law was visiting from the UK, he and Guy convinced the local sailing club to buy a keg of Propeller. They agreed, but said they would only put it on after all the Bud Light was gone. Once they put the keg on, it quickly sold out. It was an important lesson. Craft beers can sell in small towns. You just have to make them available.

Before opening the brewery in 2012, Emily says she and Henry made "huge amounts of beer in our basements and backyards and then we hosted dozens of tasting parties for friends and acquaintances and anyone that had heard about us on Facebook. We told people to invite ten or twenty people to their house and that we would provide them as much beer as they could drink as long as they filled in our evaluation spreadsheet. We collected hundreds of opinions on the beer flavours and aromas, on food pairings, on context. And we used all of that data to select the three beers that we launched with."

I meet Emily at Boxing Rock, just off Highway 103 in Shelburne. We go through the taproom to the brewery, where one of the employees is patiently zesting lemons for the company's signature Hunky Dory beer. ("Quite honestly, if I'd known what I know now I wouldn't have put lemon zest in the Hunky Dory because it's a right royal pain in the ass, and we have to do it [zest lemons] twice a week," Emily says.)

I ask her about those tasting parties, and she says they were about more than just finding out what people wanted: they also played an educational

LEFT: Zesting lemons for Boxing Rock's signature Hunky Dory pale ale.
RIGHT: Whisky barrels for aging at Boxing Rock.

role, which was important in an area where most people didn't have a lot of experience drinking craft beer: "We would bring them eight or ten different kinds of beer that we had made and we had the opportunity to talk about different styles and why this was perhaps, you know, a nice beer in front of the fire or maybe something you would want with your spicy curry. We were kind of sneakily educating about craft beer."

Talk to Emily for awhile, and the conversation moves from beer itself to the role craft beer can play in helping revitalize Nova Scotia communities. Not just Shelburne, but across the province.

"Every town wants a craft brewery," she says. "Why wouldn't you want one? Because craft breweries are more than a fish plant or a fish-processing facility. They are actually part of the community, like a third place. People come here, and they hang out! So it's not just about the beer. It's about being part of these communities too . . . I recently discovered this stat that if you add up all the beer that is purchased in Shelburne County — no matter what kind of beer — that's pretty much how much beer we make here at Boxing Rock. We make enough beer to supply Shelburne County. Give or take. I think the mathematics there are interesting to look at. And when the zombie apocalypse comes, I'm going to have enough beer to be able to trade it for all kinds of other useful things."

Brewing and rural economic development have gone hand-in-hand since the colonial era. In *Brewed in Canada*, Allen Winn Sneath writes:

> *The breweries were among the first industries to create employment in many of the settlements. Besides the brewers and maltsters, each brewery employed trained coopers skilled in the craft of building the wooden storage barrels. Horse power provided the sole mode of transport and stable help was needed to care for the horses that pulled the delivery wagons . . . Barley malt and hops were essential to the brewing process and the brewer provided the farmer with a ready market for his crops. The communities that grew up along the stagecoach routes all had inns and taverns which were the central meeting places for locals as well as travelers. In the days before refrigeration, their beer supply was readily available from a brewery conveniently located no further than a horse-drawn wagon ride away."*

Craft beer, of course, is not a quick fix to rural Nova Scotia's economic troubles. "There is no quick fix," Emily says. But at the same time, "We become an anchor in the community. I think real economic development happens by creating ten jobs at a time. If you have twenty businesses that each create ten jobs that's way better [than chasing big projects] because you're way more resilient."

Let's go back to the basic ingredients in beer.

Hops, malt, water, yeast.

Alexander Keith's small-batch brewmaster Stefan Gagliardi.

Probably the world's most famous — and most highly protected — beer yeast strain is the one used to make Budweiser. It also features in other beers made by brewing giant AB InBev, including a few made by Stefan Gagliardi. "No one knows we're using that," Stefan says. "It's really fun. I get to play with one of the most unique yeasts in the world. You can make some really good flavours with Bud yeast."

The yeast is directly descended from the original strain first used to brew Budweiser back in 1876. How serious is Bud's parent company about maintaining the integrity and security of the yeast? Well, journalist Lisa Brown — one of the few people to have been inside the company's yeast centre in St. Louis — compares the facility to Fort Knox. She describes it as "a windowless, three-story brick building that's under 24-hour video surveillance."

"Inside the heavily secured facility are five locked cryogenic tanks, each about the size of a dorm-room refrigerator," Brown continues in a story for the *St. Louis Post-Dispatch*. "Only one key exists to open the tanks, which hold the mother cultures for [Anheuser-Busch's] yeast at a bone-chilling minus 305 degrees Fahrenheit." That's -118 degrees Celsius.

Not everyone takes this ultra-secure approach to protecting yeast strains.

"Yeast is the key to making beer," says food writer Chris Nuttall-Smith during an episode of his CBC podcast *The Fridge Light*. The show starts with Nuttall-Smith and brewmaster Sam Corbeil driving north of Toronto into the woods to leave an open container of wort — unfermented beer — in the forest overnight to see what kinds of yeast it will pick up, and if any of them will be alcohol-tolerant enough to make beer. And if they'll provide decent flavours too. "Any bacteria or yeast that's present in the forest, in the trees — anywhere — will have the chance to fall into this liquid. Basically we're going to let the forest inoculate this wort," Sam says. "There are so many permutations. It's fantastic. They're all pooping out different flavours and aromas — so each one's different and unique. And you're just drinking yeast poop and farts . . . It metabolizes the sugars and poops out alcohol and flavours."

Whether it's carefully protected and tested to make sure its genetics don't change, or whether it comes from a bucket left out in the forest, yeast plays a crucial role in the flavour of some beers.

Yeast is a single-celled fungal organism. There are thousands of strains in the world — and we have harnessed some of them to do everything from fermenting beer and wine to raising our bread dough, to metabolizing plant protein for mass-market veggie burgers. Isolate yeasts and grow them in colonies and you can take advantage of the properties of specific species, and keep reproducing them, generation after generation. Escarpment Labs in Ontario (they're the ones who wound up analyzing the yeasts Sam Corbeil collected in the forest) sells yeasts used by craft breweries across the country — including several in Nova Scotia. The dozens of strains of yeast in their catalogue come with very specific descriptions of flavours, fermentation times and other qualities:

"Very prominent pineapple esters alongside a good dose of funk."

"Prominent fruity esters, leaning toward tropical guava and mango, lending well to traditional as well as modern aromatic styles."

"Wild Ontario ale yeast . . . isolated from an apple in a local orchard . . . Produces distinct clove, spice, and subtle banana and apple fruit aroma. The taste is dry, spicy and clean."

"I used to say to people I'm at the mercy of my yeast. Like, I don't know next week if I'm free on Thursday till I know whether this beer is going to be done or not," Emily Tipton of Boxing Rock told me. "To a

A community brew for Nova Scotia Craft Beer Week at the Saltbox Brewery in Mahone Bay.

chemical engineer, fermentation is interesting . . . and playing with different yeast strains is really, really, really interesting. Understanding how your yeast behaves in different [circumstances] — all of that is appealing."

Our bodies are covered in yeasts, and so are countless other surfaces — like that apple from a local orchard. "They are everywhere," says bio-chemist Russell Easy, who teaches at Acadia University. "Yeasts are ubiquitous. They settle on nearly every surface."

A couple of years ago, Russell stopped in at Saltbox Brewing in Mahone Bay to have a drink and listen to some Sunday afternoon jazz. He wound up talking yeast with Saltbox's Patrick Jardine, and soon after the pair and another Acadia biology professor, Allison Walker, hatched a plan to collect yeasts from around the province and see if they could isolate any strains suitable for brewing. One of the key characteristics is an ability to survive in an alcoholic environment. If the yeast dies when the alcohol reaches 2 per cent per volume you're not going to get decent beer out of it.

It's not the first time anyone's thought of making beer from wild Nova Scotia yeast. Back in 2017, Big Spruce Brewing of Nyanza, in Cape Breton, released what they believe to be the first local beer made with 100 per cent local ingredients — including yeast isolated from a wild pin cherry growing on the brewery's farm property.

But the Saltbox-Acadia deal is the first partnership of its kind between a brewery and a university.

There's a real enthusiasm in Russell's voice as he tells me about the first phase of the project. It started with a technician packing a lot of sterile swabs and running them over many different surfaces to pick up yeasts. Then the yeast strains were screened for toxicity, isolated and grown in colonies each made up of one individual strain whose properties could be tested.

"We swabbed the churches in Mahone Bay, the *Bluenose* [which, unfortunately, didn't yield anything useful], plants — blueberry plants, bay leaves, apple buds, partridge berries, cherries, poison ivy. My wife and I do a lot of kayaking and we swabbed at Blue Rocks too," Russell says. They even got some yeast from unwashed wool at the Ross Farm Museum. "Some of the growth on the poison ivy is kind of cool. Fizzy is one of the characteristics we look for, because that means it's producing gas and fermenting. We found some fizziness from hawthorne berries, red maple buds, and rosa rugosa leaves."

The team isolated about 300 strains of yeast, and Saltbox got fifteen or so strains to play around with. The next step is to figure out what kinds of proteins the different strains produce and how those proteins and enzymes affect flavour. "All these enzymes contribute to flavour. It's an ongoing dynamic. An incredible dynamic."

The basis for beer is malted grain. If you've ever made alfalfa sprouts at home in a Mason jar, parts of the malting process will sound somewhat familiar. When it comes to the beer industry, it takes place on a slightly larger scale than kitchen-window sprouting though.

Most beer is made with barley malt, but other grains can be used too. Like many others, I enjoy wheat beer, and I have a glass of locally made rye beer sitting next to my mouse pad as I write this.

Barley and other grains are rich in starches, and starches provide the raw food and sugars that yeasts love. Malting is a way to release those starches, making more of them available during fermentation. It starts with soaking and steeping, a process that develops enzymes in the grain so they break down proteins, in turn releasing starches.

After a couple of days of alternating soaking and resting out of the water, it's time to let the grain germinate. As it sprouts, starches and proteins continue to break down. Germination creates heat, so this stage requires a cooling process too. Finally, after four or five days, the malt is kiln-heated — with hot air blowing through it — to stop germination. As an additional step, it might also be roasted. And each step includes variables that can affect the taste of the beer.

For centuries, beer was primarily made at home (usually by women) and malting was a part of that process. But the industrial revolution also brought industrial malt houses.

The first commercial malt house in Canada was built in 1856 in southern Ontario. In much the same way that brewing went through a series of consolidations through the twentieth century, malting became more heavily centralized and industrialized.

But as the craft brewing industry has grown, there has also been a return to more traditional malting techniques, along with a focus on local and organic grain. Local malt helps provide terroir — local flavours — in a way imported malts can't.

In *Craft Beer & Brewing* magazine, writer Emily Hutto quotes Bill Manley of the US-based Sierra Nevada Brewery on artisanal malting: "Over the years, a lot of focus in craft beer has been put on hops, but too often, unique malts are overlooked . . . Now the tide in brewing malt is turning, and maltsters are focusing on varieties that can have a different impact on beer flavor . . . Working with small-scale craft maltsters is great because their malts are often handled in smaller quantities and feature older heirloom grain varieties that add complexity to beer."

In Nova Scotia, Horton Ridge Malt and Grain has supplied more than half the province's craft breweries with malt made using a traditional floor malting process. Many brewers I've talked to use at least some Horton Ridge malt and wish there were enough local supply for them to use more. Horton Ridge owner Alan Stewart, a sixth-generation farmer who went organic in the 1980s, opened the malt house — the only one in Atlantic Canada — in 2016. He malts his own grain, imports some from other provinces and hopes to eventually work exclusively with grains grown in the Maritimes. Floor malting is a lot more labour intensive than industrial malting, because it requires raking and turning the malt as it lays on the floor of the malt house, and being alert to making small adjustments.

As Alan explains in an interview in the book *East Coast Crafted*, "Most malt used by today's craft brewers is highly industrialized, in the same way that macro beer has become industrialized. We produce our malt the same way that craft brewers produce their beer, in small batches, with a much more hands on approach."

Malt is sweet, so beer needs something to play off that sweetness and add more flavour.

Which brings us to the next ingredient on our list: hops.

Hops first became popular among brewers way back in twelfth- and thirteenth-century Europe. Before then, beer "was flavoured and preserved with grut, a combination of herbs, which breweries had to buy from their local ruler, who used it to tax breweries indirectly," write Johan F. M. Swinnen and Thijs Vandemoortele in their essay "Beeronomics: The Economics of Brewing" in *The Economics of Beer*.

Mike Lancaster harvesting hops at Micou's Island.

Hops, it turned out, could also flavour and preserve beer. Even better, hops were not taxed by local rulers. This, not surprisingly, resulted in the widespread adoption of hops by brewers — followed, equally unsurprisingly, by local authorities switching from a tax on ingredients used in making beer to just taxing the beer itself.

Yeast can contribute to the flavour of beer, but hops generally have a much greater impact.

Hops have been grown in Nova Scotia for centuries. Early local sourdough starters were sometimes made with hops (sometimes written as "ups" in Acadian recipes). Hop plants are indigenous to North America, but settlers in what would become Canada and the United States introduced and cultivated specific varieties. For decades, hop production was centred on the West Coast, but a growing number of farms are now growing them in the US Northeast. And growers have begun to appear in Atlantic Canada too — including Big Spruce Brewing and Meander River, both of which double as farm and brewery — and Fundy Hops in the Annapolis Valley.

On a blustery fall day, I join a group of volunteers on Micou's Island in St. Margaret's Bay, near where I live. The island is publicly owned and managed by the local stewardship association, who organize monthly work parties. Today, one of the items on the to-do list is harvesting the hops cones hanging from a plant beside the nineteenth-century home on the island. Mike Lancaster, head island steward, hands me a pair of scissors and together we start snipping the cones. Mike and Nick Horne, another member of the association, will use the hops to brew up a batch of homemade beer — and then share the brew with stewardship volunteers.

Mike noticed the plant four years ago. "I looked down and thought, 'Is that hops? I think it's hops!'" He built a trellis to support the plant, which has seen greater yields every year. While he doesn't know what variety of hop plant it is, Mike suspects it is likely Cascade, an opinion Nick shares.

The papery cones feel almost light as air as I snip them as close to their base as possible and drop them into a plastic bag. Once we are done, Mike will put them on a drying rack at home so they don't get moldy.

Picking the hops by hand is a finicky and pain-staking process. "It's quite laden, eh, on the upper parts. It's super-concentrated," Mike says.

He's right. Even though this sounds silly, I'm struck by just how . . . hoppy they are. Within a few minutes, my hands smell like an IPA.

East Coast hop production is still tiny. Hops don't do well in heavy clay soils, or in foggy and humid coastal areas — meaning much of Nova Scotia is far from ideal. Even while promoting hops as one of a trio of crops that could be the next big thing, speakers at a series of 2013 workshops put on by the Nova Scotia government say conditions here will never allow for mass production of hops, but that "there are opportunities to supply microbreweries." As with grapes, there are areas in the province in which they can flourish — but production lags well behind the needs of craft brewers. Even at Meander River, Alan Bailey and his family, who were growing hops well before they got into the brewing business, don't produce enough to meet their own needs.

There are many variables when it comes to adding hops: whether they are wet, whole dried or pelletized; at what point in the boil you add them; whether you do a second addition. As with so much in the world of fermented products, there is a seemingly infinite number of changes you can make using a few basic ingredients in order to produce vastly different results.

Let's take a little detour from beer to talk about the other brew whose popularity has grown in tandem with local craft beer.

I'm talking, of course, about kombucha.

Kombucha has gone from complete obscurity to household word in the space of just a few years. In Nova Scotia you can buy bottled local kombucha at farmers' markets, supermarkets and big box stores, get it on tap, or fill growlers with it, craft-beer-style. One company even has taps built into the side of one of its trucks. As a wave of sober bars (serving non-alcoholic drinks) spreads across the continent and as some people question how much they are drinking, it's not surprising to see a tangy and fizzy alternative to beer like kombucha gaining traction.

A Few Varieties of Hops

Hops contain acids and essential oils that contribute bitterness, full flavour and aroma to beer. Naturally, different strains of hops produce different results. Here are a few varieties that have been used by brewers in Nova Scotia.

Cascade

Developed by the US Department of Agriculture's breeding program, Cascade has been a workhorse hop for many ales. These hops are quite resistant to hop nemesis downy mildew. After years of testing, Cascade was made available in 1972 — and took off when brewing giant Coors adopted its use. It has since gone on to flavour many a craft beer.

Willamette

Released in the mid-1970s, this variety has been described as spicy, with hints of herb and fruit. Widely grown and not very bitter.

Kombucha is a fermented tea drink, usually sold fizzy and with flavourings. It does contain a small amount of alcohol — but at about 0.5 per cent or less it's equivalent to non-alcoholic beers sold in grocery stores. The alcohol in kombucha did cause a bit of confusion in early 2018, with liquor inspectors in PEI warning a restaurant that it was contravening the law by selling kombucha that hadn't been purchased through the province's liquor-licensing agency. The agency, meanwhile, doesn't deal in kombucha because the alcohol content is so low.

The drink is fermented with a gelatinous mass called a mother, or SCOBY — that stands for the unappealing-sounding "symbiotic colony of bacteria and yeast." And it is decidedly unappealing-looking to most people: a thick, membrane-like disc (sounds yummy, right?) that floats atop sweetened tea and gradually ferments it, eating the sugars and leaving a slightly sour, tangy beverage. SCOBYs are incredibly complex little ecosystems and many of them are unique. There is no one set of specific bacteria and yeast that form a mother. Kombucha makers may drink or sell the plain tea, but most add flavourings.

Galena

Another variety released in the 1970s, Galena is high in alpha acids and is valued primarily for its bittering qualities.

Tettnang

Originating in Germany, these hops can be used in a wide range of beers, including wheat beers and pilsners.

Zeus

Another hop whose roots lie in the Pacific Northwest, Zeus is grown in Nova Scotia and is primarily a bittering hop.

Centennial

A relative newcomer, released in 1990. Similar to Cascade, but with a bit more citrus flavour. Developed at Washington State University and sometimes called a "Super Cascade."

Brenna Phillips with a bottle of her home-made kombucha.

Fruit and ginger are popular, and so are more unusual flavours and combinations, like peach blossoms or mango and turmeric.

Although some rave about it, kombucha is not to everybody's taste — I've had people tell me it seems like an unappetizing mix of tea and vinegar. But, like with many fermented products, if you do acquire the taste it gets its hooks into you, leaving you craving more, and maybe even wanting to make it yourself.

At the Up!Skilling food festival in Cape Breton, Brenna Phillips stands at the front of a room, leading a workshop on kombucha making — a beautiful array of colourful bottles each holding different flavours on the table behind her. In keeping with kombucha's hipster image, the crowd at this session is by far the youngest of any I've attended at the festival.

Brenna, the kitchen manager at an Ingonish Cafe, sports a buzz cut and a Daytona Bike Week t-shirt. "Let's start off with a kombucha sampling," she says, pouring fizzy drinks into paper cups.

"Why should we make kombucha?" someone asks.

"Because it's delicious?" Brenna replies. "I'm not going to make any health claims."

As with many other fermented foods and drinks, kombucha is brimming with bacteria that may be good for your gut. But for whatever reason, kombucha has also been touted as a cure-all that can help protect you against (or even cure) cancer, lower blood pressure and cholesterol, cure AIDS, get rid of wrinkles and on and on. On its website, the Mayo Clinic very succinctly says, "These claims are not backed by science."

In *The Art of Fermentation*, Sandor Katz says the drink is "neither panacea nor peril. Like any ferment, it contains unique metabolic by-products and living bacterial cultures that may or may not agree with you. Try some, starting with small servings, and see how it tastes and feels to you."

One of the keys to making kombucha is the SCOBY. It is the engine that drives kombucha fermentation — and with each batch you brew, it grows another layer, becoming thicker. Brenna puts on a pair of black gloves and holds up two different SCOBYs. One is young and pristine, while the other is dark and somewhat stained. A battle-hardened veteran of many fermentation cycles. "This is an older mother, but she still has a lot to offer," Brenna says. "It's very gelatinous. It really feels like a jellyfish."

Kombucha mothers are diverse eco-systems, with dozens of different species of both bacteria and yeasts on them — and their composition can vary from SCOBY to SCOBY.

In *The Big Book of Kombucha*, authors Hannah Crum and Alex LaGory go into quite a bit of detail on how the SCOBY, "the mother ship to millions of organisms," works. In short, "the bacteria and yeast in a SCOBY depend on each other, in that the by-products of the yeast fermentation feed the bacteria and the by-products of the bacteria fermentation feed the yeast."

When it comes to kombucha, as with other ferments, Crum and LaGory urge us to use our senses in assessing the health of a SCOBY and of kombucha itself. Both should have a fresh, tangy, smell. Mold is a no-no. If you see any, throw out both your SCOBY and the kombucha you brewed with it. Find another SCOBY from a reliable online source, or ask around and get one from a kombucha-brewing friend.

Mercedes Brian, who makes and sells both fermented vegetables and kombucha, says mold is "the worst thing that can happen. You have to throw it out. There's no coming back."

She remembers the first SCOBY she got from a friend, before she started making kombucha commercially. "It was little, in about a cup of liquid in a little sour cream container and I realize now it was not a very healthy SCOBY." She says the resulting brew had "lot of barnyard odours." Not good.

Today, Mercedes brews on the counter in her workshop in one-gallon jars, using essentially the same process as home kombucha makers. "I use the same method as a home brewer with a one-gallon jar on the counter, but I do it sixty times. Kombucha requires air permeating all the way to the bottom and a one-gallon jar is just the sweet spot for me. I take the empty clean jars, put my sugar in — a cup and a quarter — put my strong black tea in, then I add filtered water, and then on top of that I float the SCOBY. Over that I pour a cup and a half of finished kombucha [this helps kick-start the fermentation]. Then I put a tight-weaved cloth over it with an elastic and set it off to the side for two weeks as a minimum, or maybe a month. I go by taste."

Mercedes goes for an accessible big flavour. "I do not like thin-tasting. I do not like yeasty," she says. She removes the SCOBY before the kombucha gets vinegary, adds her flavourings and then does what's called a secondary

Make Your Own Kombucha

Kombucha is easy to make and doesn't require any special equipment. You can make it unflavoured — using just fermented tea — or add ingredients ranging from rose petals, to ginger, to orange juice for additional flavour. It's worth experimenting to find a combination that works for you.

If you are worried about sugar consumption, you may think the amount of sugar in kombucha is alarming. Don't worry. During the fermentation process those sugars will get eaten up and metabolized. You can control the sweetness of your final product by deciding when to remove your SCOBY and stop the fermentation. The longer it goes, the more sour it will get.

There are two basic techniques for brewing kombucha: batch brewing and continuous brewing. Batch brewing, as the name implies, fermentation with a bit of pineapple juice right in the individual bottles. "That gives a nice boost and a nice fizz," she says. "I make it the way I like it: big taste, a little bit sweet and a bit tart."

Any kind of tea can be fermented for kombucha, but Brenna says the ideal choice is Oolong. Some kombucha makers advise against heavily flavoured teas like Earl Grey, which might impart their flavours and odours to the mother.

It's also possible to ferment other beverages with a SCOBY. I've tried a couple of delicious coffee kombuchas, which make a refreshing alternative to iced coffee. I also fermented a store-bought bottle of root beer with my SCOBY in a misguided attempt to get my kids to try kombucha. As you can probably imagine, it was not a huge success. I'm amazed my SCOBY even survived.

The polar opposite of Mercedes making small batches of kombucha on her counter stands in the North End of Halifax. Here is where you will find the Oland plant — the largest brewery in the province. By far.

On a classically Nova Scotian grey and drizzly autumn day I head to

involves making one batch at a time. In continuous brewing, you make kombucha in a container with a spigot, replenishing the container with fresh sweet tea as you take out finished kombucha. This recipe uses the batch brewing method.

The terms "SCOBY" and "mother" are interchangeable. Kombucha mothers are stored in liquid that comes from a previous batch of kombucha. The best way to get a SCOBY is from someone who regularly makes kombucha. So many people are doing it, a SCOBY should not be hard to find. Ask around. You could also post in a fermentation forum or look for a local Facebook group for fermentation enthusiasts. I have heard of people buying SCOBYs online. I have never done this, but I suggest checking reviews if you go this route. Do not buy a dehydrated SCOBY.

When you get your SCOBY, it will come in liquid. Use some of that liquid when making your first batch of kombucha and replenish it when you are done.

Agricola Street for a visit. Back in 1905 the Oland family bought the brewery that already stood here. It was called Hayward's Highland Springs. The Oland brewery was destroyed in the Halifax Explosion of 1917, rebuilt nine years later and has seen several expansions and modernizations since then, along with changes of ownership.

Today, the Oland operation is part of AB InBev — the largest beer company in the world, with more than 500 brands and worldwide sales of over $50 billion in 2017.

The Halifax brewery makes fourteen of those brands, including Maritime

Kombucha

Materials
- 1 gallon (4 L) glass jar
- Cloth, beeswax wrap, or paper towel and rubber band to cover jar
- Resealable bottles (like Grolsch beer bottles)

Ingredients
- 1 Kombucha mother or SCOBY
- 1 gallon (4 L) water
- 4 tbsp (60 mL) or 4 to 8 tea bags of black or green tea (I prefer tea that is not heavily flavoured)
- 1 to 1 1/4 cups (250 to 315 mL) sugar
- 1/2 to 1 cup (125 to 250 mL) kombucha from a previous batch
- Optional flavourings: Juice of one lemon or orange, and grated ginger.

Method
Boil the water and turn off the heat.
Add tea and sugar and stir thoroughly until the tea dissolves.
After about 15 minutes, remove tea bags or strain out loose tea.
Allow the liquid to cool completely to room temperature.
Pour the liquid into a 1-gallon jar.
Add the kombucha from the previous batch.
Place the SCOBY in the jar. It may sink to the bottom, but it will eventually rise to the surface. (This may take a couple of days.)

favourites like Keith's, Schooner and Oland Export.

Wade Keller, who works in communications, and brewing and facilities process manager Jim Parker meet me at the brewery, and we sit down to talk beer. Jim started here as a summer student in the warehouse back in 1993 and has done half a dozen different jobs at the brewery since then. Wade is a trim-looking guy who plays recreational hockey (on a team sponsored by Bud Light) and appreciates precision. At one point, he pauses and corrects himself when he says "fewer" instead of "less."

Between them the pair tick off the beers made here: "Budweiser, Bud

Cover with paper towel, cloth or tea towel and leave to ferment at room temperature, out of direct sunlight. (A kitchen cupboard works well, but you can also place it on your counter away from a window.)

Leave to ferment for 7 to 10 days or longer, tasting it every so often, until it reaches a flavour you like. Sometimes I find a batch is done after 10 days, and sometimes it can take two weeks.

Put your SCOBY back into its container, along with a cup or so of liquid from your new batch of kombucha.

To add optional flavour

At this point, you have two options. You can bottle the kombucha and drink it as is, or you can add some more flavour to it. One of my favourite flavour combinations is lemon or orange and ginger.

Grate a couple of inches of ginger, evenly dividing it among your resealable bottles.

Squeeze the juice from one lemon or orange and divide it evenly between the bottles.

Pour in your kombucha, leaving a couple of inches of head space, seal the bottles and leave to ferment out of sunlight for a 3–4 days, or up to a week if it takes longer to get fizzy.

If all goes well, the liquid will become bubbly, so check in on it every day and open the lids to release the pressure.

Once the kombucha has reached a flavour you like, put the bottles in the fridge. You may choose to strain out the ginger, or you can leave it in the bottle.

Light, Michelob Ultra . . . Do we do Labatt Lite?" Wade asks. "I don't think so," Jim says. (Later, I check with Wade. It turns out they do make it after all, in bottles only.)

Wade says some of the trends in the beer business are counter-intuitive. Craft beer sales are booming thanks largely to flavourful, hoppy beers. So you would think that's what the market wants. But at the same time, Wade says, the fastest-growing beer in Canada is Bud Light, which isn't exactly high up there on the flavour scale. Look at online reviews and the words "watery" and "tasteless" come up a lot.

I ask Wade what he thinks about the craft beer revolution and he says he is "very careful not to put down anybody's beer" and that he "has a lot of time" and "a great deal of respect" for the people who toiled for years to get craft brewing firmly established in Nova Scotia. "At the end of the day, we make beer, which is meant to be shared and enjoyed. I mean, it's a competitive business, but we don't have to hate each other . . . I always say there are different beers for different occasions. You're not taking a double-hopped IPA with hints of watermelon and pine needles to the soccer field or the hockey game. You're taking a two-four of Bud Light, or Budweiser, or Keith's," Wade says.

And then he starts talking numbers. "When you compare all of the locally made craft beer sold in Nova Scotia at the NSLC (Nova Scotia Liquor Commission) it would be very close to the market share of Oland Export alone." And he says when it comes to overall sales, the beers made by AB InBev are almost two-thirds of the market in Nova Scotia.

"I think that there is an appetite for the local in Nova Scotia," says Ian Stewart, back at King's. "The question of whether or not locality matters . . . For marketing purposes it absolutely does."

It sure seems to matter to the people who buy Oland Export Ale, a classic regional brand made here. Even Wade seems surprised by its consistent sales, year-in, year-out.

He says the beer gets "zero marketing . . . Maybe once a year we'll throw some t-shirts in a case, yet it continues to be a huge success. It's four and a half per cent [of the Nova Scotia market]. That means out of every 100 beers sold, four or five are Oland Export. It's amazing when you think about that."

While many craft brewers and local winemakers pride themselves on terroir — the expression of local flavours and conditions in their products — multinationals take a different approach. They want their beers to taste exactly the same, no matter where they are produced.

Jim, whose jobs at Oland have included fermentation manager and assistant brewmaster, says ideally, "The aim is to make the beer taste the same across all the breweries that produce it. Now mind you, there are some malt supply differences, and that's where the brewmasters really need to tailor their brewing processes."

And it's not just taste. Jim, in his quiet and deliberate way, reels off some of the many factors, or parameters, involved: colour, sugar content, alcohol per volume, bitterness. And there are a whole slew of ways to affect them all. Carbon added to the water to remove the chlorine. Calcium carbonate or gypsum to soften it. And then there are the hops. Even different crops of the same variety of hops may produce "variations in alpha acids," (which contribute bitterness to the beer) Jim explains, and brewmasters have to compensate for that too.

Over the next ninety minutes or so, Jim shows me around the plant. While the basics of brewing beer are similar, regardless of scale, there are some differences. Oland uses adjuncts — unmalted grains like corn or rice as a source of fermentable sugar, for instance, and that's a practice craft brewers tend to avoid.

It won't surprise you to learn my preferences tend to interesting local brews. Low-carb Michelob Ultra does not appeal to me in the least. A few months ago, I had a can of Budweiser for probably the first time in fifteen years. I did not enjoy it.

But I couldn't help being impressed as Jim walked me past 200,000-litre fermentation tanks, and as I watched thousands of cans of Bud Light go

Alexander Keith's brewery museum.

by, get packed into cases and then piled onto pallets and wrapped by a robot.

And, even though this plant produces beers drunk the world over as part of a brewing behemoth, it is still the only place making Oland Export.

Wade Keller says he thinks that's part of the beer's appeal. "There's no marketing behind it, it's an organic brand that has been around forever and . . . it's only made at this brewery, it's almost all sold in Nova Scotia."

When he was a chemical engineering student living in southwestern Montreal, Stefan Gagliardi would head over to the Labatt brewery, grab a couple of two-fours, and skateboard the seven kilometres home while balancing the cases of beer, his arms locked tightly together to support them.

Then the craft beer scene in Montreal started to take off — and Stefan also discovered this beer from Nova Scotia called Alexander Keith's India Pale Ale, and he and his friends got hooked on it.

Stefan tells me this as we stand at the Alexander Keith's small-batch brewery in Halifax's historic Brewery Market — the same place Alexander Keith himself was brewing beer back in the 1820s, on Lower Water Street by the harbour. Today, Stefan is the brewmaster here, and even though he's an import from Quebec, he's spent a lot of time consulting archival materials and reading up on the history of the brewery and brewing in Nova Scotia. He points out over the cobblestone courtyard below us (now covered with a roof), which is home to a weekend farmers' market. Ships would unload hops and malt nearby. "This would have been the action spot," Stefan says.

We go down to a basement room that would likely have been a cellar, and Stefan shows me a tunnel unearthed nearly two decades ago during building renovations. The floor is sloped, allowing for barrels to be rolled more easily to waiting buggies that would drive off through the building's north arch and deliver beer to locations around Halifax. "They made a lot of beer here — not a lot by our standards, but by 1800s standards they did. From what I gather, their peak production here would have been about 8,000 hectolitres a year out of this brewery. Right now, our capacity here is about 4,000."

Keith's of course, is a part of the Oland family, now owned by the mammoth AB InBev. In 2016, the company opened a brewery here in the historic market — which means Stefan is in the funny position of brewing small-batch beer for the world's largest beer company. Ian Stewart says

Stefan has "the job from heaven" because he gets a lot of freedom to experiment but doesn't have the financial worries craft brewers face. Others are less charitable. The authors of *East Coast Crafted* say, "Some products are being brewed at the 'Historic Alexander Keith's Brewery,'

Name That Beer

The Stillwell Beer Garden on Spring Garden Road in Halifax is packed. Patrons share tables with strangers, others sit on the steps near the bar, and several stand, glasses in hand.

Stillwell was the first bar in Halifax devoted exclusively to craft beer and cider, and their summer beer garden was an instant hit when it first opened. The beers on tap and available in cans are constantly rotating and the incredible variety of styles and types of beer available are dizzying.

"I got decisions to be made between lager and ale" sings Kim Mitchell in his classic rock standard. Most beers can be described as lagers (fermented at cooler temperatures, with yeasts that sink to the bottom) or ales (fermented at higher temperatures with different yeasts, which rise to the surface). But each category includes a very large number of styles.

It is impossible to give a comprehensive listing of those styles of beer here — whole books are devoted to the subject — but here is an overview of a few different ones. Keep in mind this is a broad overview. Many styles have subsets as well, for instance, there are several kinds of pilsner. These are general thumbnail descriptions, and there are surely exceptions to each one of them — not surprising, given the huge array of beers available:

IPA, or India Pale Ale

A classic English style, with a strong, bitter flavour, and the early workhorse of the craft beer movement. It's said the beer had extra hops added to preserve it for the voyage to India during the colonial era (though some say this is more myth than reality).

Double IPA (or DIPA)

As the name implies, a more flavourful and more strongly bitter beer. Developed by US West Coast craft brewers.

and the beer's original ties to downtown Halifax are milked for all they're worth."

Certainly there is an aspect of faux old-fashioned to the brewery: copper tanks that look old-fashioned — but the copper is just cladding covering

Pilsner

Pilsner is one of the most popular styles of beer in the world, thanks to several mass-market brands (including Heineken and Pabst Blue Ribbon). But don't hold that against it. A type of lager, pilsners are crisp and tend to be light yellow to golden in colour and not very bitter.

Stout

Very dark beers, often with a sweet malty flavour. Some English-style stouts include oatmeal, while American-style stouts go heavier on the hops.

Wheat beer

Using malted wheat, which gives a fruity flavour, wheat beers are usually bright-coloured and often hazy. The proportion of wheat malt to barley malt can vary with the type of wheat beer.

Sour

Sour beers have *Lactobacillus* — sometimes introduced from yogurt with active cultures — which lowers their pH, making them more acidic. For kettle sours, the bacteria are introduced after the wort (unfermented beer) has boiled and then cooled down to a safe temperature. After the bacteria work in the wort for a few days they are killed off with heat and the beer is then fermented.

Session beer

Session beers are not a style in the way other beers in this list are. Rather, the name refers to beers that are easily drinkable and refreshing, with an alcohol content of five per cent or less. If you're heading out for an afternoon of sampling many different beers, sessions may be the way to go.

stainless steel underneath; wooden shelves filled with Mason jars holding ingredients that are just for show.

But there is some real history too. Stefan pauses on our tour of the brewery and pulls out a 1949 brewing book. "They documented everything really well. It's kind of nice. So here you have their ale recipe, and every once in a while you find a lager. I used these books to try and decipher what they were doing in those different eras. Hop dosing had already started decreasing — just looking from 1908 to 1949 to 1970 they had already dropped by probably by more than half. We can see what was popular in different eras.

"Historic beers are funny because I think it's more about the equipment that they used and the process rather than the ingredients — because replicating this recipe would be pretty boring if you just looked at ingredients. You have 8,000 pounds of Canadian malt. One kind of malt. And then three dry hop additions."

I ask Stefan about his funny, neither-here-nor-there position relative to the worlds of macro- and- micro-brewing.

He says while he has a lot of independence, he's also keenly aware of being one of a line of people stewarding the Keith's brand. He established four regular beers coming out of the brewery, and then started doing more experimentation. He's made beer with yeast from the brine of locally made sauerkraut, and one drawing exclusively on Maritime ingredients, including berries and hops from New Brunswick, and malt and honey from Nova Scotia.

"I don't think Keith's consumers were ready for that when we started, but we're starting to introduce these experiments slowly but surely," Stefan says. "A lot of our experiments are really fun to do. Like just figuring out how we can push the boundaries of fermentation and how we can manipulate it through different bacterial and yeast cultures . . . We're starting to play in that category and release the experiments. It took me a while to decide where we wanted to go with it. I didn't want to make big mistakes. I kind of took it slowly so it worked for both the brand and for where I was in terms of brewing. But yeah you'll be seeing quite a bit more of those fun experiments."

You want opinions? Craft beer people will give you opinions. Recently, I saw an online exchange in which one person listed their top five favourite beers, and another responded that the list was nearly correct, and offered an improved ranking. Fixing someone else's top five list? I'd say that's opinionated.

But one thing all the people I spoke to in the beer business could agree on was that more variety of beer, more talk of beer and more brewers on the local scene are a good thing.

Stefan Gagliardi spreads his arms out when I ask him about varieties of beer. "This is what beer can taste like," he says. "As wide as your arms can go."

5
Apple Cider
Cheerfulness and Contentment

The apples aren't much to look at. Some are piled up in bushel baskets, others tightly packed into mesh bags lying in the grass. I see Russets with discoloured skin at their blossom ends, holes where worms or other insects have burrowed into the flesh and patches of rot. It's late October, nearly deer-hunting season, and some of the mixed bags of unknown varieties look more appropriate for tempting deer than for human consumption.

Soon we will be juicing these apples and turning them into cider — a long-standing Nova Scotia tradition that dates back to the early days of European settlement.

I drop the reusable Atlantic Superstore bag I brought with me on the ground. Earlier today, I took my dogs for a walk in the woods. While they ate windfall apples on the ground, I picked the last of the old orchard fruit growing on our property. Our house was built more than a century ago, and I wouldn't be surprised if some of the apple trees nearby are a hundred years old. We've pruned some of the trees over the years, and tried some of the apples, but they are small and fairly sour. Not prime eating.

Despite it being close to the end of the season, I still manage to fill a bag, and bring it here with me — to Brian Braganza's thirteenth annual home Ciderfest.

I first met Brian nearly two decades ago, when he led a group of men on a canoe trip through the Tobeatic Wilderness Area. Brian's hair and beard are mostly grey now, but he still has a sprightly childlike quality to him. He lives on an old, rambling farm property atop one of the fertile drumlins in Newcombville — a short drive from Bridgewater on Nova Scotia's South Shore. Brian is a community-minded type with a talent and passion for bringing people together and turning what might be otherwise mundane events into memorable occasions. Friends and neighbours helped build the straw-bale house he lives in. Soon after moving to the Bridgewater area, he helped organize what would become a massive annual community Christmas dinner that involved culinary arts students at the local community college cooking turkeys, and a small army of volunteers prepping and transporting dishes in aid of getting hundreds of local residents to enjoy Christmas in a communal setting.

After he moved onto the farm, Brian pruned back some of the old apple trees on the property. And, given his community-oriented background, it's no surprise that after he found a tree bearing Golden Russet — one of the classic cider varieties — he decided to create an annual event centred on juicing apples.

Nova Scotia is full of old apple orchards, and residents have been making cider from their fruit for centuries. Long-abandoned ancient-looking apple trees can still be found along roadsides or on rural properties, dotting fields, or in areas now overgrown by woods.

Apples are not native to Nova Scotia. French settlers first planted apple trees in the Annapolis Valley in the early 1600s. One of the first varieties grown here was called the Fameuse, also known as the Snow Apple. The US Apple Association notes that it "tolerates cold winters."

In a land where making wine from grapes was not an option at the time, apples were valued not as a crunchy snack, but as a source of alcohol: hard cider.

Planting apple trees for alcohol is not unique to Nova Scotia. The story of John Chapman (aka Johnny Appleseed), who planted hundreds of thousands of trees in the northeastern United States, is often presented as some kind of wholesome children's story. But, as Matt Blitz puts it in a story for *Food & Wine* magazine called "The Real, Alcohol-Fueled History of Johnny Appleseed", "Appleseed's apples weren't for eating, they were for drinking . . . in an intoxicating glass of hard apple cider."

The cider tradition had long been established in France, and Acadian settlers happily transplanted it to what is now Nova Scotia. And they didn't waste any time. Samuel de Champlain established a community at Port Royal in 1605, with a view to settling sixty homesteaders a year there, and they brought alcoholic cider with them from the old country. In his 1605 diary, Champlain notes that the weather was so cold the French had to split their cider with an axe and divided it up among themselves by the pound.

It didn't take long before the Acadian settlers began planting their own trees. In her book *Heritage Apples*, writer Susan Lundy says a 1698

What's in a Name?

In North America, the word "cider" can refer to either hard cider, a fermented alcoholic drink made from apples, or sweet cider, fresh apple juice that hasn't been filtered.

In the UK, the word "cider" refers only to what North Americans call hard cider. It is an alcoholic beverage.

The juice coming out of the press at Brian Braganza's is fresh and unfiltered — sweet cider. Some of the folks who come to the party later ferment it into hard cider. Others will freeze their juice, while Brian processes and preserves his in Mason jars.

census counted 1,584 apple trees growing at Port Royal, with most of the fruit being used for cider. By 1715, the settlement of Beaubassin on the Tantramar Marshes, near the present-day border with New Brunswick, boasted fifty families and thirty-two acres of apple orchards.

By 1755, the year of their expulsion, Acadians had planted extensive apple orchards — approximately 18,000 trees — with some believed to have survived into the twentieth century.

Having forcibly deported thousands of Acadian settlers, the government now needed people to tend the farms and orchards they had planted. So it looked south. Charles Lawrence, the Governor of Nova Scotia, issued two proclamations encouraging New Englanders to come to the colony, where they would be given grants of both forested and cultivated land — land from which the Acadians had been removed. The first of this new group of settlers, known as the Planters, arrived in 1760. Many of their family names will sound familiar to present-day Nova Scotians: they include Chipman, Elderkin, Fuller and Whidden.

The Planters greatly expanded the number of apple trees, and introduced new varieties. Charles Ramage Prescott, a wealthy Halifax businessman who retired to Starrs Point, in Kings County, at the age of forty (his health was poor and he found Halifax too foggy), introduced many new varieties in the mid-nineteenth century.

The Annapolis Valley was and remains the province's apple-production centre. Although apple trees were planted throughout the province, in other regions the fruit they grew was usually consumed locally. In a wonderful 1973 article from *Cape Breton's Magazine*, writer Erika Du Bois of Mabou pays homage to the apple trees of Inverness County — hardly prime orcharding territory: "Orchards are certainly not a conspicuous feature of Inverness County, but these often dilapidated stands of trees contain some really delicious 19th Century apples pretty well extinct in the rest of Canada and regarded today as collectors' items. These worthy old trees have proven their toughness through half a hundred winters and still bear plentifully, if biennially. All of these old varieties are specially suited to a home orchard where flavour, quality and season are more important than the ability to tolerate lengthy shipping or gas storage . . . By heedful choice, prudent Cape Breton farmers who planted these trees provided themselves . . . with fresh fruit for ten months of the year — no small achievement in our fickle climate."

Nova Scotians began exporting apples in 1849, nearly a century after the Planters arrived. The development of the apple barrel, first produced in 1863 in New Ross, allowed fruit to be shipped safely and led to a dramatic increase in exports.

An 1887 document in the Nova Scotia Public Archives' Chipman Family Papers collection shows the prices being paid for "sound well-packed Canadian Apples" in London (some fetched double the prices of American apples). The list includes familiar names — Northern Spy, Gravenstein and, of course, Golden Russet — along with now largely forgotten varieties such as Blenheim, Baldwin, Greenings, Vandevere and Red Streak.

Although the old varieties have now disappeared from large-scale commercial production, which has been dominated by the Honeycrisp for the last two decades, some can still be found in old orchards, while others are being actively brought back.

In a *Saltscapes* magazine article, writer and slow food advocate Brian Kienapple introduces us to octogenarian apple grower Marion Inglis, a descendant of Bishop Charles Pippin, who developed the Bishop's Pippin apple. Inglis takes Kienapple into her twenty-five-acre orchard near Tupperville, in the Annapolis Valley. Here she shows him the remnants of the old Acadian cellars that would have been used to store apples, and collects a basket full of apples with now unfamiliar names such as Tolman Sweet, Bough Sweet, Nonpareil and Astrachan. Most of these varieties are known as juice or cider apples — particularly the Nonpareil, which originated in France in the 1600s and went on to become popular in England.

The apple industry boomed in the nineteenth century, with ships carrying apples loading up in then-busy ports like Canning (which was called Apple

Tree Landing) across the Atlantic to England. Apple farmer Larry Lutz of Scotian Gold noted in a 2015 presentation to the International Fruit Tree Association Conference that by 1931, Nova Scotia farmers were harvesting nine million bushels of apples a year, with 80 per cent of the crop being exported to Europe — mostly Britain. But with the formation of what was then called the European Common Market, Canada's preferential treatment disappeared, and apple exports to Britain plummeted. Older varieties fell out of favour, and farmers removed and burned thousands of trees. Lutz says about 155,000 trees were removed from the Annapolis Valley between 1949 and 1959.

Look at the top apples grown in Nova Scotia in the post-war era, and, unless you're an apple aficionado, most of the names will be unfamiliar: Ben Davis, Stark, Wagener and Baldwin were the top four. The more familiar Gravenstein and Golden Russet — one of the most coveted cider apples — are next on the list, at under 10 per cent of the crop each.

By the time insurance adjuster turned apple farmer Keith Boates got into the business, in 1960, Nova Scotia apple-growing was at a turning point.

Cider Apples

The English and French have been drinking cider for a very, very long time. The Romans are said to have encountered cider-drinking Britons in 55 BCE, and in ninth-century France, Charlemagne ordered that his estates have cider makers on hand.

So it's no surprise that many of the best cider apple varieties come from the two traditional cider making regions of Somerset in southwest England, and Brittany in northwestern France.

Here are some types of cider apples being grown in Nova Scotia:

Dabinett

A traditional English variety that cider maker Jay Hildybrant says also grows well in Brittany. He says it "has this rich feel, nice complexity, beautiful tannins."

"The apple business in Nova Scotia had been quite vibrant until the Second World War, with a lot of exports to the UK, and we hoped that it would be revived. Before the war, the main market in the UK was for cooking apples used to make pie — varieties like Ben Davis, Stark, Wealthy and Northern Spy," Boates says.

"When we first owned the farm, a lot of it had already been converted from the old culinary apples, but I realized we couldn't make a living from big old trees that had been grafted over, and we had to keep up with the new varieties. I almost went broke planting a new orchard — a lot of McIntosh, Cortland and Red Delicious."

Throughout the Annapolis Valley, other apple growers were doing the same. But they still were struggling to make a living from their orchards. All that changed in the mid-1990s, when the industry's new saviour appeared on the scene: the Honeycrisp. That orchard Boates planted, filled with McIntosh, Cortland and Red Delicious? "Most of it is gone now," he says, "because we've redeveloped it again with new varieties like the

Golden Russet
The basis of much Nova Scotian cider. The comprehensive Cider School website calls it "one of the better American varieties." It has very high sugar content.

Yarlington Mills
A traditional English cider apple whose juice is bittersweet.

Ribston
A relative newcomer (introduced in the early eighteenth century) from Yorkshire. Features an aromatic flavour.

Northern Spy
A familiar eating apple in Nova Scotia, this is a North American variety with high acidity, and it is a staple of many local ciders.

Frequin Rouge
A key French cider apple whose juice is sharp and bitter.

Honeycrisp." It soon became the most widely planted apple in the province.

While the Honeycrisp has become ubiquitous, it is not an ideal cider-making apple.

Cider at Home

Hard apple cider is among the easiest fermented drinks to make at home. Of course, a little experience and skill will give you more consistent results, but you can get a perfectly drinkable cider quite easily.

Because of the high sugar content in apples and the naturally occurring yeasts on the fruit, fresh apple cider ferments very easily. You can literally leave it on your counter and let it start bubbling away. If you are happy with a slightly sweet and uncomplicated cider, you can make one with no ingredients or special equipment. If you want a drier, more mellow cider and you have the patience to wait several months, you will need a bit of equipment, but the process is still quite straightforward.

You can either buy juice or press it yourself. Raw, unpasteurized juice will ferment faster but may be hard to find because of food safety concerns. (There have been some cases of *E. coli* contamination linked to unpasteurized cider recorded.) But even pasteurized sweet cider will ferment if left alone. Boates Farm cider undergoes UV pasteurization, but will nonetheless begin to ferment after ten days or so. You can also buy sweet cider (the dark brown stuff, not the clear, bright yellow juice) from the supermarket. Just make sure the juice doesn't contain chemical preservatives such as sodium benzoate, because they kill micro-organisms and will prevent fermentation.

If you are pressing your own apples for juice, try to use a variety of apples for a more interesting flavour.

One of my go-to books for making various wines is a delightful English book called *First Steps in Winemaking*, by C. J. J. Berry. (My copy has completely fallen apart through heavy use.) While Berry includes detailed descriptions for making many fruit wines, for apple cider he simply has this to say: "Collect the juice in a jar, stand it on a tray in a warm place (about 70° F / 21° Celsius) and add yeast. Invert a small glass over the top of the jar. For a few days the jar will froth over and must be kept topped up, but when the ferment quietens fit an air-lock and proceed as for any other wine."

Pretty simple.

Brian Braganza works the apple press.

Jay Hildybrant, cider maker and one of the co-owners of Chain Yard Cider in the North End of Halifax says, "When you bite into a Honeycrisp, it's got a lot of water, a lot of sugar, no tannins and no acid." Tannins and acid being two of the qualities you look for in a cider apple.

"They seem kind of thin to me," I tell him.

"That's exactly it," he answers.

Brian Braganza's not entirely sure about what kinds of apples he has. "It's one of those old properties — back there, there are probably six or eight trees, and three or four over here," he says, pointing. "There are Russets, there's some Gravenstein. I don't know all of them. That little tree over there doesn't give very much. Like, last night it had two apples. But the Russet — the big one there — gives quite a few. The Russets are the most plentiful."

Taste any of the apples from these old trees — or any of the other apples people like me have brought this afternoon, and you're not likely to be impressed. They may be overly tart, or a bit mealy. But blend them together, and it is magic.

While Brian pours juice through a funnel into jugs, Kathleen Naylor works the cider press. "Have you tried some yet? If you press a bunch out of one bag you can taste the difference really clearly," she says. "I try to mix it up a bit. I don't know what kind of flavour the Russets give, I just know if you play with it you can taste the difference."

Kitchen-Counter Cider

Ingredients
• Unfiltered apple juice

Method

Take a container of juice, or fill one with pressed juice, leaving a bit of headspace. Leave the bottle or jar uncovered, but stretch a piece of paper towel or fine fabric such as cheesecloth over it to prevent any insects from getting in. (As a bonus, this will also allow wild yeasts in the air to contribute to the fermentation.)

Place the container holding the juice on a tray or in a bowl, because it will likely start to ferment quite vigorously and will overflow.

Once the fermentation has slowed down, cap the juice, refrigerate and enjoy the bubbly, tangy cider. Consume within a week.

Those old Nova Scotia orchards with the unprofitable varieties? Those are the ones people who make cider for a living are most interested in.

To understand why, it helps to know a bit about what makes cider tasty.

Just as we don't make wine from table grapes, the ideal cider apples don't necessarily make for the best eating. In fact, some of them may make downright unpleasant eating — including crabapples, which are known in the business as "spitters." As in, they taste so bad you spit them out. But some of those spitters and similar varieties are vital to cider making.

As with many fermentation processes, the keys to fermenting cider are — at the simplest level — yeast and sugar. If you're using pure apple juice and not adding any sugar to it, the sugar comes straight from the apples. Through the fermentation process, yeasts consume these sugars and convert them into alcohol. But sweetness needs to be balanced by the acidity of tannins and other flavours. And that's where traditional cider varieties come in.

Ask John Brett about these varieties and he gets very passionate and animated.

During the 1980s and 1990s, John made a name for himself as a documentary film director and editor. (He remembers "drowning myself in cider" bought at corner stores in Montreal after late nights spent mixing sound at the National Film Board studios.) In the early 2000s, there wasn't a lot of good-quality cider available in Nova Scotia — so he decided to start making some. He teamed up with apple grower Andrew Bishop of Noggins Corner Farm, whose family first planted fruit orchards on their land back in 1760, and together they formed Tideview Cider.

"We were focused on using the traditional varieties that grew here and that we determined were the best for cider making" John says. And "the basis for any real, authentic cider from this part of the world is an apple called the Golden Russet."

Russets are very sweet, have a balanced flavour and allow you to produce a cider with an appropriate level of alcohol. But Russets alone won't produce a delicious cider, because they don't have the bite of tannins. John says ideally, he would have gotten his tannins from "the traditional English or French varieties that they would grow just for tannin: Tremlett's Bitter, Bulmer's Norman, Fréquin Rouge, or Médaille d'or." Those varieties are not readily available in Nova Scotia, so Tideview turned to Northern Spy,

Your Basic Dry Cider

Kitchen-counter cider can be made in very small batches. A longer fermentation to produce a more traditional dry hard cider requires more effort, so I suggest making a larger amount — enough to fill a 1-gallon (20-litre) carboy (also called a demijohn). This recipe produces a dry cider that is not bubbly.

Materials
- Glass or plastic carboy (1 gallon / 4 L) jug
- Cheesecloth or other fabric
- Large bowl or other container
- Airlock
- Food-grade plastic tubing
- 6 standard wine bottles
- Corks and hand corker

Ingredients
- Enough unfiltered apple juice to nearly fill the jug
- Package of yeast for winemaking (optional)

Method

Start the same way you would with kitchen-counter cider. Fill your jug and cover it with cheesecloth or fabric. Place it on a tray, because the fermentation will be vigorous at first.

You can use the naturally occurring yeasts in the juice or add yeast. If you are adding yeast, buy it at any local home winemaking shop or online. Any number of commercial yeasts will work well, though they don't all produce the same results. Follow the instructions on the package for the appropriate amount of yeast.

Wait several days or more until the vigorous fermentation has settled

Jonagold and crabapples. "Different crabapple varieties are probably the best source, a lot of them being completely inedible," John says.

Tideview produced its first ciders in 2004. They were sold in wine bottles, were bubbly like a sparkling wine and in many cases had been aged a year.

down and the juice is no longer actively bubbling. At this point, the level of liquid in the bottle will have dropped. Top it up with water (if it's only a bit lower) or fresh juice, then carefully wipe the top and neck of the bottle so it's clean.

Place an airlock on the top of the jar. Airlocks are simple devices that hold a bit of water and let air escape without letting flies or contaminants in. You can buy them online or at winemaking supply shops for just a few dollars. Let the cider happily bubble away in a warm place. I like to place the bottle in my office because it's sunny and warm and I find the regular "bloop" sound of the cider bubbling quite relaxing. Eventually (this could take a couple of months) the bubbling will stop or slow to a near-stop.

Next, rack the cider. Racking is the process of getting rid of all the sediment that will have settled at the bottom of your fermentation jug. I place the jug on my kitchen counter beside the sink and use a piece of food-grade plastic tubing to siphon the liquid into a bowl. You can simply suck on the tube to get the liquid flowing, place your bowl in the sink (or on the floor) and allow the cider to flow out of the fermentation jug. Stop the flow by pinching or lifting up the tube before you reach the sediment.

Now wash the carboy (or whatever other bottle you are using) to get rid of the sediment, pour the cider back in, fit your airlock once more and leave it for another month or two.

After that it will be ready to bottle and enjoy. Buy bottles from a wine shop, or reuse your own bottles (just wash them well first). Use natural or synthetic corks (natural ones are cheaper and work fine) and fit them into the bottles with a corker. These are simple machines, usually with two levers, that exert enough pressure to force the cork into the bottle.

Store in a dark, cool spot, with the bottles on their side.

The cider will keep for years, but it will be at its best for six to eight months.

Yield: About 6 x 750 mL standard wine bottles

John was a familiar sight at local farmers' markets, standing behind a table lined with attractive-looking cider bottles. A decade later, he sold his interest in the company to partner Andrew Bishop, who continues to produce cider under the name Noggins Farm. John hung onto the Tideview name, and has considered getting back into the business.

The main reason he got out of it? Economics. At 15,000 litres a year, the company's production was, he admits, "tiny." In contrast, the fermentation tanks at Chain Yard hold 8,000 litres apiece. Getting bigger would have meant investing much more money than the partners had, in order to buy larger tanks and a bottling line. And at the time, the cider business hadn't yet taken off in Nova Scotia. John doesn't feel bitter about the business taking off after he left it. "I'm pleased. Very pleased at how much it's grown. It was reasonable to think it would hit here because it was a wave, and it had gone right across North America. And things always hit here a little later."

He also hasn't left the cider business altogether. For now, he is growing apples at his orchard in Cunard, near Greenwich in the Annapolis Valley — by the Cornwallis River, which he describes as "a big saltwater estuary."

John knows a lot about apples, but not so much about growing them. So he selects the varieties he wants to produce and orchardist Josh Oulton takes care of maintaining the trees. "We're putting in the last fifty trees by the end of next week," John says on a late spring day. "We'll have about 550 trees, which is about as big as I want to make it.

"The neat thing about these old cider varieties is they all have wonderful names and great stories. So this is good if you're in the cider business. I'm hopeful we'll either start Tideview up again as a small operation producing maybe 50 to 60,000 litres per year, or we'll press the juice and sell it to all these new cideries and just help the industry mature. We'll help them make better cider by having better fruit available."

I ask Brian Braganza if there is an underlying philosophy to inviting dozens of people onto his farm every year to press apples, or if he just wanted to get some juice.

"No, no!" he says, recoiling from the suggestion. "It was about community. About bringing people together. It's about having people on the land, being on the land — and it's about celebrating the Earth and what it gives us. The bounty in the fall. The potluck dinner after. There are lots of apple trees on the property so we can celebrate the fall, make cider, have people over to help with that, have a potluck and make it a great party. And it's all inter-generational, which is a large part of it for me. It's not just about the cider. It's about everyone working together, adults and kids."

Sitting on a large rock in the warm sun — it's going to get close to 20 degrees here today — an elementary-school-aged girl in a pink shirt and leggings tosses away a partly rotten apple. "Wait!" Kathleen Naylor, who works in student services at the local community college, calls out. "This is good enough. Just cut that bad part off." The girl slices it away with a knife, then quarters the rest of the apple and drops it into a big plastic bucket of water, where someone will wash it before carrying the apples to a creaky-looking old cider press a few yards away.

"As long as the apple isn't rotten, everything goes in: seeds, core, everything," Kathleen says.

Over the course of the afternoon, more people arrive. Middle-aged couples, families with young children, teens and parents who have been coming for years. All bring apples — picked from trees on their properties, bought at roadside stands, collected from old, abandoned orchards now reverting to woodlands. Eventually, about two dozen people will be here, transforming this mismatched collection of fruit that wouldn't get a second glance in a supermarket into delicious apple cider.

Brian is the ringmaster, keeping an eye on kids, changing the water in the apple-washing buckets, supervising juicing in the press he bought from

Brian Braganza's Ciderfest is a community event that brings people together.

a neighbour soon after he moved in. It seems like a bit of a Willy Wonka contraption: boards hammered together in a frame, a wooden bucket with slats and an angled trough through which the juice flows into a bucket below. A rusty electric motor connected to an extension cord drives the mechanism, while a squeaky shaft screws a plate down into the bucket as pressing continues in order to squeeze out every last drop of juice.

Kathleen and her partner, Jody Conrad, have been coming to Brian's Ciderfest for years. Wearing sunglasses and sitting in the heat, Jody says, "I feel like I'm fermenting just sitting here."

Kathleen describes to me how the afternoon is likely to play out. "We'll press a bunch of juice, then the machine will break down and a bunch of people will stand around and scratch their heads and figure out how to get it going again. And then the wasps will gather because of the juice, and the dogs will try to eat the wasps."

"We're not used to working in this heat," Jody says, and someone else adds, "Remember the times it would be cold and raining and we'd be doing this under a tarp?"

As the Nova Scotia apple industry expanded — and then boomed, in the 1800s, growers and processors needed to find uses for their less-than-perfect apples. Making cider was one solution. Cider apples were cast-offs.

In a history of the Nova Scotia Fruit Growers Association, Julian Gwyn notes: "In a letter to the Central Board [of Agriculture] written in 1842, Dr. Charles Cotnam Hamilton of the East Cornwallis Agricultural Society says many 'orchards within a few years have been totally engrafted and are now producing apples of the most valuable kinds, whereas before they were very inferior and considered only fit for making cider and feeding to hogs and cattle.'"

Anne Hutten, in *Valley Gold* — her history of apple-growing in Nova Scotia — says apple growers were constantly looking for ways to use waste fruit. They built evaporators to dry apples (leading to widespread fires), experimented with cider vinegar and started producing fresh juice in the 1930s.

She says one of the early efforts at making cider came from an Englishman named R.W. Arengo-Jones. "He had registered the name Scotian Gold for his light, sparkling cider. The drink itself remained unsuccessful, but the name went on to become one of the top brands in the apple industry."

Overall though, cider never became a dominant drink, and apples had many other uses. Jay Hildybrant of Chain Yard says, "Apples have always been a principal component in Nova Scotia's export sector but they also played a major role in the culinary world here on the east coast. Pies have always been and continue to be produced on large levels and a great amount of juice is packaged and sold here too. So the apples have always been here for diverse applications." With the growing interest in craft cider though, more orchard-owners like John Brett are planting increased numbers of trees and growing apples specifically for cider. "The shift from home cider makers to industry-sized producers was a natural progression, using the apples available and challenging growers to produce cider varieties as opposed to culinary or cooking apples," Jay says.

He also believes that the cider business has benefited from the craft beer explosion and the maturing of Nova Scotia's wine industry. People have gotten used to the idea of local flavours in beer — and that's carried over to cider. At the same time, cider makers benefit from advances in winemaking. As Jay puts it, "We now have the ability to introduce a unique creativity in tandem with proper winemaking knowledge to the whole process . . . As a result, the craft side of the industry is flourishing."

Bulwark Cider, one of the new companies driving Nova Scotia's cider revival, is forty-five minutes away from Brian's farm, near New Ross. The November day when I visit is as crisp as a freshly picked Cortland. Nearby, a makeshift farm-stand sells bags of carrots, apples and other fresh produce grown in the Annapolis Valley. The Christmas tree farms and U-picks are welcoming early customers for the holiday season.

At first, I drive right past the big red building. There is no sign outside Bulwark, and I carry on farther down the road until I cross the county line and realize I've gone too far. Then I remember the red building — didn't it have large tanks set up outside? — and turn the car around.

Co-founder and current owner Germain Bergeron meets me wearing his Bulwark Cider hoodie, and we walk up the outdoor staircase into his office, which overlooks the cider production area. As soon as I go through the door, I'm hit with a powerfully pungent, yeasty smell.

A wiry man with piercing grey eyes, and a shock of semi-upright grey hair, Germain is animated and passionate about his business. He didn't get into cider out of a love of making the stuff — Germain describes his original role as "marketing, purchasing, strategy, planning." It was his business partner Dominic Rivard (who has since sold Germain his interest in the business) who took care of making the cider itself — a role filled at the time of my visit by peppy young cider maker Alexandra Beaulieu Boivin.

Jay Hildybrant — co-owner and chief cider maker at Chain Yard Cider.

Germain grew up in Jonquière, Quebec, and remembers his father bringing home German ciders for Sunday-night dinner and sharing them with the family. "It was a way of getting us accustomed to drinking a bit of alcohol and was an entry into the wine world too."

Even though he may not have a direct hand on production, Germain is clearly proud of his company's products. He calls up a chart on his computer showing me the regulations governing what products can call themselves cider in various jurisdictions. In some places artificial flavours and heavily watered-down juice are okay, much to Germain's dismay.

The company was founded in 2010 as a producer of fruit wines, under the Red Barn label, but turned to cider quickly, producing its first batch in 2012. Seven years after its founding, Bulwark accounted for 20 per cent of the cider sold in Nova Scotia.

The cider presses here are several orders of magnitude bigger than the

Cider press at Brian Braganza's.

one sitting in Brian Braganza's yard. Stacks of large wooden boxes filled with apples from Scotian Gold — a grower-owned co-op that supplies the company — are tipped into large vats where they are sprayed with water, then they travel up a conveyor to the gleaming press that will transform them into juice. Bulwark starts pressing apples during the late-summer harvest and continues making juice monthly, right through until June. They go through about a million pounds of apples a year: Golden Russet for tannins, tart Northern Spy and the sweeter Cortland, Honeycrisp and McIntosh. "Sweet, and a bit of tartness as well," Germain explains. "It gives us a nice complexity in the blend."

Like many cider companies, Bulwark has a basic cider (they call it Original) which they sell alongside others using the base as the foundation.

And then there's the People's Cider — an experiment in old-fashioned cider making that's reminiscent of Brian Braganza's cider party.

Cider maker Alexandra Beaulieu Boivin greets me in her tidy lab. It's a quiet spot compared to the bottling plant next door, where 3,000 bottles rattle off the line every hour, and feels snug compared to the large room filled with fermentation tanks. Alexandra describes her job in the simplest terms as "fermenting juice . . . We get the apples and press them here and then I ferment it. My job covers everything from when we get the juice to when we bottle."

When you have liquor stores and tap rooms to supply, consistency is important. But part of the fun of fermenting is experimentation, and that's where smaller projects like the People's Cider come in. Bulwark asks locals to go through their properties, find old apple trees and bring some of them in. In the company shop, located right next to the road, a sign-up sheet has the names and contact information of people who contributed apples, along with the amounts they brought in: ten pounds, two bushels, five 25-kg feed bags. Alexandra combines all these apples into a limited-edition cider — one that will taste different every year — and then makes sure everyone who contributed apples gets some free. The first year, the company held a dinner at a local restaurant to launch the beverage, and invited everyone who gave apples. "The dinner was really fun, really magical," Alexandra recalls. "I was very anxious when people were trying the cider. You bring in apples, you want a good cider!"

Alexandra gives me a taste of last year's People's Cider, which has a sweet and pleasant pear-like taste ("I think we got quite a bit of Russets," she says) and pours a bit of this year's into a small glass and invites me to smell the aroma. "I wouldn't drink it because we are still doing some trials on it, but I think it's going to be really, really, really good."

Born in Trois-Rivières, Quebec, Alexandra studied biochemistry and pharmaco-economics in Montreal before getting interested in wines and doing her sommelier training. She started off working at a winery in Nova Scotia before moving on to cider.

Like many people who have caught the fermentation bug, she makes all kinds of fermented foods and drinks on her own time: ginger beer, sourdough bread, kimchi, kombucha, elderflower wine and homemade beer.

Making drinks like the People's Cider allows her to tinker and experiment. "Normally, you get the juice and then you decide what you want to do with it. Which yeast are you going to use, based on the juice that you have? What adjustments do you have to make? Does it need more acidity? Does it need more sugar? With this one, I don't really like to touch it too much. I just added the yeast. The flavours of wild apples are so interesting. If you're using commercial dessert apples, you may have to do a bit more with them, because the juice is less interesting. You have to add a little acidity, add a bit of tannins, tweak it a little bit. But for this one I did nothing, nothing. There is a deepness of terroir in wild apples. It's deep. There is much more flavour there than in a Honeycrisp."

The People's Cider isn't just a way of making a unique drink — one that's different every year. It's also a way of identifying old orchards and finding out what's growing in them.

Jay at Chain Yard Cider is also on the lookout for old orchards whose fruit can be used for cider making, and working with orchardists to grow traditional varieties.

He jokes that Chain Yard, which opened in May 2017, is "the oldest cidery in Halifax." Unlike other operations, which tend to be close to apple country, Chain Yard is in the heart of the city, and boasts both cider-making facilities and its own tap room.

"Now that we have this cider explosion, we've been contacting lots of orchardists and they're willing to start programs to grow these apples. Apples that give more of a backbone, more complexity to the cider." One of those apples is the Dabinett — an old variety long-used for making hard cider and known to produce a bittersweet juice. "It just has this rich feel, nice complexity, beautiful tannins," he says. That means having growers graft these varieties onto their trees, and finding old, disused orchards. Jay mentions one property that some friends bought, "and they had no idea what they had. So they called me in to take a look, and there was a lot of beautiful stuff out there."

Standing in a cavernous space in the North End of Halifax, surrounded by the tanks where his current batches of cider are aging and fermenting, Jay smiles as he remembers how his fascination with cider began during a stint as a bartender in Ireland.

"I was living close to a lot of unusual orchards — orchards which were pretty overgrown, but were still being used. And every Thursday night, these older gentlemen would come in, about four of them, and they'd sit down in the far corner, order pints of Guinness, and bring in these little jars they'd be drinking from. Eventually, I approached them and said, 'What are you guys trying here?' And it was scrumpy. Scrumpy is a very farmyard kind of cider: a lot of crabapples, wild apples, that sort of thing. Very rich, very funky, with almost cheese-like notes. They would taste it and smell it for hours. Most people wouldn't like it but I developed a taste for it. I got into cider shortly after."

Fermenting apple juice is a relatively simple process. It can be as easy as placing a container of juice in a warm place for a few days. Try that with some unpasteurized fresh apple cider, and pretty soon you'll have bubbles in it. It could even be pretty tasty.

But that's clearly not a reasonable strategy if you're making a commercial product that requires some consistency.

Jay shows me around the production area at Chain Yard, where fermentation tanks line one wall, sharing space with barrels aging smaller batches of cider. There is also a small lab area, where he can keep an eye on the fermentation and aging processes. A warm, yeasty aroma fills the air.

Cider makers generally use commercial yeasts to produce consistent results. Like most cideries, Chain Yard buys apples from growers and has them pressed off-site. Every other week, about 8,000 litres of juice sloshes in and goes into one of the fermentation tanks.

Juice varies, of course, so Jay conducts tests on it to determine things like

Scrumpy and Perry

Like all early ciders produced in Nova Scotia, scrumpy (cider made with local wild apples and sometimes crabapples) and perry (a cider-like drink made with pears) were primarily household affairs. But, unlike apple cider, these drinks have remained that way.

Jay Hildybrant has occasionally made both scrumpy and perry at Chain Yard, and a few other producers have experimented with them as well. He says he believes "scrumpy has been prevalent in Nova Scotia for many years, but its creation and circulation remains somewhat esoteric since it is rarely commercial and is usually made in small batches by hobbyists."

Jay says proper perry is hard to find as well. There are two reasons for that: pear trees can be challenging to grow on a commercial scale, and unlike cider apples, many of which can do double-duty for eating, "the fruit needed for a proper perry is usually unpalatable." So perry remains a drink produced for sale only occasionally.

the level of nutrients, tannins and sugar. Once he knows what he's dealing with, typically he adds "enzymes the juice wants" along with yeast.

Any yeast will convert sugar to alcohol, but not all yeasts are equal.

Alexandra from Bulwark explains the choice of yeast like this: "The yeast will always give you a result, but different yeasts will use different products in the juice to feed themselves. Depending on the amino acids that are in the juice, the content of the juice, the vitamins — the yeast will give you different byproducts. It's those byproducts that give you differences in flavours."

When I ask her about her favourite yeasts, she laughs. "It takes a long time to find your favourite yeast that works really well with the juice that you start with. So that's kind of a secret that winemakers keep. Nobody talks about that."

Once the fermentation is underway, temperature is key to the process. Chain Yard uses tanks with a cooling jacket that can be filled with glycol to lower the temperature of the juice. Lower temperatures equal slower fermentation. "So let's say we're working with a particular variety and I want a very cool, long ferment, I could drop that temperature right down," Jay explains. "Sometimes we work with techniques of stressing the yeast out a little bit. If the yeast works well at say anywhere from 15 to 20 degrees, towards the end of fermentation you might bring that down to 13 or 14 just to make it stress a little bit. That lets unique flavours come through. The temperature control allows us to have more diverse fermenting procedure which is kind of cool."

All good things come to an end, and when it comes to yeast, that applies to the fermentation process too. The yeast can only tolerate so much alcohol (the amount varies depending on the strain). When he wants to stop the fermentation, Jay introduces a bit of sulfur dioxide to kill off the yeast. Foundation, one of the company's signature ciders, ferments for two to three weeks. After that, he adds bentonite — a clay-based binding agent — to the now-alcoholic juice. It binds with solids and drops them to the bottom of the tank. Most ciders are then filtered ("we want to make sure they're nice and clean and have no issues whatsoever," Jay says), and from there the cider is moved to a pressurized tank called a brite tank, which is where it gets carbonated.

Ciders can be aged for as little as a few weeks, or as long as a year. If they are sold at a price similar to beer, they tend to be aged for less time than ciders sold in champagne bottles at prices comparable to some wines.

As afternoon turns to evening, the tap room at Chain Yard Cider starts filling up with people drinking pints and flights of smaller glasses with a variety of ciders while nibbling on appetizers.

Since the cider revival remains relatively new, the tap room regularly sees people curious about trying their local cider.

In addition to his standard ciders, Jay gets particularly excited when he talks about his limited runs, barrel-aging and wild ferments.

Twist an apple off the branch of a tree, look at it and you may see what looks like a dusting of extremely fine white powder. Those are wild yeasts. To get batch after batch of consistent-tasting cider you can't rely on those yeasts to ferment your juice. That's because there are seemingly endless varieties of yeasts out there, and they have different properties — for instance, when it comes to alcohol tolerance.

Wild fermentation — using those wild yeasts instead of the always-consistent commercial strains — can be deeply satisfying, but is also risky.

"They're always going to be different. We had one product called Kings Are Wild. It is one of the most beautiful wild ferments I've tried. Mother Nature made it — I just helped it along. It's great," Jay says. "We get a lot of people asking when it's coming back, and we say it's not. It's not coming back. You might get something close somewhere down the line. Part of the fun is having that really unique experience."

Because they are micro-organisms, yeasts get everywhere. To make sure yeast in the air at Chain Yard doesn't mix with wild yeasts, Jay keeps juice he plans to wild-ferment sealed in the tote it arrives in, connects a hose, and hermetically seals the fermentation tank into which it is being drawn. "Then I bring the temperature up to a healthy, say 16 or 17 degrees so the yeast can feel comfortable, and then I give it the nutrients that it needs."

Thanks to DNA testing, it's possible to find out just what those wild yeasts are. Jay remembers an "absolutely beautiful" wild-fermented perry (cider made with pears) and sent it off for testing. It turns out it was half a dozen different yeasts mingled together. "What we have found is Nova Scotia has some amazing indigenous yeasts," he says.

John Brett credits Hanspeter Stutz with re-launching the cider industry here. Stutz owned the Grand-Pré winery, and John says, "cider is a fruit-based fermentation like grapes, so it made a lot of sense for someone like him who was in the grape fermentation business to also deal with cider. Being Swiss, and having seen ciders in different parts of Europe, he thought there was a market."

Several years later, Germain Bergeron and Dominic Rivard saw that market too — all the way from Thailand, where they lived and owned a winery. John Brett describes Dominic as "the real deal — a winemaker who did what he said he was going to do." Dominic moved to Nova Scotia to set up Bulwark, and Germain arrived soon after.

Germain says, the craft cider revival they are part of taps into an old Nova Scotia tradition of small-scale home cider making. "If you go to rural Nova Scotia and talk to people, almost all of them will tell you that their grandparents used to have cider in their basements. They were all producing it and drinking it in the wintertime."

On his Wines of Canada website, Robert A. Bell says by 1775 one of every ten farms in North America had its own cider press, and there is no reason to think the situation was any different in Nova Scotia.

Before widespread water purification, mild alcoholic beverages like cider were widely consumed. Even children drank them. Ed Coleman, a long-time

Picking and packing apples, 1941.

chronicler of Annapolis Valley life and history, notes that even temperance campaigners who railed against the evils of alcohol saw cider as wholesome. Coleman cites an 1831 almanac in which the Nova Scotia Temperance Society gives cider its blessing — up to a limit. He writes, "Wine, in moderation, said the Society, brought strength, vigor and provided nourishment. Cider and Perry (in moderation of course) were also recommended since they brought one 'cheerfulness and contentment.'"

In his spiral-bound self-published memoir, *Sauerkraut, Codfish, and Apples*, Earle K. Hawksworth recalls living with his aunt and uncle when he was a teenager, on their South Mountain farm near Annapolis Royal, at the peak of the temperance movement. He writes, "The Women's Institute and Women's Temperance Union were vigorous organizations in those days and my aunt was active in both. This did not prevent my uncle, or indeed other men of the community, from maintaining ample supplies of cider in their cellars, some sweet and some hard." One spring, Earle and a local boy named Everett Strong were preparing the fields. "I was to drive the horse in marking out rows for planting," Earle writes. "It was a very hot day and Everett helped himself to some hard cider that was kept in the farm cellar. I, too, refreshed myself with the drink, not having any experience with cider, sweet or hard. We both became quite tiddly. Soon I became nauseated and developed a splitting headache. By this time Everett had gone home . . . When I surveyed the plot the next morning I realized how very inebriated we must have been."

Hydrographer and cartographer Mark McCracken grew up in Berwick, in the Annapolis Valley, and remembers his aunt Karen and uncle Cam's cider. Karen and Cam moved to the valley from Ontario, but they tapped into a centuries-old tradition by making cider.

Mark says his uncle Cam would help an apple-farmer friend press juice for cider and get some in exchange. "There used to be a distillery in Bridgetown called Acadian Distillery, and they would put the apple juice in barrels from the distillery to ferment it. When there was a group of people at Karen and Cam's place, the cider would come out — and some evenings there was a lot of cider. It seemed to do funny things to people — more so than other forms of alcohol. There would be times when you'd get up the next morning and there would be someone lying on the living room floor and you didn't remember them going to sleep there — and they wouldn't remember it either."

Alcoholic and non-alcoholic ciders were among the mainstay beverages made by Nova Scotia's Roue family. Their business was located at Wood's Wharf, near the bottom of Salter Street in Halifax. The Roues were in the carbonated beverage business from 1879 until after the end of the Second

World War. (William J. Roue, the famed naval architect who designed the *Bluenose*, was part of the family and ran the business for a number of years.) The Nova Scotia Archives has a collection of Roue family papers, including recipes, tips and price lists. Some of those recipes — like the one for making cider with saccharine — are probably best not attempted today. In a catalogue aimed at beverage houses, the Roues advertised "Fermented apple juice, made from sound ripe apples and bottled fresh from the press, with the addition of pure carbonic gas for its preservation . . . brilliant as Champagne, yet containing no trace of alcohol." A case of a dozen quarts ran two dollars.

The same page offers sparkling crabapple cider, slightly more expensive at $2.25 per case, and described as "an excellent substitute for light, dry Wine," and Golden Russet hard cider ($2.75 per case) described in wonderfully fragrant tones:

> *Made from hand-picked apples, fermented and treated in accordance with most approved methods for Wines. It is far superior to any cheap Champagne . . . With every barrel of bottled Cider we pack six finely engraved thin crystal champagne glasses, for which we make no charge; one quart bottle will just fill six of them, or a pint bottle will fill three. Handsome glasses promote sales and proper sizes insure profits.*

One of Nova Scotia's most successful and notorious ciders (or apple drinks, if you are a purist) was Chipman's Golden Glow, aka Chippy's, Golden Glow or just Glow.

In *Valley Gold*, Anne Hutten describes the origins of Golden Glow. Lewis Chipman, or Lew:

> *"who died in 1980 at the age of 93, began making his special cider in his kitchen, at Chipman Corner. The year was 1939,*

possibly 1940. The Prohibition years (1921 to 1930) had helped popularize the easily available local cider, and Chipman decided to supply some of this ready market. He labeled it "Apple Sauterne." It was clearly alcoholic, and he acquired a listing with the Nova Scotia Liquor Commission.

A period of two years during which he was out of production coincides neatly with the rumor that he was bootlegging and lost his license. But by 1943 he had moved to Kentville . . . The name 'Sauterne' was outlawed, and he changed it to 'Golden Glow.'"

The Chipman family opened Nova Scotia's first commercial winery in Kentville in 1941, under the name Chipman's Apple Products, later changed to Chipman's Wines Limited. The winery burned down a dozen years later. It was rebuilt and business ran independently until 1983, when it was sold to the BC-based Andrés Wines — one of the giants of the Canadian wine industry. Andrés shut down the Kentville operation and started making Golden Glow at its plant in Truro, until the product was discontinued in mid-2000s. At its peak, it sold 50,000 gallons a year in Atlantic Canada.

Golden Glow was the signature Chipman product. Sold in a jug, it boasted a low price point and 15.5 per cent alcohol per volume — making it the drink of choice for teens and college students throughout the province.

In the first issue of *Old Trout Funnies*, his classic 1970s alternative comics, Cape Breton-based writer/illustrator Paul MacKinnon includes a villain called Captain Glow. Cape Breton University professor Ian Brodie, describes him as 'a Captain Hook-type figure' who carries a jug of 'Golden Equalizer' — "so named because it made everyone equally stupid." One of Glow's henchmen, a character by the name of Bad Onion, leans in from the margins of one of the comic's pages and tells us, "Glow is all you need!" Captain Glow uses the drink to subdue the local population, before a massive Glow explosion ends his attack on the good people of Cape Breton.

Writer Alison DeLory, who works in advancement at the University of King's College, not far from where she grew up in the South End of Halifax, laughs out loud when I ask her about drinking Golden Glow in her teen years, during the late 1980s. "We drank it in high school because it was cheap. It came in a moonshine kind of jug, and I think it cost thirteen dollars. Three or four of us would go in on it, so you could get drunk for three dollars. We drank it purely for economic reasons."

Golden Glow, she remembers, compared favourably to skimming off a bit from each bottle in your parents' liquor cabinet and drinking the resulting hooch.

"It's a nostalgia thing for me and my friends. It was the cheap drunk we'd groan and laugh about at the same time."

Germain Bergeron didn't grow up in Nova Scotia, and knows little about how Golden Glow tainted the reputation of cider for decades. ("I think there was a product called Glow Cider maybe twenty years ago?" he says. "It was sort of an entry-level product.")

John Brett says when he launched Tideview Cider, the legacy of Golden Glow "was a bit of a problem. Because for very many local people of my generation, the first and worst hangover they ever had was on Chipman's Golden Glow. So the word "cider" didn't conjure up nice thoughts. At all. People thought it was just rot-gut. It was actually easier to sell it to younger people, because they had no association with Chipman's Golden Glow."

At Brian Braganza's, the cider-pressing part of the day is winding down, soon to be followed by an old-style potluck and music.

Cate de Vreede is one of the last arrivals, pulling up with her pre-school aged son, Dylan. Before long Dylan, who is wearing a ball cap printed with green tractors, is eating an apple from one of Brian's trees and squatting atop

Bottles waiting to be filled with cider.

the cider press, screwing down the plate onto the bucket with all his strength while his mother watches.

A motley collection of containers waits to be filled: four-litre glass jugs, pop bottles and a significant number of growlers from local craft breweries — a sign of the burgeoning local beer industry.

Brian won't personally end up with much sweet cider. "I probably get four of these four-litre jugs out of it," he says. But that's not the point. The afternoon is about connecting with neighbours, producing juice together, and celebrating one of the oldest crops grown in Nova Scotia — one that's had people raising glasses to each other for hundreds of years.

6
Wine
Finally Bearing Fruit

Gabrielle Perlat was hoping to leave the grapes on the vine a bit longer. But bugs have forced her hand. She moves quickly up and down rows of vines laden with white grapes, harvesting them and filling up a Rubbermaid-style box. When the box is full, she drags it down to the end of the row, grabs three more empty boxes and runs back up the row to start over.

Gabrielle is the operations manager at the Petite Rivière winery on Nova Scotia's South Shore — not far from where the first wine grapes in the province are said to have been planted over 400 years ago. She and Christian Perlat, the winery's vineyard and cellar manager (and her husband), monitor the grapes regularly during the season. Now they've found sour rot on some of the grapes. If it spreads, it will ruin the grapes for winemaking, so Gabrielle has to move fast to harvest the healthy fruit — especially since the sky is threatening rain.

Gabrielle Perlat hand-harvesting Cayuga grapes at the Petite Rivière estate vineyard.

Snip, snip, snip. I can't see much difference between the healthy grapes and those with sour rot, but Gabrielle can spot them immediately.

I leave her and walk the few steps to the winery, where Christian is getting ready to press a shipment of L'Acadie Blanc grapes grown nearby in Barss Corner. (Like many wineries, Petite Rivière grows grapes and buys some from other growers.)

Donald Hann, a young assistant in a *Duck Dynasty* shirt and a ballcap that reads "Happy happy happy" carefully power-washes equipment ahead of the pressing, then starts feeding grapes into a gleaming de-stemmer reminiscent of a small wood chipper. Christian — whose family in France has made wine for generations — spots me as he prepares the press near the mouth of the cellar. He calls out an enthusiastic "Bonjour!"

Petite Rivière co-owner and winemaker Barbara Thomson is also in the cellar, feeding yeast nutrient to barrels of fermenting red wines and monitoring their temperatures to ensure a slow, cool fermentation. A former interior designer, Barbara jokes that she and her husband/business partner Sean Sears hadn't fully realized how much work they were getting into when they bought the place. "We were looking for a vineyard but hadn't really thought through what that meant — that there was a winery attached to it."

For the most part, winemaking in Nova Scotia is a small-scale affair. Most wineries produce a few thousand cases a year. And it's labour-intensive work.

Christian is using a small press that he will monitor closely as it squeezes the juice out of these grapes. Pressing just this one batch is going to keep him busy well into the evening. "I'll be here till 10 tonight," he says.

Barbara turns to him and says, "I'll have to get you a pack of toothpicks," and Christian pops his eyes wide cartoonishly. "I've been up forty hours over the last two days already," he says.

The hydraulic press comes to life — its metal plate, fitted inside a wooden barrel, slowly descending. Christian starts it off at 100 bars of pressure and will very gradually work it up to 500, but he can't get there too fast. Use too much pressure and the juice will spurt out the sides and be lost. Use the right amount, and the grapes are pressed through a filter that captures the skin and seeds, the juice gently collecting at the bottom of the press before being filtered and then pumped into a large

Christian Perlat (left) and Donald Hann (right) tend the press at the Petite Rivière winery.

tank, where it will ferment. A whiteboard in the cellar notes which grapes are in what tanks, and other key information like tank temperature and litres of juice. Each grape gets its own distinctive treatment. "You can't mix the different yeasts," Barbara says. If she's feeding nutrient into a tank, she has to be careful not to then use it in a tank with a different yeast, contaminating it. So it's important to know what's where. Right now, most of the tanks hold Léon Millot and Luci Kuhlmann grapes. "L'Acadie" is written on the bottom line of the board, for the grapes Christian is pressing right now.

Christian separates layers of grapes, using straw mats called "scourtins." After the juice in each layer has been pressed out, what's left is called a cake.

Press, pause, check, up the pressure, press again. Christian observes the press closely, and whenever the flow of juice drops to a trickle, he ups the pressure a little more. Each time, a little more juice comes out. "C'est un travail de patience," Christian tells me. A job that requires patience.

After half an hour or so, Christian walks across the cellar, grabs four wine glasses and fills them up with freshly-pressed juice. Without saying a word, he hands one to each of us.

"Oh, that's good," says Donald. "Better than the red we had last week. That was sweeter. It was like drinking sugar."

I take a sip. The juice is complex — sweet, with a hint of tannins. We all sip it quietly. Then Barbara says, "It's so nice. So fresh."

A tractor pulls up from the field with a bin brimming with recently harvested Cayuga grapes.

"Apparently we have a *huge* Cayuga crop," Christian says to Barbara.

"Yes. Big, beautiful, juicy grapes."

People have grown grapes in Nova Scotia for centuries. And they've been drinking wine for almost as long. Making wine though? That's another story.

The colonists who made the journey to New France were likely wine drinkers back home. And they may have thought they could grow grapes and make wine just as easily here.

It wasn't quite that easy.

The first vineyard in Nova Scotia is said to have been planted near Bear River in 1611, less than a decade after the first French colonists arrived, by an apothecary named Louis Hébert. French settlers also tried to grow grapes in the LaHave valley, where Monsieur Isaac de Razilly, Governor of Acadia, planted a vineyard in the early 1630s. But after he died in 1636, serious attempts to grow wine grapes in Nova Scotia came to an end and wouldn't be revived for centuries.

Grapes do grow wild here. And if you like, you can try making wine

Making Country Wine

You can turn almost anything into wine. Over the years, I have made wines from dandelions, apples, crabapples, pears, elderberries, white currants and kiwis — on their own and in various combinations. In Nova Scotia we have an abundance of fruit and flowers that lend themselves to winemaking.

"Country wine" is the term for wines made with fruit other than grapes, and these wines have a long and storied tradition. There are several wineries in the province making fruit wines, and some have been at it for decades.

The steps for making wine are not complex, particularly if you are making a small batch. I recommend buying a 5-litre demijohn (or carboy). This is enough to make half a dozen bottles of wine. If you are not happy with the results, cook with the wine or turn into sangria. No great loss.

When I first decided to explore winemaking, I was put off by the precision of many of the recipes and instructions I found. These typically included dire warnings about how the wine would be ruined if everything that came into contact with it was not meticulously sterilized. It seemed like an almost militaristic approach to eradicating all the indigenous yeasts.

from them. But don't expect to enjoy drinking it. They have a quality often characterized as "foxy." A euphemism, I presume, for "largely undrinkable."

Without access to wine, French settlers turned to less palatable beverages. A 1664 book on New France by colonist Pierre Boucher describes who drank what: "Wine in the finest of houses, beer in others, and a drink known as bouillon, drunk communally in all homes; the poorest drink water, which is very good and abundant in this land."

That "bouillon" being drunk by people who couldn't afford wine? Essentially, it was like the hooch that grows on sourdough starter. Colonists made a leavened dough, dried it, then broke off an egg-sized piece and put it in water — where the yeasts in the dough would multiply and cause it to ferment, giving the beverage a tangy taste.

So it was a relief when I chatted about winemaking with Sandor Katz and realized he felt the same way when he started to learn about fermentation and making wine. "It was all about sterilizing everything, using these selected strains of yeast, measuring the specific gravity. It was very, very technological." Sandor said there was nothing particularly bad about that, but it contrasted with his experiences walking through West Africa decades ago. "Basically, every village we went to, we were met by people who greeted us with some kind of homemade alcoholic beverage: palm wine, date wine, sorghum beer, millet beer. And later when I was reading this [winemaking] literature . . . I was thinking I'm pretty sure the people in these little villages didn't have potassium metabisulfite tablets to sterilize everything. How was it that these people, who had such limited access to technology, were making such wonderful beverages when the literature I had access to was telling me you needed all this technology in order to do this?"

With that in mind, here is a basic recipe for a berry wine. I used this one to make wine with currants from the garden, but you can substitute other berries.

Country Wine

Materials

- Very large bowl or food-grade plastic bucket
- Rolling pin or other tool for crushing fruit
- Glass or plastic carboy (1 gallon / 4 L) jug
- Cheesecloth or other fabric
- Colander and long-handled spoon for stirring
- Airlock and food-grade plastic tubing
- 6 standard wine bottles
- Corks and hand corker

Ingredients

- 3 lbs (1.4 kg) of currants or other small fruit
- 1 gallon (4 L) water
- 1 package yeast
- Pectic enzyme (optional)
- Yeast nutrient (optional)
- 2 1/2 to 3 lbs (1.1 to 1.4 kg) sugar

Method

The first step is the hardest: Pick over the fruit and remove any stems or hulls. Get as many as you can and don't worry about getting them all.

Now crush the fruit. You could use a wooden or marble rolling pin, potato masher or drink muddler. Another option is to put the berries in a large bowl and crush them with your (washed) hands. Whatever method you use, make sure you can hang onto the juices.

Put the fruit and any juice released in the crushing process into a container made of glass or food-grade plastic.

Boil water and pour it over the fruit, submerging it. Cover the container with a piece of fabric held by elastic. (Fruit flies are not good for your wine!) Leave it to cool during the day or overnight.

Add yeast, following the instructions on the package. For many of my country wines I use Lalvin EC-1118 yeast, which originates in Champagne, is very versatile, easy to find and can survive in environments of up to 18 per cent alcohol.

Berries, like currants, are high in pectin, which can result in a cloudy wine. Adding pectic enzyme will help clarify the wine. It is cheap and any wine shop should have it. (Adding pectic enzyme is optional.)

Unlike grapes, berries don't provide as much nutrition for the yeast. One way to remedy this is to add yeast nutrient. Some winemakers add a bit of lemon juice as an additive, others buy a commercial yeast nutrient. If you use nutrient, follow the instructions on the package.

Cover the container again, and let stand overnight or until the next day, stirring often.

Put the sugar in a pot and cover it with some juice from your container. Whisk or stir the sugar until it is dissolved (heating it slightly — and gently — if necessary). Now add the dissolved sugar to your juice.

Stir several times a day for 4 to 5 days, or until the most vigorous bubbling has ended. Make sure to cover the container. Use a container that has lots of extra space, so the frothy mixture doesn't overflow its side.

Once your wine has settled down, strain out the fruit. Pour the strained wine into a well-cleaned carboy. You should have a bit of headspace but not too much. Add a bit of water if necessary. Place an airlock on the carboy and leave it to ferment in a warm place for 2 to 3 months. You will see bubbles passing through the water in the airlock at a fairly rapid pace at first, then more slowly.

After a few months, it's time to rack the wine. Racking is to get rid of all the sediment that will have settled at the bottom of your carboy. I place the jug on my kitchen counter beside the sink and use a piece of food-grade plastic tubing to siphon the liquid into a bowl. Stop the flow by pinching or lifting up the tube before you reach the sediment. Dump out the sediment, rinse or wash the carboy, then return the wine to it and fit the airlock once again. Leave it for 7 to 9 months, then bottle. Use natural or synthetic corks (natural ones are cheaper and work fine) and fit them into the bottles with a corker. These are simple machines, usually with two levers, that exert enough pressure to force the cork into the bottle.

Store in a dark, cool spot, with the bottles on their side.

Fruit wines tend to not age as well as grape wines, so once your wine is bottled, start enjoying it soon.

Yield: About 6 x 750 mL standard wine bottles

Mmmm, delicious.

Some residents of New France were willing to pay exorbitant premiums for wine though. In 1753 to 1754, more than 7,000 barrels of Bordeaux arrived in Louisbourg to be sold at prices ranging from four to seven times what they would fetch back home.

The English colonists who followed the Acadians also planted grapes, but the varieties they grew were more suitable for eating than making wine.

That's not to say nobody tried making wine though. The Nova Scotia Archives do have a recipe for grape wine, likely hand-written by Rosina Jane Uniacke, whose husband, James Boyle Uniacke, served as Nova Scotia's first premier under responsible government. It is not a particularly precise recipe (it begins with the instruction to "take any quantity of ripe grapes you please,") but it follows the same basic process we would use today for making homemade wine from fresh fruit: cover the fruit with water, let it stand a few days, squeeze and strain it, add yeast and sugar, leave to ferment for a few days while stirring often and then rack into another container (in this case a cask) with a fining agent to get rid of sediment. "It will be fit to drink or to bottle in about nine months," Uniacke writes in her careful hand, before going on to a recipe for pickled cauliflower.

So if you want wine and don't have grapes, what do you do? Make wine with whatever else you have at hand.

The MacGregor Miller Collection in the Nova Scotia Archives includes two folders filled with recipes collected by the South Shore's Miller family between 1816 and the mid-1880s. Many of these recipes are for wines: blackberry wine, raspberry wine, currant wine, ginger wine, rhubarb wine. The archives also include other hand-written recipes for quince wine, gooseberry wine, cherry wine — even parsnip and turnip wines.

"Take a good many turnips, pare and slice them, put them in a cyder press, and press out all the juice very well . . ." starts the turnip wine recipe in Rosina Jane Uniacke's handwritten recipe book from November 12, 1849. I've eaten turnips, and I imagine you have too. Trying to press juice out of them to make wine does not seem particularly enviable.

Picking berries for home winemaking was (and is) a long, labour-intensive process. Louisa Sarah Collins was eighteen or nineteen years old in the summer of 1815 when she wrote a diary chronicling her daily life on her family's Colin Grove farm east of Dartmouth. "I have been picking currants from nine this morning till four this afternoon. We have got a large washing-tub full of wine," she wrote. Later, she refers to spending the whole day making wine from them.

Hard, hard work.

On an unusually hot and sunny summer day, I exit Highway 101 near Wolfville. There are indications everywhere that this is wine country: roadside signs with the distances to nearby wineries, vineyards spread out in neat rows on hillsides washed by cool breezes from the nearby Minas Basin and a brightly painted tour bus that shepherds visitors from winery to winery all afternoon.

Keep driving down the valley for another fifteen or so kilometres and you come to Agriculture Canada's Kentville Research and Development Centre (formerly known as the Kentville Research Station) where dedicated scientists spent decades trying to develop wine grapes that would thrive in Nova Scotia.

It's a task that must have often seemed, well, fruitless.

Kentville researchers began their quest to grow wine grapes in Nova Scotia in 1913. In their definitive *Wine Lover's Guide to Atlantic Canada*, Craig Pinhey and Moira Peters describe looking through the station's 1913 to 1917 logbook, which recorded the types of grapes planted and how the crop fared. "Much of it did not do well," they write, drily.

Donald Craig joined the Station in the 1940s. He was mostly interested in strawberries and rhododendrons, but he started experimenting with grapes too — and doggedly kept at it.

Kentville researchers tried breeding their own varieties, but also worked on seeing how hybrids imported from elsewhere would handle the Nova Scotia climate. One of these hybrids was the pedestrian-sounding V 53261, which was developed in Ontario where it failed to flourish. Craig decided to give it a shot here. He planted some vines in the research garden and waited to see how they did.

The vines took. Eventually, V 53261 was renamed L'Acadie Blanc, and became the foundational grape of the Nova Scotia wine industry.

By 1976 it looked like the researchers might be getting close to success when it came to developing grapes and techniques to produce truly Nova Scotian wines. The *Nova Scotia Times* ran a story by John McCormick

Nova Scotia Grape Varieties

Dozens of varieties of locally grown grapes make their way into Nova Scotia wine. For years, it was accepted wisdom that classic varieties (known as *vinifera*) like Chardonnay and Pinot Noir couldn't be grown here. Now we know they can.

This list leaves **vinifera** aside to look at a few of the hybrid grape workhorses of the Nova Scotia wine industry.

White Grapes

L'Acadie Blanc

Often called Nova Scotia's signature grape, and sometimes compared to Chardonnay for its ability to blend well with other varieties.

Seyval

A white grape that ripens early — making it a good choice for cool climates. "Very nice in blends," according to wine writer Sean Wood.

Vidal

The grape of choice for making ice wine. The vines can produce grapes even after late spring frosts, and the grapes' tough outer skins can withstand the -8°C temperatures needed to freeze them on the vine.

that year under the excited headline, "Developing New Wines for Nova Scotia!" McCormick says the research station was growing about fifty varieties in the Annapolis Valley on a test basis: "Foch, a French hybrid — ruby-red table wine produced from a black grape — has bright prospects. So have DeChaunac, another French hybrid — reddish-brown wine from a purple grape, and Vineland 53035, a dry white table wine — from a cross between French and North American varieties."

Could a wine industry grow in Nova Scotia?

Roger Dial and Hans Jost were about to appear on the scene to show that it could.

Sean Wood was there at a pivotal moment in the birth of the modern Nova

Red Grapes

Baco Noir

A fruity, aromatic grape developed by crossing a French variety with a type of grape indigenous to North America. Many older Baco Noir vines were destroyed in the 1980s, when Canadian growers were paid to remove them as part of a plan to upgrade the industry. But Nova Scotia seems to embrace grapes others are skeptical about, and a few wineries produce high-quality Bacos.

Léon Millot

Another grape that does well in cool climates, Léon Millot was developed in France over a century ago, and is very resistant to fungal infections — an advantage in Nova Scotia's cool, damp climate. It is related to Maréchal Foch and Lucie Kuhlmann, two other grapes well-established in the province.

Maréchal Foch

An intense, dark and aromatic grape, used on its own, or blended. The Sainte-Famille winery in Falmouth says it has the oldest Foch vines in Nova Scotia.

Scotian wine industry. Sean grew up in London, England, moved to Montreal to study history and came to Nova Scotia in 1969 to do a Ph.D. at Dalhousie University. He never finished the degree. Instead, he got interested in wine, writing the curriculum for the province's first sommelier program, penning a wine column for seventeen years, and authoring a book on Nova Scotia wineries.

On the day I meet him, Sean is seated on a sunny pub patio in South End Halifax, enjoying a glass of craft beer. He tells me how he met Nova Scotia wine pioneer Roger Dial at Dalhousie, where Dial taught Chinese politics and political science.

The pair were part of a group who would get together and drink wine on Sunday afternoons. They called themselves the South Street Sippers. "There were, to put it bluntly, not many good wines available locally at the time," Sean says.

And locally produced wine? Forget it. A 1982 price list from Nova Scotia's Port of Wines shows all of eleven Canadian whites and three reds available. None are from Nova Scotia.

"Roger had this crazy idea of making wine in Nova Scotia. We all thought he was nuts," Sean says. Dial had worked as a salesman and general manager for the Davis Bynum winery in California. He had also written extensively on wine. So when he heard that Agriculture Canada scientists were experimenting with grapes and that his Dalhousie colleague Norman Morris, a professor of economics, had vines growing on his property, Dial was intrigued.

Dial heard the Kentville Research Station was experimenting with a variety that hadn't done well in Ontario — this would be the lowly V 53261. Sean recalls, "Roger got hold of some of these grapes and decided to make some wine. He served the result to me blind and said, 'What do you think this is?' I said, 'I can't quite place it, but it tastes sort of like Chardonnay.' And that was what subsequently became L'Acadie Blanc . . . We started getting enthusiastic about it, and gradually one thing led to another, Roger bought the property and eventually set up the [Grand Pré] winery."

Wine Tidings magazine took notice, and ran an article in 1982 on Dial, calling his operation the "heart, albeit in the development stage, of a Nova Scotia cottage wine industry." At the time the story was written, Dial was growing an astounding sixty varieties.

Meanwhile, across the province, Hans Jost — who came from generations of German winemakers — was planting vines of his own. Donald Craig of the Kentville Research Station was one of the driving forces here too. It was Craig who convinced Jost to try planting grape vines — 400 vines in 1970 and 4,000 more two years later. "It soon became evident that the Josts would turn from beef and hog farming to grapes and wine," write Peters and Pinhey. An understatement, considering his company would soon start a decades-long run as the largest winery in the province.

Some forty years later, Craig's son Colin sat on the patio at Jost, having lunch and enjoying a glass of wine. All of a sudden, he says, "It hit me that all of what lay before me existed because of my dad. Had he not asked Hans to try vinting some of his grapes I would be looking at strawberry fields rather than vineyards."

Growing grapes and running a winery require patience (among other qualities). It can be years before you can produce wine — and typically wine quality will improve as vines age. But in the meantime, you have to make a living.

Sean says, "The first generation — remember, these are the pioneers — were pushing string uphill. They had a lot of skepticism to deal with, a lot of trial and error in getting to what they did." To make a living, Nova Scotia wineries would bring in juice from elsewhere, ferment it here and sell it. "Oftentimes it was not very good stuff," Sean says. On the one hand, the revenue from these wines helped keep the early wineries afloat while they developed their own home-grown products. But on the downside, they created a poor reputation for Nova Scotia wine that the industry has only really shaken off in the last decade or so.

Sommelier Jenny Gammon, who works for wine retailer Bishop's Cellar in Halifax, says she still sees some of the old prejudices against Nova Scotia wines from people who come into the shop.

"There are people to this day who say, 'I don't like Nova Scotia wine. I tried it, I've had it, and I don't like it.' I'm like, okay, tell me about what you tried. And if it was not in the last five or ten years, it's a good opportunity to start sharing the story of how fast things have grown and where we are now versus where we were in the past."

Jenny calls Nova Scotia's wine industry "a scrappy upstart."

"Some parts of the world have a 500, 600, 800-year head start on us. So we have to be gentle with ourselves here in Nova Scotia. In Burgundy, for example, there's lots of writing and fond recollections about how the monks basically did split tests and trial and error for hundreds of years. That's why the concept of terroir is so very elevated in Burgundy. Because the monks had nothing but time on their hands and a passion for winemaking. They could ask why the soil over here is slightly different than it is over there, and three more generations that came after them could ask the same question."

Rachel Lightfoot, who studied winemaking at Brock University and works for the family-owned Lightfoot & Wolfville — one of the newer wineries in the province — says, "We are still a very young, new region but for me what's so exciting about Nova Scotia is that we have an incredibly distinctive terroir. It all goes back to that geography, the fact that we are influenced by our proximity to the coast for example, and we have a very cool climate which leaves a lot of really wonderful natural acidity in our grapes. That translates into wines that are really fresh. I like to use the word vibrant. They have an energy and a tension about them."

Ask Bruce Ewert about his wines, and the owner of Nova Scotia's only certified organic winery starts talking about the soil.

"We are encouraging a living soil," Bruce says. In his vineyard, on a sunny July afternoon, he walks me through rows of L'Acadie Blanc grape vines bearing still-immature fruit.

Bruce points to small mounds of soil under the vines.

"You'll see we've turned the soil this year underneath the vines and we're tilling every second row, but we're not using herbicides or pesticides — and the reason for that is we have delicate organisms down here at the root zone. And there's a bit of symbiosis there: the micro-organisms live off a little bit of the sap, the sugars from the vine, and in exchange they help the vines take up nutrients."

Bruce is an engineer turned winemaker who honed his skills in Australia, California and B.C.'s Okanagan Valley, learning the art of making traditional method sparkling wines — fermented in their bottles the way winemakers in Champagne have been doing it for centuries.

He used to work for Canadian winemaking giants Peller Estates — at one point making their Hochtaler brand, which the company markets as a "popular priced product" and wine writer Beppi Crosariol has called "frightful." Bruce says, "I used to make 110,000-litre blends at a time. That was a three-month supply. One hundred and ten thousand litres. And we could standardize it across the country. I don't miss those days . . . Now I make 2,000 cases a year, and I'm much happier."

Bruce arrived in Nova Scotia in 2004 with his wife, Pauline, and their three children, and opened L'Acadie Vineyards. The Nova Scotia Wine Industry was transitioning out of its early days, and Bruce saw not only a lot of potential for the industry, but also an opportunity to make wines the way he had always wanted to: using certified organic grapes and traditional processes.

Owner and winemaker Bruce Ewert at L'Acadie Vineyards.

Pointing to his vines, he says, "Those roots are three feet down now and they've worked for every inch. There's an old saying: 'A stressed vine makes a good wine.' We don't have any issues with drought now that the roots are that deep, and we are getting those mineral flavours. And because this is an ancient seabed, we get a little bit of saline in our wine too."

As we walk between the vines, Bruce and I talk over the sound of the trimmer his son runs a few rows over. Just over a month earlier, a late-season frost caused extensive damage to fruit crops — including grapes — in the

L'Acadie Blanc — Nova Scotia's Signature Grape

L'Acadie Blanc took an unusual route to becoming one of the mainstays of the Nova Scotia wine industry.

For one thing, it wasn't developed in Nova Scotia. L'Acadie Blanc came out of what was then known as the Vineland Horticultural Research Station in Lincoln, on the shores of Lake Ontario. Breeder Ollie A. Bradt created the hybrid variety by crossing the Cascade and Seyve Villard 14-287 varieties. As with all newly minted grapes, it began its career under the banner of an uninspiring combination of letters and numbers. In this case, V 53261.

From that unassuming beginning a couple of thousand kilometres away, this hybrid would go on to become "Nova Scotia's best varietal and a signature of the region," in the words of sommelier and writer Mark DeWolf.

The Vineland research station sent ten of the vines to Nova Scotia to see how they would do in the cooler climate. Local wine pioneer Roger Dial took up the challenge. He described the grapes as "this damn thing, this cast-off variety from Vineland," according to writers Moira Peters and Craig Pinhey, in their *Wine Lover's Guide to Atlantic Canada*. But the vines thrived. Dial rechristened V 53261 as L'Acadie Blanc. "It hadn't done well in Niagara," Sean explains. "But it took to Nova Scotia terroir just like it was made for it." The grapes ripened well, withstood pests and could survive temperatures as low as -25° C.

For an industry as young as Nova Scotia wine, it may sound funny to call any grape traditional — but if there is any one that can make a solid claim to that title, it's L'Acadie Blanc. In addition to being made into wine on its own, it is one of the core grapes that go into the province's signature Tidal Bay wines and is also a staple of many other blends made in the province.

province. "It wasn't just a frost event, it was a freezing event," Bruce says. He leans down toward one of the plants and gently cradles small grapes in his hand. "On this shoot alone there are three clusters. That's a good sign."

Just over 10 per cent of the wine sold in Nova Scotia is made here. Historically, one of the reasons for that is the grapes themselves. They haven't been especially marketable.

L'Acadie Blanc, Cayuga, Luci Kuhlmann, Maréchal Foch, Léon Millot, Seyval Blanc: these aren't exactly superstar grapes when it comes to name recognition. As Christian Perlat of the Petite Rivière winery tells me, "More people in Nova Scotia are ready to buy a bottle of Pinot Noir than one of Léon Millot."

And what's true of Nova Scotia is even more true of the export market.

Remember the struggles to find grapes that would grow in Nova Scotia's cool climate? The first grapes to successfully be grown and turned into wine in the province were hybrids. The majority still are. These are grapes from plants that are cross-bred, often with indigenous grapes for winter hardiness, and for qualities like resistance to disease.

In the world of wine, there is a sharp distinction when it comes to grapes. On one side, *vinifera* — the classic varieties first grown in Europe. You likely recognize some of the most famous members of the family: Chardonnay, Pinot Noir, Riesling. On the other side, the hybrids.

Traditionally, these are the grapes you grow when you can't grow *vinifera*.

If you want to get Bruce Ewert going, ask him about the *vinifera*-hybrid divide.

He has nothing against *vinifera* — as he speaks to me he points to where he is planning on planting "a little bit of Pinot Noir and then some Chardonnay." But turning to his L'Acadie Blanc vines again, he says, "I would never put this at the back of the bus. Ever. I will always revere it."

And the old prejudice about not being able to grow *vinifera* in Nova Scotia? It turns out that's not true either. Nova Scotia is a province of varied micro-climates. I live in Glen Margaret, where it is regularly five degrees warmer than spots less than ten minutes away. I've called nearby friends and chit-chatted about the sunny day only to learn that their homes are engulfed in fog, or that snow is coming down hard.

Depending on soil type, micro-climate, slope, proximity to water, winds and other factors, growing *vinifera* happens to be very doable — even if the first French settlers had a hard time doing it.

Sean Wood remembers visiting friends in Bear River years ago, when, as far as he knew, nobody in Nova Scotia was growing *vinifera*. "I looked across the river and thought, that looks like a vineyard." He walked over to check it out and met Bear River Winery founder and then-owner Chris Hawes, who Sean calls "a wildly interesting character . . . very much an experimenter who does things his own way."

Sean found Hawes on his tractor and went over to speak with him. He remembers, "Nobody in the wine game knew about this guy. I introduced myself and said, 'What have you got growing here?'

'Oh, I've got Auxerrois, I've got Chardonnay, Pinot Noir,'" Sean remembers him replying. He was floored.

Vinifera, it seems, could be grown in Nova Scotia.

The first winery to make a real splash with *vinifera* was Benjamin Bridge — just a few minutes down the road from Ewert's L'Acadie Vineyards, in the Gaspereau Valley. Founders Gerry McConnell and the late Dara Gordon, a husband-and-wife team, wanted to see if they could make wines that would make an impact on the world stage. They hired famed wine consultant Peter Gamble, and the late Raphaël Brisebois, a sparkling wine expert from Champagne, France.

They went to work, and eventually McConnell called Sean Wood. Sean takes up the story: "Gerry invited me to the property. They had planted some vines, and there was an old barn Gerry wanted to turn into a winery. When I arrived, Gerry and Peter were there. We went down to the storage cellar in this part of the barn, and they served me this wine. And I thought, this is unbelievable. It was like good vintage champagne. It was outstanding. It was a eureka moment."

A couple of years later, Bruce Ewert would buy his property, and soon the Gaspereau Valley and Nova Scotia would develop a reputation for high-quality sparkling wines.

No matter what kind of wine you're making, you're going to need yeast — the natural yeasts growing on the grapes if you're wild-fermenting, or purchased yeast.

And there is a yeast for every occasion.

Your local wine-kit shop probably has a rich selection of yeasts. And if not, you can go online and choose from hundreds of strains. Yeast is so easily (and cheaply) available, it's hard to believe that different strains were only identified less than 150 years ago — and that the ability to isolate, propagate, preserve and sell yeasts is quite recent.

It was Louis Pasteur who first confirmed that wine fermentation took place thanks to yeasts found on the skins of the grapes (before that, there was some question over whether the yeasts were found inside or outside the

Making It Bubbly

Nova Scotia is known for its sparkling wines. But not all wines are made to sparkle the same way. Nova Scotia wineries use three different techniques to get those bubbles.

Traditional Method

This is the most time-consuming, labour-intensive and complex method. After fermenting in tanks or barrels, the wine is bottled and then fermented again in the bottle. The yeasts used for traditional fermentation need to have a thick cell membrane because they have to withstand going into an already alcoholic environment. But that's not the end of the story, because the sediments formed by the yeast eventually have to be removed from the bottle. The process of moving this sediment, or lees, up to the neck, is called riddling, and it involves gently turning the bottles, necks angled downward, a quarter turn a day for twenty days. This moves the sediment into the neck of the bottle. Freeze it, uncap the bottle carefully and out comes the sediment. Then it's left to age further in the bottle.

grapes — not to mention the question of whether or not yeasts were even living organisms).

During the late nineteenth century, scientists started identifying and cataloguing yeasts from all kinds of different sources — ranging from elm tree branches to dried truffles and to less savoury media such as rotten wood, intestinal mucous and the urine of a person with diabetes.

Combine the ability to identify the effects of different yeasts with the ability to reproduce them and you have a winemaking revolution on your hands.

A 2014 article in the magazine *Decanter* calls yeast "the unseen hand in every wine." You can pick yeasts that will give your wine a woodier flavour, yeasts to pump up the aroma of the grapes and yeasts that reduce acidity. All this is possible because yeasts do not all transform sugar into alcohol in exactly the same way.

"The classic description of Meursault [a wine produced in Burgundy]

Charmat Method

The Charmat method is not as old as the traditional method, but it has been around for over a century. As with the traditional method, two fermentations are involved. But in the case of the Charmat method, the second fermentation takes place in a pressure tank and does not last as long as traditional bottle-fermentation. The wine is then clarified, and sediment removed. Rachel Lightfoot of Lightfoot & Wolfville explains the technique means "you can keep your time on the lees much shorter" resulting in a more fruity and aromatic wine.

Carbonation Method

This technique involves injecting carbon dioxide into the bottles to produce bubbles. It's suitable for making fruity wines, often from grapes with strong flavours.

is nutty and buttery," writes Benjamin Lewin in *Decanter*. "Want your Chardonnay to taste more like Meursault? Use CY3079 yeast, which increases the impression of hazelnuts and brioche."

There is a constant tension in winemaking between how much of the final result comes from the grapes — from the vineyard — and how much results from decisions made after the harvest by winemakers.

Should they add some additional sugar (a process called chaptalization)? Will the wine be fermented with the indigenous yeasts in the air and on the grapes, or with added yeast? And if added, what kind?

Ideally, wine is an expression of time and place. The flavours vary year to year, but they embody the land where the grapes were grown, and the year the wine was produced. In an interview on CBC Radio's *The Current*, B.C.-based winery owner Matthew Sherlock put it like this: If you standardize your wines too much, you lose the sense of "where they are grown and when they are grown."

Jenny Gammon warns that the focus on grapes can lead people to forget how much of the winemaking process happens away from the fields and in the winery. At one extreme is what she calls "that dominant style of California Chardonnay, where it tastes like popcorn kernels and butter — that was a very manufactured style." But even if you are trying to just bring out the best in your grapes, there are still plenty of decisions to make in the winery.

"Are we going to press it and have the juice come out like a white wine? Or are we going to press it, let the juice come out and then let it soak on the skins and seeds?" Jenny asks. "And the fermentation — where does that happen? In stainless steel or in an oak barrel? And then they're always monitoring the temperature, making sure the conditions are right to create the style of wine they want."

Bruce Ewert compares winemakers like himself and many of his Nova Scotia colleagues to shepherds. "When you think about it, a shepherd has a lot of responsibilities. You think they're just lying around relaxing, but they're responsible for protecting the herd of sheep from wolves. Sometimes you have to move to a different pasture, and you need to make sure they have enough food. So you could think of winemaking as trying . . . to coax the wine in the direction you want it to go without," he pauses, folds an arm in front of his chest, "putting it in a headlock."

Rachel Lightfoot uses the shepherding analogy also. She says one of L&W's underlying philosophies is "not mucking about too much with the wines and shepherding them through . . . We often say we are wine growers rather than winemakers. You can't make great wine from bad fruit. When you have really terrific fruit it allows you to shepherd it through to the bottle."

Bruce Ewert's Minimalist Orange Wine

As Bruce Ewert and I discussed his process for making wine at L'Acadie Vineyards, he told me he sometimes does small-batch "carboy winemaking" for himself. "I've just got something off in the corner and then I taste it."

I later asked Bruce if he had a recipe for this kind of simple wine, and he shared a technique for making an orange wine from L'Acadie Blanc grapes.

Orange wines, sommelier Jenny Gammon explained to me, are "also called skin-contact whites. Usually, white wines don't soak on the skin and seeds, but for orange wines they do. That gives them a certain amount of colour — these are white wines that have some tannin."

Bruce's "in the corner" wine is "not really a recipe" he says, and it's about as simple as you can get: "Wild ferment organic L'Acadie on skins and stems for a month, pushing down the cap weekly. Press with cheesecloth into a carboy so that it's full with no airspace. Allow to settle and preferably let sit over a winter at 2–5 C. Rack and bottle."

Wineries that really want to play up the terroir aspect of their offerings may avoid adding cultured yeasts altogether, and just ferment them with the indigenous yeasts on the grapes. After all, that's how wine has been made for most of the history of humanity. Or, as Rachel puts it, "If you want to showcase your sense of place, why not let the microflora from that place do the work instead of an isolated strain?"

The downside to these wild ferments is that the risk of spoilage is higher, and results are less consistent. (It's estimated that before the appearance of standardized yeast strains, 20 per cent of the wine produced had to be thrown out.) But in a world in which so much has become standardized and homogenized, that may be an advantage.

"Oddly enough," Bruce says, "this whole fermented foods interest here in Nova Scotia has caused people to finally understand what we do. The kombucha crowd. They get it. Twenty-year-olds. Twenty-five-year-olds. They get it. They want transparency, and they want to know what's in the wine and what isn't."

Down by the Tidal Bay

Back in 2010, the Winery Association of Nova Scotia (WANS) started exploring the idea of a signature style of wine for the province. So they hired celebrated Canadian wine consultant Peter Gamble to help develop it.

The result was Tidal Bay. Launched in 2012, Tidal Bay is the name given to wines produced by wineries belonging to WANS, using a blend of specific varieties of Nova Scotia grapes grown according to a particular set of standards.

"Tidal Bay is Nova Scotia's signature white wine blend — that's the elevator pitch," says wine expert Jenny Gammon, of the Bishop's Cellar wine shop.

On an early September afternoon, the liquor store in Bayer's Lake, on the outskirts of Halifax, sees a steady flow of customers. At the back of the shop, near a fridge filled with local craft beers, an NSLC employee offers samples of three different wines: two reds from California and the new Benjamin Bridge Tidal Bay. A man who appears to be in his sixties pauses, and the woman behind the counter asks him if he is familiar with Tidal Bay. "No," he says. "Just looking for a bottle of wine for the Missus." She tells him it's made from a blend of Nova Scotia grapes, that it's light and refreshing and that it goes well with seafood: "What grows together goes together," the employee explains. He takes a sip, nods and, sold on the taste, walks off toward the cash with a bottle in hand.

"We say there's nothing better for wine drinking and appreciation than having a wine industry in your backyard," Jenny Gammon says. "When people can taste the wines they want to know more, drink more, learn more, taste more. We are the latest in a long line of regions that have benefited from that."

Before going on the market, Tidal Bay wines also have to submit to a blind taste test by a panel of experts, to ensure they are of high quality. Sean Wood has served as one of the tasters on those panels. He says the "whole point about Tidal Bay is to demonstrate what is unique and distinctive about Nova Scotia terroir: aromatic, crisp, light, with alcohol content no higher than 11 per cent, and with some mineral character. And it is distinctive. My wine-writing colleagues from elsewhere would say yeah, this is pretty much unique."

Writing on the Bishop's Cellar website, Alanna McIntyre explains that the blend of grapes in Tidal Bay varies, "but some of the star grapes are L'Acadie Blanc, Vidal, Seyval with lesser amounts of supporting varietals like Ortega, New York Muscat, Riesling and even Chardonnay."

7
Bread
No Such Thing as a Perfect Loaf

The starter has been sitting on my kitchen counter for a few days now. It's fall, the weather is cool and I hesitate to fire up the wood stove this early in the season. So the house is a bit chilly. My starter is a mixture of wild yeast drawn from the air, flour and water. It will kickstart the bread I'm about to bake and give it a richer flavour. If this were summer, the starter might have started bubbling happily within twelve or twenty-four hours. But now it is a bit sluggish.

That's okay. I can give it time.

I stir a few more grains of instant yeast into it — cheating maybe, but I'm okay with that — stir it again, cover and leave it once more.

The next day it's ready to go. Nothing dramatic. No big, frothy bubbles. But I can see the starter is active — a few bubbles in the surface of the coarsely cut, locally milled whole wheat flour.

It's time to make the bread.

I add more flour, water and a bit of salt, stirring with a Danish dough whisk — a simple whisk with a circular head that allows the ingredients to come together quickly and incorporates air into the dough as I stir it. Soon, the dough is too thick to stir. I toss the whisk into the sink, sprinkle a bit of flour onto my counter, then turn the dough out onto it and begin to knead. (See the recipe for "Not Very Instagrammable Bread" on page 232 if you want to make this loaf. Danish dough whisk not required.)

I push the heels of my hands down into the dough, pushing it forward,

Sourdough-ish: Pre-ferments

Nova Scotia Community College baking instructor Suzanne Benoit says everyone who comes into the program asks about working with sourdough. But sourdough can be complicated. So she has her students wait until the second semester of their program before they tackle it. During their first semester, they work with pre-ferments.

Put simply, pre-ferments are techniques that give you a head start on bread baking, but without the complexity of feeding and maintaining a sourdough starter. (The "Not very Instagrammable Bread" recipe on page 235 uses a pre-ferment.)

Essentially, a pre-ferment is a way to start part of your bread ahead of time, giving it time to develop before you add all the ingredients. These techniques have several advantages, including boosting flavour, better keeping power and more developed gluten. All of these are possible because the fermentation process makes the dough more acidic, and because the organic acids that naturally develop in pre-ferments add more complexity to the flavour.

Pre-ferments like these are a fast and easy way to add a bit of oomph to your bread without having to master sourdough making first. Here are some common ones:

Biga

A biga is like a mini-bread dough. Mix water and flour at a two to one ratio (two parts flour to one part water) and add a small amount of yeast. The dough will be stiff, but as you leave it for up to twenty-four hours it then pull it back with my fingers, rolling it back and forth, over and over again with this motion. Occasionally, I vary the pattern — folding the dough in from the sides, pressing it down and repeating, or closing my hands into fists and digging my knuckles into the dough, moving them with a rhythm that makes me think of paddling a canoe solo across the smooth waters of a lake.

At its best, the practice of baking bread can be grounding, elemental and deeply satisfying.

will turn softer and more beautiful and begin to rise. To bake with a biga, break it up into little pieces and drop them into warm water in a mixing bowl, using whatever amount of water your bread recipe specifies.

Poolish

A poolish is sort of like a more watery version of a biga. For a poolish you use equal parts water and flour, plus a bit of yeast. The poolish is ready to use when you see a lot of bubbles forming near the surface, a process that can take anywhere from overnight to twenty-four hours.

Sponge

A sponge gives you some of the advantages of biga and poolish, but without having to wait as long. Baker and cookbook author Marcy Goldman calls sponges "a low-rent approach" that "produces rather phenomenal results." Here's how it works. Choose the bread recipe you want to make, mix together a portion of the flour and water from your recipe (cookbook writers use a variety of proportions) along with most or all the yeast. Then let it rise anywhere from an hour to several hours, until the dough puffs up nicely. You can control the timing to suit your schedule by using less yeast or by varying your water temperature. If you mix up a sponge using cold water, it will take longer to rise than one made with warm water. Once your sponge is ready, punch it down, combine it with the remaining ingredients and follow the recipe for the rest of the bread-making process.

On other days, when my dough has too much liquid, making it a ragged mess, or when it's dry and hard and resisting any effort to shape it, I don't feel quite as romantic about this whole process.

When my three kids lived at home, baking sometimes felt like a chore — muscling 20 cups of flour and water into enough dough to make the five or so loaves my family would go through in just over a week. Then there are the days when the bread surprises you, springing beautifully in the oven into gorgeous, perfect-looking loaves. Sometimes it's over-baked. Sometimes it's under-baked. Sometimes a big gooey mess of rye dough comes together into chewy but airy loaves. Sometimes (well, maybe just once), you use cumin seeds instead of caraway and bake odd-tasting loaves that really don't work well at all with strawberry jam. And sometimes the best thing to do is compost your bread, or chop it up into cubes for croutons, or whirl it up in the food processor and turn it into breadcrumbs.

But today, it works. It works well. Unless I do something stupid — like put it on for its final rise in the pan (a stage called proofing) and forget about it so that it sinks or turns into a goopy mess — this is going to be good bread.

Although I enjoy the rhythm of kneading, I don't enjoy it for too long. I glance at the clock on the gas range behind me: 11:33. I'll knead until 11:40. That will give the gluten — the long, elastic strands that give the bread its loft — plenty of time to develop. Once I'm done, I drop the dough into a ceramic bowl, gently rub a little olive oil over its surface, flip it over, cover it and leave it to rise on the counter.

It's hard not to get nostalgic and romantic about bread. Whether you are baking for the first time or the five hundredth, there is something about the process of manipulating simple ingredients and yeast — whether wild or store-bought — to create a food that is a staple in so many cultures, with roots that go back millennia.

"Bread is an immediately approachable food from the second you smell it to the instant you slice it. And it is satisfying," says food writer Simon Thibault. When I get together with him, he is working on a book about whole-grain baking and is recently back from two conferences on whole grains. "Especially here in Nova Scotia. I mean, we lived on bread as colonists. We lived on bread products, no matter what. That's just all there is to it."

In a *Saltscapes* magazine story from 2010, written by Donalee Moulton, Chef Daniel Dennis of Eskasoni laments that traditional Mi'kmaw cuisine is in danger of being lost. But one of the foods that has survived is traditional Mi'kmaw bread — often served fried. I've seen its name spelled in English as "looscuniguen," "lusknikn" and "luskinigan." It's also sometimes called four-cent bread, because of the cost of the ingredients.

In the same story, Nora McCarthy-Joyce of the Native Council of Prince Edward Island describes the bread as "a heavy bread that is flat, often cut in squares and served at all traditional cultural gatherings as an important part of the feast," adding that if it is fried in oil it's called fry bread. Fry bread continues to be popular today and is the base for the popular Mi'kmaw tacos you can find at powwows throughout the region.

About forty years ago, the North Queens Heritage Society published a cookbook of traditional recipes and remedies with the wonderful title, *Granny Picked Blueberries While the House Burned*. The book includes a recipe from a Mrs. Edward Labrador for looscuniguen "Indian bread." It involves gently mixing four parts flour to one part fat, adding a bit of salt and baking powder and then pouring in and stirring water until the dough is soft. The dough is then baked in a pan in the oven or on the coals of an open fire. I imagine that before the development of baking soda (which some lusknikn recipes use) and baking powder, the bread would have either been left to rest, which would cause it to rise slightly from wild yeasts, or perhaps it was leavened using wood ash. Ash is alkaline and contains compounds that act in the same way as baking soda — creating carbon dioxide that produces leavening. Historical recipe expert Sarah

Lohman says ash leavener (called pearlash) was commonly used in North America from about 1780 to 1840. It was used in other places as well. I have old recipes from Greece for Easter cookies which use ash instead of baking soda.

Fry bread only became a part of the Mi'kmaw diet after contact with Europeans. As Mi'kmaw history expert Dr. Ruth Holmes Whitehead points out, that's because the pre-contact Indigenous population did not cultivate wheat or other grains. Although, she says, once a population "can digest wheat, you really start to crave it."

Wheat arrived in North America with the French settlers who set up a habitation at Port Royal, in what is now Nova Scotia, in 1605. The next year Marc Lescarbot, a Parisian lawyer who spent a year at Port Royal, oversaw the planting of the first European grains in North America: wheat, rye and barley, sown in fields where the grass had been burned off. Making bread from the grain must have been no easy task, with the wheat for bread being ground by hand.

By 1607 though, the settlers had built the Lequille grist mill, in what is today the village of Lequille, not far from Annapolis Royal, on Allains River. The mill would have made grinding grain faster and a lot easier — making it much more practical to bake bread for the dozens of colonists at Port Royal.

Acadians continued to grow a variety of grains — mostly wheat, barley, oats and buckwheat — for use in bread and crepes or pancakes. As settlers grew more grains across the province, the need for more mills arose. At first they were powered directly by rivers,with the current turning water wheels, and by turbines in the river generating electricity.

No matter where you find yourself in Nova Scotia, odds are there was once a grist mill not too far away. Farmers could only travel so far to take their

Balmoral Grist Mill Museum.

grain to be ground — generally, as far as they could travel by horse and cart within a day. Even in urban centres you can see signs of grain-growing and milling from the not-too-distant past. Walk along the Shubenacadie Canal trail, just a stone's throw from downtown Dartmouth, and you will come across an old millstone propped up by the water. It comes from a grist mill and bakery built in 1792 by loyalists Lawrence Hawthorne and Jonathon Tremain. A historical plaque at the site says the enterprise "supplied His Majesty's forces in Nova Scotia, Newfoundland, Bermuda and the West Indies, as well as the civilian population of this region. This enterprise led to the development of a substantial grain-growing industry in Nova Scotia." Head out of town via Cole Harbour and you'll pass a Methodist chapel built in 1825 with another (smaller) millstone on display just outside.

One of the few (if not the only) working mills left in the province is the Balmoral Grist Mill Museum, in the fittingly named community of Balmoral Mills, about halfway between Earltown and Tatamagouche. It ran commercially until the 1950s, before being converted into a museum.

Built in the mid-1870s by brothers Alexander and John McKay, whose father was a miller as well, it was one of eight grist mills within a radius of about forty kilometres. The brothers started off with a building that housed both a sawmill and a grist mill, but decided to separate their operations, with John keeping the sawmill and Alexander running the grist mill, located just down the river. That turned out to be a lucky decision for Alexander, because soon after the sawmill burned down.

Kaleb Fifield is the seventh man to serve as miller here, a role he took up in the summer of 2018. Kaleb is young, late twenties probably, with old-fashioned sensibilities. He seems right at home explaining the history and workings of the mill and firing up the machinery to mill flour three times a day — more often if there's greater demand.

Kaleb demonstrates how to use a quern — the hand-powered contraption used to grind grains before the era of the grist mill. Two small millstones sit one atop the other, with a handle affixed to the top one. He shows me how you would pour a handful or small scoop of grain at a time into a hole (or eye) in the top stone, then crush it into flour through the circular motion of the mills, turned by someone holding the handle. It's a painstaking process that would typically take about twenty minutes to grind enough flour for a loaf of bread — and that's not taking into account interruptions caused by piling in too much grain at a time, which pushes the stones apart. The results would have been quite coarse, resulting in a not particularly refined loaf.

The grist mill, on the other hand, is a technological marvel, and Kaleb seems to delight in explaining the ins and outs of its workings. The turbines that once ran the mill are no more. Today it is powered with electricity from the grid. Still, when I stand on the lower level of the mill and Kaleb turns on the works, I can't help but be impressed as the massive machinery — wooden gears, wheels and belts rumble to life, all in the service of turning the massive, 2,000-pound stones above me, their weight and furrows working to transform wheat into flour. It's easy to feel a connection to those who stood here a century ago, waiting as their grain was milled.

Because the area around Balmoral Mills was settled largely by Scots, its main output was not wheat flour. The mill has four different sets of stones and could grind oats (for oatmeal,the mill's main commodity) along with wheat (white and whole) and buckwheat. Kaleb says that diversity helped the mill stay viable for as long as it did. That and the fact that the millstones are big enough for him to make up to two hundred pounds of flour an hour.

There may be a lot of romanticism to homemade bread, but even 175 years ago, the process required to produce flour was a heavily industrialized one for its era. The millstones at the Balmoral grist mill were shipped from France in sections, while the balancing units that keep them, well, balanced, were manufactured in London in 1859 (at 48 Mark Lane, near the Thames — today the site of a trendy-looking café). And milling was hard, repetitive work, with the miller operating the machinery for hours a day and taking the stones apart to clean and sharpen them every couple of weeks. "Right now, they're actually quite terrible from a milling perspective," Kaleb says. "They're quite flat and the grooves aren't very deep anymore. You can tell that they were rubbing on each other at one point."

Not all mills were finely calibrated, and not all millers equally skilled. In his memoir, *The Rooster Crows at Dawn,* Lee Zinck remembers his family

Quern for manually grinding grain at the Balmoral Grist Mill Museum.

travelling by boat from Blandford to take barley to a mill on a small river in the community of Western Shore. "When the grain went passing through it was ground into coarse flour, but before making bread, the housewife had to pass it through a fine sieve to remove the chaff and other course fibres. The result was barley bread with no vitamin-enriched white flour mixed with it. So two things could happen when eating this bread: one either lost a tooth or suffered a mild case of indigestion."

The grain milled at Balmoral no longer comes from local farmers but from a distributor in New Brunswick. Still, it's grown in the Maritimes. Kaleb feeds some Red Fife wheat into a hopper. After a few minutes of rumbling and grinding, a small amount of coarsely ground flour appears on a wooden tray by the millstones.

I buy two small bags of flour and head home.

Acadian camp cook from Saulnierville Station baking bread at mid-morning, August 1950.

Acadians, Scots, Germans — no matter where they came from, the people who settled Nova Scotia baked bread. Look through old cookbooks or community recipes, and a few types of breads appear over and over: oatmeal or porridge bread, a basic white bread, brown bread with either whole wheat flour or white flour and a good amount of molasses and breads including buckwheat or barley flour.

Emily Walker's book *A Cook's Tour of Nova Scotia* offers a recipe for one of these staple breads from my own little community, "the picturesque village of Glen Margaret," as she calls it. "Glen Margaret Oatmeal Brown Bread" is made with rolled oats, shortening, molasses, salt, brown sugar, yeast, sugar, water and white flour.

Porridge in bread adds a bit more oomph when it comes to its nutritious quality and helps it last longer — an important consideration in the summertime when bakers might do a large number of loaves at a time in an outdoor, wood-burning clay oven, one that you wouldn't fire up every day.

Few staples seem to encapsulate so much of our food history and culture as bread. In his book *Pantry and Palate*, Simon Thibault has a recipe for a cornmeal molasses loaf (aka anadama bread), versions of which appear as hand-written recipes in the notebooks of people from many Atlantic Canadian communities, including Acadians and the African Nova Scotian descendants of Black Loyalists.

I've made Simon's bread recipe, and it's delicious. But I'll admit to a complicated relationship with these standard Nova Scotia breads. On the one hand, there is something comforting about them (even for someone like myself, who did not grow up here). On the other, I can understand feeling stifled by them if that's all you grew up with, and wanting a good, hand-folded classic sourdough baguette instead.

Bread in general is complicated, Simon says.

We are in his apartment in the North End of Halifax, surrounded by jars of various kinds of locally grown flour on a shelf in his kitchen, stacks of pots, pans and baking dishes piled up on wall-mounted shelves, and shelves and shelves full of cookbooks. (There's also a section of wall filled with kitschy religious art, which Simon says he comes by honestly from his Acadian upbringing.)

As we talk, he stirs a strawberry-rose compote he's testing, along with a plum paste, offering me a taste of each. Both are delicious.

The bygone tradition of regular baking leaves us feeling nostalgic for an era in which fresh bread came out of the oven regularly. But, Simon points out, what may seem tinged with nostalgia from our perspective was a whole lot of hard work. While we may have lost some of our baking traditions, developments like instant yeast and store-bought bread "emancipated women from their kitchens to a certain degree. So, you can't neglect that . . . We now generally live in a time where the idea of baking bread is not viewed as a chore but rather as a form of pleasure."

On the one hand, we idealize baking bread. On the other, many people are scared to try it, thinking it is too difficult or complex. What if it doesn't rise? What if I under-bake it? Or over-bake it? Or if it comes out rock hard?

I've been baking bread for more than thirty years, and in that time very, very few loaves have not turned out at all. Some had sticky, ragged doughs that were hard to work with. Some sprang beautifully in the oven, giving them a beautiful loft. Some have been enjoyably dense and chewy. And a few, yes, have wound up in the compost or as croutons or breadcrumbs.

But if you bake a batch of bread and it doesn't work out, you'll know within a few hours, or — if it's a recipe with more steps and a longer rise — a few days. Compare that to making a batch of wine and waiting a year or so to find out if it is any good.

Simon says many readers with little baking experience successfully tried the cornmeal molasses loaf in his book, or made the white bread. "It's the easiest thing ever. Du bon pain blanc [good white bread]. Good. Even my own mom, who in her later years had attempted three different times to make bread and it never worked — she made the cornmeal molasses bread and it did work. That was pretty sweet."

He adds, "If you're a person of average wages and time, you can make bread pretty easily. Whether you use a bread maker or mix it yourself, from start to finish you can have a loaf of bread in the house in three hours. Which is pretty cool! Everyone loves warm homemade bread. Find me a person who doesn't, and I'll be amazed. For some people, it's a connection with their family past. You can't deny that."

Simon says one of the downsides of the increased popularity of home baking is its tendency to become almost competitive in the age of social media. Bread, unlike some of the other foods in this book, photographs really, really well. (I'm sorry, but no matter how delicious kimchi might be, a photo of a gallon jug filled with the stuff generally looks at best unappetizing and at worst like something you might have to clean up off the floor.)

One of the downsides of people sharing photos of their bread online is that many of us seem to be trying to make the same bread: a classic French sourdough with large holes, the kind made popular by San Francisco-based chef Chad Robertson through his Tartine bakery and books. "One thing I find super-fascinating — and I was also a victim of this — is how we as North Americans view bread in the twenty-first century, especially with Instagram culture. We all want that big open-hole crumb, that Chad Robertson Tartine-esque beauty," Simon says. The breads may be gorgeous, but they are also hard to make. "We are limiting ourselves to breads which are aesthetically pleasing. That bread is pretty! It's fun to eat on its own, straight like that. But have you tried spreading butter on it? It's a pain."

I go back to check the bread I'd left rising earlier. Many recipes call for a first rise of ninety minutes or so, but, as with all things related to bread baking, that can vary. It's been about an hour, and the bread hasn't risen much. I leave it again, then come back about forty-five minutes later. It looks better now. Not light and airy but puffed up enough that I think it will make decent bread. I punch it down, divide the loaves, put them in baking tins, then leave them on the stovetop to rise again. They'll be nice and warm here as the oven heats up.

Wheat was among the earliest crops planted in Nova Scotia. A few years before Confederation, wheat was the second most important field crop in Eastern Canada, its production peaking in 1901. As agriculture developed on the Prairies, wheat production in Eastern Canada fell off a cliff. By 1950, Nova Scotia was producing just 45,000 bushels of spring wheat. New Brunswick was producing twice that amount and PEI grew four times more than Nova Scotia.

The two varieties of wheat that were most widely grown in Nova Scotia were Selkirk and Acadia. Acadia is a spring wheat developed in Saskatchewan, at the federal government's Indian Head Experimental Farm. It came from a cross between two different strains first tried in 1934. The researchers at Indian Head tested it in small plots until 1952, when it was made available to farmers in Eastern Canada. An Agriculture Canada pamphlet from that year describes the wheat as "mid-season, strong strawed, high yielding and moderately resistant to stem rust and leaf rust, bunt, black chaff, and some forms of root-rot. It is semi-resistant to loose smut."

Acadia was not popular in the West, where it wasn't considered as high quality as other varieties that could thrive there. But it served local needs well.

Eventually though, wheat production in the Maritimes cratered, as flour from other regions became cheaply and readily available.

But by the early 2000s, heritage varieties were getting ready for a comeback. In a 2004 story for the magazine *Rural Delivery*, writer Jennifer Scott details the early days of the heritage wheat revival in the Maritimes, which included renewed interest in growing Acadia wheat. Artisanal bakeries appeared on the scene, making delights like sourdough baguettes available. At the same time, consumers showed a growing interest in both local and organically grown produce, and the Speerville Flour Mill in New Brunswick — using reconditioned old millstones to mill flour the old-fashioned way — was expanding its operation. The time was ripe for Nova Scotia farmers to dip their toes back into the world of wheat, despite the challenges of a short, damp growing season.

While local wheat may not be easily available in every supermarket, more farms are growing it and experimenting with heritage varieties like Acadia and Red Fife (which was developed in Ontario in the mid-1800s). Simon Thibault has some "amazing" local bread flour in his freezer, and his shelves hold locally grown buckwheat and spelt. Simon does not see the rise of local grains and local food in general as a trend, but as essential for the Nova Scotia economy. "The reason the local movement has worked in this province is because it's not just a form of lip service or some bourgeois lofty ideal. It's rooted in small, local and rural communities ensuring their economic survival. You're buying from your neighbour because you know your neighbour, and your neighbour will have enough pride in their product to make sure it is worth buying. Otherwise, they know they will not survive."

I forget to set a timer to remind me to check my bread as it proofs. Suddenly, an hour later, I remember and race downstairs. Fortunately, the loaves have not over-proofed. When that happens, instead of having a lovely rise, they get flabby and fall in the middle. The result? Not good. I pop the bread in the oven, set the timer this time, and leave it to bake.

You can make bread with any number of ingredients. But, as with beer, you can also keep it to essentials and just use a handful of them: In this case, water, flour, salt and yeast whether in the form of purchased yeast or wild yeasts in a starter. (There are saltless breads, like those famously made in Florence, but they are an exception, and while they taste good they keep poorly.)

Foolproof Pan Grease

My early bread-baking bible was *The Laurel's Kitchen Bread Book* — a hippyish whole-grain baking book first published in the early 1980s. I rarely turn to the recipes in this book anymore (though there are some very good ones), but it does offer one five-star tip that I have used for decades and shared with many friends.

If you are using a tin to bake bread (as opposed to, say, baking directly on a stone) you will need to grease it. You can slather on cooking oil or butter, but if you don't use enough your loaf will stick, and if you use too much you wind up with a greasy bottom to your loaf.

Enter what the *Laurel's Kitchen* authors — Laurel Robertson, Carol Flinders and Bronwen Godfrey — call "the best release product in the business." It's dead simple, works every single time, and lasts forever in your fridge.

No matter what kind of bread you make though, you'll need to find a way to leaven, or rise it.

In his memoir, *Sauerkraut, Codfish, and Apples*, Earle K. Hawksworth recounted many of the wonderful foods that came out of his mother's kitchen in Scarsdale, Nova Scotia. But Earle, who was born in 1916, recalled that "of all the food available to us, Mother's home-baked bread was my favorite. Oft-times she made her own yeast using grated potato, flour and hops grown in the garden, as the base. This mixture stood in a crock behind the kitchen stove and was 'Built up' every few days. A measured quantity was added to white or whole wheat flour or a mixture of both, and combined with sugar, salt and shortening. We ate great quantities of bread, mostly freshly baked . . . I would cut a thick slice from a loaf, preferably the heel, smear it with clotted cream and maple syrup or molasses and enjoy . . . It was most satisfying to a hungry, active boy."

This leavening, a mix of potato, flour and hops, seems to have been a common way to make bread rise in the days before industrial yeast was widely available.

Here it is: combine two parts vegetable oil with one part lecithin. (You can find lecithin at most supermarkets, often in the natural foods section.) Mix them together, either in a small food processor, or simply stir with a fork or spoon. I don't know how the science works, but the combination of lecithin and oil is a far more effective way to grease your tins than oil alone. Use sparingly and your bread will pop right out of the tin once it's done. The release product works well for all kinds of baked goods — cakes, muffins, cupcakes — not just bread.

You use very little of this each time, so there is no need to make a huge amount. I usually do a half cup of oil with a quarter cup of lecithin. Store in a jar in the fridge. It will not go bad.

Make (and Keep) a Sourdough Starter

I loved baking day at my grandparents'. They lived in the mountains of Lakonia, a rural region on the southern Greek mainland.

My grandparents had once made their home in the village of Krini, where my grandfather was the village priest, but after a house fire they moved to what was supposed to be a temporary home outside the village. They stayed there for the rest of their lives.

In the courtyard outside the main building (which had only a kitchen and a bedroom), a wood-fired oven was built into the wall. Here my relatives, either my grandparents or visiting aunts and cousins, would bake massive quantities of bread, some to be eaten fresh, and some to be baked again and left to harden into rusks that could be kept for months with no refrigeration. When you live in a hot climate, you don't want to be firing an oven up to 500-degree temperatures too often. Making rusks (known as paximadi) instead of bread meant less frequent baking.

The leavening for these breads was my grandmother's sourdough. Because of the extreme heat and lack of refrigeration (my grandparents did not have electricity), the sourdough starter was not kept in a jar as starters typically are in North America or northern Europe. Instead, flour would be added to the starter, so it was almost like its own little loaf of bread. Then it was broken up into smaller pieces and left to air-dry on linen towels. When it was time to bake with it again, all you had to do was rehydrate the starter, feed it with some fresh flour, and let the dormant yeasts wake up and start their leavening action again.

Several years ago, my cousin passed some of this dried starter on to me. I rehydrated it, baked with it for months and thought of my grandmother every time a new batch of loaves came out of the oven. Beautiful. A connection with the past, with family history (who knows how many generations back the original starter went?) and delicious bread too.

And then I killed it.

Not deliberately, of course, but through bad management, and because I somehow had gotten the misguided impression that I needed to add salt to it before drying it out. Salt and yeast do not tend to get along too well. Yes, we use salt in our bread dough, but it can slow leavening and too much of it can out-and-out kill the yeast.

Despite my misadventures, sourdough can actually be quite easy to make and keep.

Some bakers and bakeries are happy to give away starter. At Birdie's Bread Co. in Dartmouth, owner Jessica Best says, "We give starter to those who are dabbling at home. Spread your starter love around the world."

If you don't have a source of starter and want to make your own, one of the classics is the one Chad Robertson of San Francisco's Tartine Bakery has popularized. (The *New York Times* says "it has reached cult status.") Robertson starts by mixing a kilogram (2.2 lbs) each of white and whole-wheat flour, then taking 100 grams (a little less than half a cup) of warm water, adding an equal amount of the flour mix and mixing until you get a thick batter. Then you cover it with a towel and let it sit for a few days, until it starts to bubble and look a bit lively.

Now comes the counterintuitive part. Each day, you throw out about three quarters of this mixture, then add equal parts (around 50 grams, or 4 tablespoons) of water and your flour mix. Keep feeding it for a week or so, until you notice a consistent rising and falling action and it starts to smell pleasantly sour.

At this point, you're ready to bake with it. Follow whatever sourdough bread recipe you are using. Once you're done baking, go back to feeding your sourdough daily. If you're not going to bake for awhile, stick it in the fridge where it will happily live for weeks, maybe even months, and then pull it out and start feeding it again a week or so before you want to bake with it.

Why throw out so much of the starter in the early days? It's so you don't wind up with a huge amount of starter, and because "keeping the volume down offers the yeast more food each time you feed it; it's not fighting with quite so many other yeast cells to get enough to eat."

You'll notice that some recipes say your starter will be ready to go in a week. Others may say longer. The process — harnessing wild yeast to leaven bread — varies tremendously based on factors ranging from your environment to your flour. Your own time-frame may be a bit different. In his classic *Beard on Bread*, famed writer James Beard writes that his starter was much more successful in Connecticut, Long Island and Massachusetts than it was in New York. And even within New York City, he said its performance varied between neighourhoods.

Lee Zinck, a contemporary of Earle Hawksworth's, remembered his mother using the same mixture: "The biggest problem was making yeast starter from hops and potatoes, a process that involved days. So care had to be taken to have a fresh supply of yeast on hand at all times [the starter here is called yeast]. Kept in a tightly corked stone jug and stored in a cool place, it would keep fresh for months."

In researching *Palate and Pantry*, Simon Thibault found an old recipe for this starter, but with the hops referred to as "ups" — written out the way Francophones would pronounce the word, dropping the "H." In her cookbook *La cuisine de Chéticamp (Chéticamp Cooking)*, Ginette Aucoin also refers to this classic Nova Scotia starter. The book, published in 1980, compiles old recipes popular among Acadians of Chéticamp. Under the heading "Bread Making As It Once Was," Ginette describes the process of using "ups" to make starter. "They needed a product called 'ups' which grew in their gardens. It was used in a manner similar to the yeast cakes we use today. They made beer with this 'ups' and added it to the bread; the dough was kneaded around midnight before going to bed and then around 5 A.M. it had to be kneaded again." The whole process took two days.

New England settlers had their own version of the hops starter. It was made with hops, rye, corn and water. After it fermented, the leavening was cut into cakes and left to dry in the sun. These cakes could then be reconstituted for future use.

In a wonderful and long-out-of-print book called *The Blessings of Bread* (my copy is a discard from the Mississauga, Ontario, library system), writer Adrian Bailey describes how the appearance of Fleischmann's yeast supplanted these traditional starters. It was "a reliable product" that was "skilfully marketed, replacing many of those raising agents generally known as 'starters' of which sourdough . . . is the most ancient type."

In an age in which people can get very fussy over their sourdough starters — weighing precise amounts of flour and laying out quite specific times —

it is refreshing to read Bailey, writing in the mid-1970s, say "Practically anything will make a starter." The simplest technique is to mix up your bread dough, add a bit of honey and leave it overnight to ferment. Or, he says, "You can make a starter out of flour and milk, or flour and water; rye flour plus water and a slice of onion; flour, water, sugar and hops; corn meal, beer and tea leaves." Wild yeasts are everywhere. Our starter is just giving them an opportunity to concentrate in one spot and go wild, eating and excreting organic acids and carbon dioxide, until they finally bite the bullet in the oven during the baking process, having completed the task of raising our bread.

Properly cared for, a sourdough starter can last decades — even generations. And each starter has its own unique characteristics and flavours. If you've ever had a bread that tasted like home, it could be because of its starter. Simon Thibault says not all that long ago, some women in Nova Scotia would have been given sourdough starter when they got married. "That's just the way it went. Because you wanted to take that taste of home with you. Good or bad, instant yeast took that away for a lot of people."

The kitchens are bustling at the Nova Scotia Community College Akerley campus. I keep stepping aside for students heading to and from the ovens. A beautiful-looking brioche dough rises in a container on the table in front of me, while nearby a student carefully weighs individual portions of dough on a digital scale, making sure they are all the same size before she starts shaping them into bagels. Across the aisle another student puts the finishing touches on a batch of cannoli, piping a chocolate-ricotta mixture into shells she fried earlier.

Over a decade ago, our friend Shelley Taylor brandished a loaf of locally made sourdough bread from the La Vendéenne bakery and said, "These people have made life in Nova Scotia much more pleasant."

At the time, Vendéenne was one of the few bakeries in the province making traditional French-style breads. Now it seems, sourdough and other artisanal breads are everywhere — in shops and at farmers' markets from one end of the province to the other. If your taste runs to sourdough whole grain breads, including Danish-style rye, Jess Ross has you covered. (She bakes her bread in a 15,000-pound wood-fired stone oven fueled by wood she chops herself.) Former Vendéenne baker Laurent Marcel, originally from France, has opened his own shop, selling a mix of classic French breads, both yeasted and sourdough. Across the province — from the Annapolis Valley to Cape Breton, at small bakeries or farmers' markets — there is no shortage of delicious and varied local breads to choose from.

Many of the bakers making these breads learned their craft at the NSCC Boulanger and Baking Arts program — at one time the only one of its kind in Canada. (The program's final year was 2018 to 2019; students in the new program replacing it still learn the same baking skills, but spend less time proportionately on bread.

Jessica Best is one of those grads. After finishing the program, she made bread for a local restaurant, then opened her own business, called Birdie's Baking Co. "Birdie" is what her grandfather called her, back home in Newfoundland.

We sit at a table in the bakery on a Sunday afternoon, when the shop is closed. Although the space is relatively new, it has a cozy, comforting feeling: books about bread, pictures of Jessica's grandparents, bags of locally grown Acadia wheat flour for sale (freshly milled by Jessica using the mill she had shipped here from Austria).

Like many bakers, it doesn't take long for Jessica to get philosophical about bread. "It's a part of daily life. I find that fascinating. It's not like working in a restaurant where people come in for an experience a couple of times a year and it's a special thing. We're part of people's everyday just plain grind. I love that. People have their bakery and they go there every day and you're not trying to service a gazillion people. It's very much community oriented."

She sees the rise of small bakeries like hers not just as part of a food trend but also as a relatively affordable way to bring a little more pleasure to daily

LEFT: Baker Jessica Best of Birdie's Bread Co.
TOP: The flour mill at Birdie's Bread Co.

life. And she thinks the backlash against wheat may be waning. "People are tired of feeling crappy," she says. "I think crappy bread is bad. Wheat is not bad. Most wheat is a stripped product." It's had the bran and germ removed, and if it's white, the flour was likely bleached too. That's a very different product from the flour Jessica makes herself in the shop — seated at her mill, feeding locally made flour into it and then scooping up the fine yellowish-brown flour. "I never make health claims, but I do have one customer in particular who told me she hadn't had bread in ten years and she was so excited she could enjoy it again. It's that fermentation process. Wheat is a product that needs things done to it, and the fermentation process helps with the digestion process."

We walk into a cool room at the back of the shop, where Jessica lifts the lid on a plastic tote, revealing its aromatic, bubbly contents: about fifteen litres of sourdough starter. You could call it the beating (or at least rising and falling) heart of the bakery.

Sourdough is tricky stuff. As recent NSCC Baking Arts grad Isabelle Lalonde told me, the performance of sourdough can vary wildly depending on many different factors: "It's mostly about temperature, time of year, and elevation. Your elevation from the water plays a big role in how quickly things will ferment and bubble." (Good news for Nova Scotians: being closer to sea level is better than being up in the mountains when it comes to fermenting and baking.) "I have a baguette recipe that changes depending on what time of year you do it," Isabelle says. "You had to add different amounts of yeast, let it sit longer."

At Birdie's the sourdough is the basis for a whole raft of delicious breads. I ask Jessica about her workhorse loaves. She says, "Our most popular one by far is our country sourdough. It's what I recommend if you've never had any of our bread . . . Pretty neutral. So that's our white sourdough, with 20 per cent of our milled flour and 80 per cent unbleached all-purpose. We do that [and] we do a whole-wheat Acadia loaf. That's mostly Acadia flour. We do a 100-per cent rye. We do a currant and coriander that's the same base as our country sourdough. And we do a seeded one every day which is nice, and an oat porridge."

"Well, that's a classic Nova Scotia kind of bread," I say.

I pull my two loaves out of the oven, flip them out of the pans and tap the bottoms. I hear a satisfying hollow sound. I don't weigh the loaves, but they feel substantial. This isn't a light, airy bread. But it is going to be good. I put

Bag of freshly milled Red Fife flour at the Balmoral Grist Mill Museum.

the loaves on wire racks and leave them to cool for several hours.

A few months ago, it seemed like every loaf of bread I made had some problems. Sourdough loaves that were tasty and toothsome but flat, flat, flat. The white bread I over-proofed and baked anyway — resulting in a saggy, crumbly loaf. I worried that I had lost my ability to bake decent bread.

That's the thing with bread. You can bake a pretty good loaf fairly easily. It is satisfying and gives you a sense of fulfillment. But getting consistently good results can be tricky. Jessica encourages people to bake at home and says many home bakers give up too soon if they're not satisfied with the results.

"You've got to screw it up a lot before you don't screw it up anymore, and people get really discouraged when they screw it up," she says. "I was

Not Very Instagrammable Bread

Here is the recipe for the bread I baked using coarsely ground Red Fife flour from the Balmoral Grist Mill Museum. You can use any hard, whole-wheat bread flour. As with many bread recipes, you may find you have to adjust the amounts if your dough feels too wet or too dry.

The resulting loaves are hearty and tasty, but unlikely to win too many awards for beauty.

Materials

- Small-to-Medium sized bowl for starter
- Medium-to-Large bowl for bread dough
- Wooden spoon for stirring
- Dough scraper (optional)
- 2 Bread pans

Ingredients

Starter

- 1 cup (250 mL) unbleached white flour
- 1 cup (250 mL) lukewarm water
- Pinch of yeast (Just a couple of grains will do, or skip the yeast altogether, or add as much as half a teaspoon if you want a faster rise.)

Bread

- 5 1/2 cups (1.4 L) whole-wheat flour, divided
- 1 tsp (5 mL) instant yeast*
- 2 tsp (10 mL) salt
- 2 cups (500 mL) lukewarm water

Method

Starter

Put flour in the bowl, sprinkle the yeast on top and stir it in. Make a well in the centre, add water, and stir until the water is thoroughly incorporated. Work the mixture with your hands if you need to, to make sure the ingredients are well-mixed.

Cover with a damp towel, plastic wrap or reusable wrap and let stand overnight.

Check the next day. The starter should show lots of little bubbles at the surface. If this hasn't happened yet, wait a bit longer until it starts to bubble. Don't worry. It will.

Bread

Mix half a cup of flour into your starter.

Add the yeast and salt, stirring well with a wooden spoon or similar tool.

Add 2 cups lukewarm water, then 5 more cups flour, one cup at a time, stirring after each addition until you have a stiff dough, at which point start working the flour into the dough with your hands. The rate at which the water will absorb flour depends a lot on your flour. Take it slowly, and if your dough looks like it is getting too hard stop adding more flour (even if you haven't used all 5 cups).

Turn the dough out onto a counter or table and knead for 10 minutes.

As you knead, the dough should become softer and silkier. The best description I've read for knowing when to stop is when it feels like a baby's bottom. (If you don't quite get there, that's okay.)

Shape your dough into a ball and put it back in the mixing bowl. If you like, gently rub a little bit of olive oil on the top, then flip the ball of dough over and rub the residual oil from your hands onto the side now facing up.

Cover and leave at room temperature or in a slightly warmer place (near a woodstove works well) for 90 minutes.

The dough should more-or-less double in size. Check it after 90 minutes. If it hasn't risen enough, leave it for another 30 to 45 minutes.

Check the dough again. If you are not yet ready to bake, punch it down and leave it to rise again for 45 minutes to an hour. (You can repeat this process a few times until you are ready.)

Once you are ready to bake the bread, punch it down and turn it out onto the counter.

Pre-heat the oven to 425°F (215°C).

Divide the dough into two using a dough scraper or a knife.

Kneading dough.

Grease two bread tins (see "Foolproof Pan Grease" on page 222 for my greasing suggestion).

Press one ball of dough to flatten it with the heels of your hands, then work it into a ball and roll it slightly to elongate it. (It should be about the length of your bread pan.) Drop it into your bread pan.

Repeat with the other ball of dough.

Leave in a warm place, covered by a towel or plastic wrap, to rise in the pan. (This is called proofing.) I find the easiest thing is to put the loaves on top of the kitchen range while the oven is heating. If your oven has a "proofing" setting, use that.

Leave the bread to proof for half an hour — it should rise some more but not sag.

Place in the oven and bake for 10 minutes at 425°F (215°C), turning the loaves once after 5 minutes. (You can skip this step if you have an oven that heats evenly — mine doesn't.)

Turn the temperature down to 325°F (165°C) and bake for another 20 to 25 minutes. To test if it is done, turn a loaf out of the pan and tap the bottom with your knuckles. It should make a nice hollow sound. If it feels a bit soft or doesn't sound hollow, bake it some more.

Baker Jessica Best says one of the most common mistakes by people making bread at home is under-baking. If you are in doubt, bake it a little longer. And, whatever you do, don't fuss too much over it.

"I think the number one thing people do wrong when they're trying to bake sourdough bread at home is paying too much attention to it. You have to just leave it alone and let it do its thing to a certain degree. Provide the right environment for it, and it will do its own work. You just have to manage the elements around it. You're not making this thing. It's making itself . . . Chill out, leave it alone."

*I use instant yeast, which can be added directly to the bread dough without first being mixed into water to activate it. If you have a different kind of yeast, follow the instructions on the package. If it needs water to activate it, adjust the recipe accordingly. For example, if you sprinkle your yeast into half a cup of water, then add 1 1/2 cups to the rest of the flour mix instead of 2 cups.

in junior high when I baked my first loaf of bread — and one of my friends told me I should sell it to the army for ammo. Now, that wasn't very nice! The only way to do it right is to do it wrong a few times."

And remember, it's never going to be perfect. And that's okay.

"There's no such thing as a perfect loaf of bread," Jessica says. "It's dynamic and it's changing. You've got to take the flaws with it. Appreciate the flaws. I think if you feel like you've got it to the point where it's perfect, shut 'er down. You're Wonder Bread. Congrats."

8
The Dairy Best

Cheese and Other Fermented Milk Products

I'm going to tell you a story, even though it makes me sound like a food snob. It was 1998, and my family and I had just moved to Nova Scotia from Montreal. We loved it here: living on the coast, huge forested area behind our house, friendly neighbours and a lovely little local school. A great place to bring up our kids.

Although I'd looked forward to leaving Montreal for our new life on St. Margaret's Bay, as we counted down the months before our move, I started feeling nostalgic for the things I was going to miss: going to Montreal Canadiens games, cycling along the Lachine Canal, walking on Mount Royal, favourite restaurants, visiting parents and relatives.

Here is one thing I did not think I was going to miss: good cheese.

We lived fairly close to the Atwater Market, which boasted two fine cheese shops. Not only that, one of them would regularly offer three-for-$10 deals — usually with cheeses that were on the verge of being past their best-by date but were still very good. Want some Basque ewe's milk cheese? How about some raw milk blue? No problem.

A few weeks after moving to Nova Scotia, I found myself standing in front of the fridge at the Atlantic Superstore in the Bayers Lake industrial park, looking at row after row of uniform rectangles of white and dyed-orange cheese. The selection? Mild Cheddar, medium Cheddar, marble, light Cheddar, mozzarella, low-fat mozzarella, a few types of processed cheese and some slightly more exotic cheeses — Havarti, Edam, Monterey Jack — that probably tasted almost indistinguishable from the Cheddars.

Writer and cheesemaker David Asher has called this kind of Cheddar "The most bastardized and industrialized cheese of all . . . An 18th-century inhabitant of Cheddar would hardly even recognize the plastic-wrapped rubbery orange blocks bearing the name of their town as cheese."

"How am I going to live here?" I thought, scanning the rows of cheese, before spotting the supposedly extra-old cheddar and dropping a block of it into my cart.

In my defence, I'm not the only one who has felt that way.

Chef Ron Muise spent years living in Europe, including time in Bath, England, where his home was around the corner from what he describes as "probably the best cheese shop in the world at the time." Then he returned home to Cape Breton with his wife, Christa McKinnon, to live on her family's farm. "I think it was the first week after I moved back," Ron remembers. (He is speaking to me while standing partway up an old apple tree on the family property, picking apples for cider.) "I was invited to a wine-and-cheese party, and the cheese was Kraft marble and sliced-up mozzarella. I was like, okay." So he started taking cheesemaking courses, with one over-riding goal: "I wanted to make stuff I wanted to eat." (As I write this, Ron is "on hiatus" from cheesemaking but hopes to return to it.)

And Willem van den Hoek — the cheesemaker knows as "That Dutchman" — recalls that soon after he and his wife, Maja, emigrated from the Netherlands to Nova Scotia in 1975, people here "were all excited, because the local cheese plant [in Salmon River] had developed a new kind of cheese. Which was . . . Marble cheese! Cubes of white cheese and cubes of orange cheese pressed together — and there you had a new cheese!"

Things are a bit different now. The Salmon River cheese plant shut down in 2014 after nearly fifty years in business — and while supermarket cheese fridges are still dominated by row after row of bland offerings not unlike those available when we moved here, a handful of intrepid small-scale artisanal Nova Scotia cheese producers are managing to make a living making a range of interesting products with milk from cows, sheep, goats — and even water buffalo.

Cheese is the solution to a problem faced by anyone with dairy animals: What do you do with all that milk? Today, of course, you can sell it. And thanks to refrigeration, it will keep. But for most of human history, milk had an extremely limited shelf-life. If you wanted to consume it, you had to transform it into a more stable food. How do you do that? By turning it into cheese. Other milk products, like yogurt and kefir, will also extend the life of milk, but they keep nowhere near as long. Demmarest Haney, a Cape Breton homesteader whose family owns goats and a cow, says, "We make a lot of cheese when the animals are producing milk. As opposed to having four gallons of milk, you can have a pound of cheese. It's a lot easier to eat a pound of cheese than drink four gallons of milk."

It's a solution humans discovered a very long time ago. In August 2018, Italian researchers announced they had found traces of the oldest solid cheese ever found — made about 3,000 years ago — in a tomb in Egypt. Within a month, another team found evidence of cheesemaking in Croatia dating back 7,000 years ago, to the Neolithic era. As the BBC explains, "Cheesemaking was a breakthrough technology which transformed humanity. More portable and longer lasting than liquid milk, it enabled early farming to spread into cooler central and northern areas."

By making cheese and yogurt, early humans not only developed a way to store milk in a longer-lasting form, they also made it more palatable. At the time cheese was first made, most adult humans would have been lactose-intolerant, and so mostly unable to drink milk. That's another problem cheese, yogurt and kefir all solve. During fermentation, the lactose in milk is converted by bacterial action into lactic acid. The result is a food much lower in lactose — meaning even those with some intolerance to lactose can consume it safely.

The process of turning milk into cheese and the ingredients involved are

What's Raw Milk and Will It Kill Me?

There are few food controversies more divisive than the question of raw milk. Raw milk is milk that has not been pasteurized to kill the bacteria it contains. In Canada, it is illegal for consumers to buy raw milk, and Health Canada is unequivocal in its condemnation of drinking it. After an outbreak in Ontario of illness linked to the practice, the agency warned that "drinking raw (unpasteurized) milk increases the risk of contracting a serious foodborne disease such as *E. Coli*" and reminds readers that "the sale of raw milk has been strictly prohibited under the Food and Drug Regulations since 1991."

Some argue that regulations against raw milk are rooted in outdated fears of cows transmitting tuberculosis through raw milk, or date from times when dairy farmers practised poorer hygiene and didn't feed their cows properly. Others argue that food safety measures like pasteurization are a key part of the reason why there are so few illnesses and deaths connected to milk.

Cheeses can be made with either raw or pasteurized milk — and even though drinking raw milk is illegal, raw milk cheeses are allowed.

That's because as cheese ages, it gets more acidic through fermentation. This, combined with salt, inhibits the growth of harmful bacteria like *E. coli* and *Salmonella*. So commercial cheesemakers are allowed to make and sell cheeses with raw milk, as long as they relatively easy to describe. But the variety of cheeses we can make through slight changes to ingredients and techniques is astounding: fresh cheeses like ricotta, soft-rind Camemberts, thick and creamy blue cheeses, hard and salty Parmesans, Indian paneer — and on and on and on.

Of course, nobody knows exactly how humans discovered milk could be turned into fermented products, but we have some good ideas. Raw milk left in pottery vessels will clabber — it starts to ferment on its own, because of the live bacteria it contains. It also begins to coagulate, or separate. In his book *Cheese and Culture*, Paul S. Kindstedt writes that the rise of cheesemaking

are aged for at least sixty days. As is often the case, Quebec is an exception. Cheesemakers there sell soft cheeses made with raw milk and aged for a shorter period of time.

In his *Art of Natural Cheesemaking*, David Asher argues that raw milk from well-treated cows raised in clean conditions is perfectly safe and that banning soft cheeses undermines traditional cheesemaking in favour of industrial processes. The Oldways Cheese Coalition (motto: "Curds, Cultures, Communities") in the US campaigns for traditional raw milk cheesemaking and says it is important to carry "these time-honoured recipes into their modern production."

While some say raw milk cheeses better showcase local terroir, Willem van den Hoek, aka That Dutchman, says he switched from raw to pasteurized milk years ago. "You don't really notice the difference unless you really know your stuff." He says his aged cheeses have a rich flavour "that's pretty damn good and it's pasteurized. So, I don't know. And the so-called raw benefits? Meh, I don't know."

As for Health Canada, while it notes that raw milk cheeses are legal, its "advice to pregnant women, children, older adults and people with a weakened immune system is to avoid eating cheese made from raw milk as it does present a higher risk of foodborne illness than pasteurized milk cheeses."

Who is right? Who is wrong? That's not for me to decide. What I do know from years of following this issue is people on both sides have very strong opinions, and few are likely to change their minds.

corresponds with the discovery of firing ceramics with high heat — making them better suited to storing and transporting food. He says, "The fragility of the coagulated milk and its tendency to separate into solid curds and liquid whey when stirred would have become quickly evident, and it was only a matter of time before Neolithic pastoralists discovered that adults were able to consume the curds." (Remember, most adults at this time were lactose intolerant, but could eat curds because the fermentation process reduced the amount of lactose in cheese.) They soon developed perforated pots and baskets to use as sieves — efficiently separating curds from whey. Around the same time, humans discovered they could coagulate milk more efficiently by using rennet (the lining from the stomach of a young calf or kid).

These discoveries literally changed the course of human history. As Kindstedt puts it, "The enormous value of milk processing and the competitive advantages that it offered must have been recognized very quickly because cheesemaking (and butter making) became common throughout the Fertile Crescent shortly after the beginning of dairying . . . By around 4500 BC Neolithic Near East culture dominated the Mediterranean basin, most of Europe, and the Middle East, extending all the way to the gateway of India. Even more important from the standpoint of cheese history, wherever these peoples migrated cheesemaking followed, and humanity was now one step closer to the development of a dizzying array of diverse cheeses."

The sign by the side of Highway 2 in Upper Economy shows a bearded man holding two wheels of cheese encased in a yellow rind. Dozens more wheels line the shelves beside him. "Fine artisan cheeses," the sign says. "Award winning. Featuring our Dragon's Breath."

Just past, at the first road on the right, an understated sign with a crest points the way to That Dutchman's Cheese Farm: "Always open" the sign says.

Turn right and drive half a kilometre, past a park with emus, donkeys, rabbits and other animals, and you'll come to a modest building with a stunning view of the Bay of Fundy. You've arrived at one of the key spots in the story

Old sign at That Dutchman's Cheese Farm.

of contemporary artisanal cheesemaking in Nova Scotia. This is where Willem and Maja van den Hoek — back-to-the-landers from the Netherlands who decided to try their hands at rural Canadian life during the early 1970s — started making Gouda.

"When we started up, we didn't know anybody else making cheese. The feta folks [Holmestead Cheese] started up a bit later, in the same time-frame. Then a couple of years later, some Dutch people sold some cheese out the back door. There wasn't much going on," Willem tells me.

Some people wax romantic about tradition and art and experiences when you ask them about their livelihoods — especially in the food business. Willem is not one of those people. We sit at a table at the Seaport Market in Halifax, the place crowded with Saturday-morning shoppers. Willem has left a lone employee to staff his stand for an hour or so while he chats with me, taking the occasional bite from a dish of stir-fried noodles and vegetables he picked up from another market vendor.

"Why the cheese business?" I ask him.

"It was just practical. I like cows . . . I wanted to make a living and I like to make cheese. There's no romantic BS . . . We did not have some idealistic dream about making cheese. We just wanted to live in the sticks and that was a way to do it. Make a little cheese."

Willem and Maja went back to the Netherlands to learn the art of making Gouda — at the time, Willem says, there were about 1,000 dairy farms in the country making their own Gouda. Back here in Nova Scotia, Maja and Willem were the only ones. That meant a lot of work — and not much access to cash. Willem recalls approaching a Mr. Lord at the Bank of Nova Scotia in Truro for a loan. He turned up for his meeting at the bank wearing slippers and shorts.

"I told my story and the banker said, 'You'd better stop there. Because the more you tell me the worse it gets.' But then he said, 'I never lost money on a Dutch immigrant' and he lent me the money. He just didn't want to know too much."

In the early days of the business, Willem wasn't "That Dutchman." He was "That Damn Dutchman." An old wooden sign from that era still stands on the farm property. In a later iteration, fellow Dutch immigrants complained, he dropped the word "damn" in favour of "That ★@★&! Dutchman." (This may not be the exact string of characters he used, but you get the idea.)

Willem says he and Maja started the business "without permission. That's unthinkable now. I was pretty casual, I suppose. I'd see an inspector maybe once a year. They are a lot more on top of it now."

From the shop in Upper Economy you can look through a large glass window speckled with salt stains at cheeses in various stages of development. Five dozen wheels in a tank soak in brine — the small ones for a day and the larger ones for three. Their next stop is a set of shelves where they begin aging. Another fifty wheels sit here, where they will be covered in a waxed rind. Finally, they will move to the aging room in the basement.

I ask Willem to describe the aging room. "It's just a big room with a lot of cheese. About $100,000 worth of cheese. And then we have a section for blue cheese which is isolated from the rest."

The oldest cheeses in the room are fifteen years old, and while Willem says Gouda that old is delicious and comparable to a higher-fat Parmesan, "there is no market for it."

Thirty years ago, it was an uphill fight trying to convince people to buy

Gouda curing in brine before it is aged at That Dutchman's Cheese plant in Upper Economy.

local cheese. Now, customers are looking for new flavours. The open fridges in the Upper Economy shop hold Gouda not only in mild, medium and old forms, but also in a slew of flavours. Stinging nettle Gouda. Sun-dried tomato Gouda. Jalapeno Gouda. Garlic Gouda.

I watch as visitors from Quebec point with delight at some of the flavours: "Look — nettle-flavoured cheese!"

Willem says, "It's no different than how ice cream used to be only vanilla and now we have everything under the sun. In a way, we're in the entertainment business. People come for the experience, and they like to try the different flavours. It's a form of entertainment."

After two decades of making Gouda and smeerkaas — its spreadable counterpart — Willem started experimenting with a blue cheese. "I do like experimenting," he says. "It took a couple of years to get it right." The result was the van Hoeks' signature Dragon's Breath Blue — a tangy blue cheese encased in black wax. Fifteen years after it was launched, Willem still seems surprised by its success. Now, the van Hoeks are experimenting with a new Camembert-style cheese, but blue cheese spores have a habit of getting onto everything nearby.

"Our Camembert-style cheese is starting to get some blue on the rind," Willem says. But he doesn't seem terribly concerned. "It has to find its own place. I like to work with the conditions we have. The cheese is doing what it wants instead of us telling it what to do. I'm not going to fight to get something perfect in an artificial environment. I don't want to go there."

As for his own tastes? "Wine, bread and a hunk of cheese. I eat bread and cheese. Either very mild or very old — I don't care for medium cheese. I've been eating it for forty years."

If you want someone who waxes poetic about cheese, David Asher is your man. The author of *The Art of Natural Cheesemaking,* David is in Nova Scotia to lead workshops on his traditional — but now uncommon — cheesemaking techniques. About twenty of us gather at the Nova Scotia Community College's waterfront campus in Dartmouth as David leads us through a day that combines practical tips on making fresh cheeses like mozzarella and longer-ripening Camembert-style ones. The group ranges from those like me who are curious about making cheese to a professional cheesemaker who has come to see if she can pick up some new ideas. David preaches the gospel of raw milk, although, unlike other raw milk advocates, he doesn't believe in drinking it: "I think milk should be turned into cheese," he tells the class. "You are allowing the milk to live out its destiny."

Even making the simplest of cheeses can take a few hours. So it's not long into the workshop before David starts pouring gallons of non-homogenized cow's milk into a large stainless-steel pot, stirring gently and frequently, and discussing the history of cheesemaking and its techniques.

David is an evangelist for returning to home-and-farm-based artisanal cheesemaking. The kind that was destroyed with the arrival of large, industrial dairies. He believes in using raw (unpasteurized) milk and decries the creep of industrial cheesemaking techniques into books for home use, which call for what he sees as an over-emphasis on sterilization and use of plastic and stainless-steel tools to avoid unwanted bacteria. "If you wish to make cheese according to industrial philosophies, you should lean toward plastic and steel because they are more amenable to these methods," he writes in *The Art of Natural Cheesemaking.* "If you wish to make cheese using more traditional methods, choose wood or other natural materials that respond best to natural cheesemaking . . . Work with whatever you've got, and the cheese should turn out just fine!"

David argues that if you follow time-honoured techniques, the right bacteria will flourish — particularly if you are using raw milk. Understandably, not everyone is enthused by David's approach. When I talked to Ron Muise, he told me he thought David's techniques were "an example of how to do things wrong" and that they are "not beneficial or safe."

There are thousands of types of cheese in the world (the website *cheese.com* boasts information on "1831 specialty cheeses from 74 countries"), but most start from a few simple ingredients.

If you are going to make cheese the first thing you'll need is milk. (I'm going to leave vegan cheeses aside here.) It's illegal to buy raw milk for home cheesemaking in Canada — much to David Asher's dismay. As with any prohibition there are, of course, people who skirt the law. I have heard of several small farms willing to sell raw milk to those they trust. But I've never bought it and I'll assume that you aren't buying it either.

Try to buy the freshest milk you can, and if you have access to non-homogenized milk, buy that. In Nova Scotia, the only source of pasteurized, non-homogenized cow's milk is Fox Hill (who also make their own delicious cheeses). Non-homogenized milk will produce stronger curds. You can make cheese with homogenized milk, but you may have to add calcium chloride to strengthen the curds, and even then the results won't likely be as good as those non-homogenized milk will produce.

Besides milk, the other key ingredients in cheese are culture, coagulant and salt.

Let's start with cultures.

If we want to turn milk into cheese, we need to add culture. Cultures are substances teeming with bacteria that will help transform the milk. As with other forms of fermentation, one of the keys here are bacteria that convert sugars into lactic acid. These bacteria lower the pH of the cheese as they multiply, crowding out other organisms and allowing the cheese to age gracefully into a delicious Brie, or Parmesan, or Gouda or any of hundreds of other varieties.

Cultures come in two broad families: mesophilic and thermophilic. How do cheesemakers decide which to use? It has to do with the temperature of the milk. Some cheeses require that milk be heated to warm, but relatively low temperatures. For those cheeses (generally softer ones), you need a mesophilic culture. Harder cheeses like Parmesan and Gruyere require heating milk to a much higher temperature. They take a thermophilic culture. ("Thermophilic" derives from the Greek words for loving heat.)

You can order freeze-dried cultures online — most of them come from one of only a few large producers — in packets. Just like winemakers can vary the flavour of their wines depending on their choice of yeast, so too cheesemakers can influence the flavour and texture of their cheese through their choice of culture.

And — again, as with winemaking — you can choose to avoid commercially manufactured cultures altogether and introduce bacteria to your cheese with yogurt, buttermilk or kefir. David Asher likes kefir, because, he tells us, its "microbial community is very similar to raw milk."

At our workshop, when the milk he is heating reaches the temperature he wants, David stirs in the kefir, then leaves it for an hour or so, so the bacteria can start multiplying before the next step.

Milk is a complex product, made up of nearly 90 per cent water, along with lactose, proteins and minerals. The proteins fall into two different families: casein proteins and serum (or whey) proteins.

Remember Little Miss Muffet, who sat on her tuffet, eating her curds and whey? When we make cheese, we want to separate these proteins from each other, turning our milk into curds (which we use for making cheese) and whey — which makes a great fertilizer or soup stock. When the pH of the milk is lowered, the curds part from the whey. For a simple, fresh cheese like fromage blanc or paneer, you can lower the pH with citric acid, vinegar or lemon juice. But firmer or aged cheeses require a coagulant. Coagulants contain enzymes that (as the name suggests) coagulate the milk into curds. As David Asher explains in his book, "Enzymes, like chymosin, fit into their partner proteins much like a key fits into a lock. And when the match is right, the key turns, the lock is opened, and the protein's form changes. Chymosin fits perfectly with casein, the most common milk protein, and when the conditions are favorable (the milk is warm and acidic), rennet changes the shape of the casein, causing it to coagulate, settle out of the milk, and form into curd."

Rennet is the classic coagulant. Used for millennia, it is made from the lining of calf's stomach. You can also use other coagulants, like vegetable-based "rennets" often derived from mushrooms.

About an hour after adding culture to the milk, David picks up a large Ziploc bag, tears it open, and removes a thin, papyrus-like item from it. He unfolds it and holds it up so all of us in the room can see it. It's part of the lining of a young calf's stomach, salted and cured. A source of real rennet. As he passes it around the room, each of us feel the papery stomach and smell its cheesy, earthy scent.

A piece of stomach like this will last a long time. David rips off a tiny piece to use today — just a little corner, maybe a centimetre square.

Rennet is powerful stuff. Usually, you dilute it, then mix it carefully into the pot of milk. Once David adds it, he covers the pot with a lid, then wraps it in a blanket and leaves it another hour for the curd to form. Even though we all know this is the next step, there are plenty of oohs and ahs an hour later as we look at the milk and see it seemingly magically transformed into this jelly-ish mass.

Now it's time to cut the curd. We take turns crisscrossing the pot with a knife, which increases the surface area and releases more whey. Then we gently stir the curds so that even more whey comes out. Less whey means a richer, dryer cheese.

For some cheeses the curd is cooked at this point in the process. Since we are making a Camembert-style cheese, we skip that step and flip the curds into cheese molds — round baskets that will give it shape. Flip the forms over a few times in the next twenty-four hours, cover the cheeses with salt (which inhibits the growth of bacteria we don't want) and then wash the rind with a brine regularly. Age it in a cool place, and within a few weeks, or months, depending on your tastes, you should have a tasty soft cheese.

It took me a couple of years from the time I learned this technique from David until I tried it at home. But when I did, it provided a thrill like few other foods I've made in my kitchen. There truly does seem to be something magical about watching a pot full of milk turn into three small wheels of cheese, and carefully tending to it — washing its rind, keeping it at the right temperature — for weeks, until it reaches the right flavour.

My homemade Camembert-style cheese pressed and ready to age.

Nova Scotia may not have had the plethora of cheeses that developed in other parts of the world (the late French President Charles de Gaulle famously complained that it was impossible to govern a country that made 246 different kinds of cheese), but farmhouse cheesemaking was part of daily rural life. Traditionally, cheesemaking (and dairying in general) was women's work. In *Cheese and Culture*, Paul Kindstedt writes that women dominated cheesemaking for centuries in rural England. Then, men began to promote the idea of scientific and industrial cheesemaking. They studied the women's techniques, but developed repeatable recipes that standardized ingredients and processes for particular varieties. Soon after, women who made cheese came to be portrayed as "backward, narrow-minded, and having a natural aversion to learning new techniques."

The first cheese factory in America opened in 1851. It took another twenty years for the cheese factory trend to hit Nova Scotia, but once it did, it caught on fast. Between his terms as a member of the Nova Scotia legislature and the federal House of Commons, businessman Avard Longley co-founded a cheese factory in Paradise, in the Annapolis Valley in 1871. Another opened in nearby Williamstown the same year. Documents from the Nova Scotia legislature record acts of incorporation for The Paradise Union Cheese Manufacturing Company, the Nictaux and Wilmot Cheese Factory and the Onslow Cheese Manufacturing Company — all passed on April 4, 1871.

(The Paradise factory quickly became a local landmark. An 1897 history of Annapolis County says Paradise "well deserves the name it bears," singling out, among others, its school, church and cheese factory.)

Other cheese companies followed, including the Brookfield Creamery and Cheese Manufacturing Company (1884) and the Little River Cheese Manufacturing Company (1892) near Nine Mile River — built at a spot in East Hants still known as Cheese Factory Corner.

The Little River Cheese Factory was founded by farmers for an eminently practical reason, as local historian Ralph Whittier explained to a meeting of the East Hants Historical Society some eighty years later: "To manufacture cheese as a means of disposing of their milk." The factory ran seasonally, producing nearly 26,500 pounds of cheese during five months in 1892. (That took "139 tons four hundredweight and 77 pounds of milk" — the factory kept very precise records.) Just two years later, the factory's cheesemakers, a Mr. and Mrs. Townson, left, and despite hiring a new cheesemaker, production plummeted. Over a three-month period, the factory produced just over 1,500 pounds of cheese. It shut down soon after, and the building itself collapsed in 1910.

Benjamin Starratt was one of the founders of the Paradise cheese factory, but he seems to have had regrets later in life about his role in industrializing cheese production. An undated, typed, yellowed, legal-size sheet of paper in the Nova Scotia Archives bears Starratt's thoughts, apparently published in the Bridgetown *Monitor-Sentinel*. (Paradise is very close to Bridgetown.) He recalls how dairying was hard work, especially for the women who did most of it, but that it "was one of the most important branches of farming and one of the most profitable . . . All the milk was manufactured at home. The farmer's kitchen in the summer days was the scene of busy activity. There were very few large dairies — not more than half a dozen in the County numbering twenty cows. Nine cows was considered a good dairy, but there were many of them. In some of the localities every farmer made cheese."

Horse-drawn Woodlawn Dairy carriage.

Starratt goes on to describe the process for making cheese: "In the summer, much of the milk was made into cheese. The night's milk was strained into a big tub to which the morning's milk was added and in up-to-date dairies a cheese was made every day. The curd was placed in hoops and pressed in strong hand presses operated generally by a lever, after which they were placed on shelves greased with fresh butter, well rubbed and turned every day. This was really the heaviest part of the work. Later in the season when the weather became cooler skim milk, cheese and butter would be made. The milk would be 'doubled up' that is, two or three days milk would be made into one cheese." (The process of leaving milk out overnight — now frowned upon — is called clabbering. Through fermentation, the raw milk begins to get sour and to thicken. It can then be used as a culture for making cheese.)

These cheeses were not just destined for local consumption. Starratt writes that their main market was Halifax, to which they were sent "by water in Captain Peter McKay's fast sailing schooner."

After admitting to his own role in launching the cheese factory in Paradise, Starratt questions whether the industrialization of cheesemaking really constitutes progress: "Since the introduction of factories, cheesemaking at home has gradually died out, factories springing up in every direction . . . Of course, they are a great relief to the wives and daughters of the farmers, but whether they have been a real advantage is a question that admits of argument."

As industrial cheesemaking displaced farmhouse dairies, one of the results was greater uniformity in types of cheese. In writing about New England, Kindstedt says, "Almost overnight the factory would come to dominate cheesemaking in America, and overwhelmingly the new American factories would produce one cheese variety: Cheddar." There were a couple of factors driving this development: the popularity of Cheddar in England, an important export market, and the development of industrial, scientific, Cheddar-making processes. Kindstedt has a chart showing farmhouse cheese production cratering to nearly nothing between 1850 and 1930, while the industrial production line of the graph rises dramatically.

Similar trends likely played out locally too. Then, Kindstedt says, American cheese developed a poor reputation in the late 1800s thanks to practices including replacing milk fat with cheaper lard. Canadian factories were among those that stepped up, and Canadian exports helped feed England's rapacious appetite for Cheddar.

While the David Asher approach is not for everyone, as an amateur I found it refreshing. I'd bought cheesemaking books in the past and been intimidated by the instructions to, for instance, bleach all surfaces in the kitchen before starting. Cheese is an ideal medium for the growth of bacteria, especially as it ages. The goal of sterilization is to ensure only the bacteria you want — the ones you introduce through your cultures, grow in your cheese.

Demmarest Haney stresses that cleanliness is important, but that "there's a line. I am meticulous with the cheese supplies . . . I scrub the hell out of them. It's not the kind of 'it's all good' hippie approach I might try if I'm making granola or something. But I'm not going to go through my whole kitchen with bleach."

Fermentation guru Sandor Katz would agree. Speaking at a workshop in Halifax, he said, "Household sterilization is a fantasy. The jar is in your oven, but then it's on your counter cooling down. It's a fantasy because the air in your house is not sterile."

For someone like me, the stakes are not high. If I decide to make some cheese and age it in a Tupperware-style container in my basement, I will be disappointed if it doesn't turn out. But that won't be a disaster.

If you are a commercial cheesemaker though, you need a bit more control over your processes.

Lyndell Findlay welcomes me into her cramped cheese plant in the basement of what was once a small home on Robie Street in the North End of Halifax. She's on the verge of moving to a new, much larger location, and she clearly can't wait — not only because she will have more space, but because it will be federally inspected, meaning she will be able to sell her cheese across the country.

Lyndell says cheesemaking is "about career number five for me." She came back to Canada after eight years overseas with the UN High Commissioner for Refugees, where she worked as a protection officer for vulnerable people, including refugees, in Darfur, Congo and Myanmar. After her return here, she took a trip to the Magdalen Islands, where she ate wonderful cheese — and became intrigued by the idea of cheesemaking. After a chance meeting at a dinner party in Florida, a farmstead cheesemaker from Ohio invited her to intern with him. She signed on, did courses in artisan cheesemaking in Vermont along with the internship, and then came to Halifax and started up her company, Blue Harbour Cheese. Her slogan, "Embrace the blue" reflects her mission: "to win everyone over

Lyndell Findlay in her office at Blue Harbour.

to blue cheese." (That's an ambitious goal, considering, she tells me, that the market share for blue cheese in Nova Scotia is about 5 per cent.) Before launching, she experimented at home, "doing little batches of a kilo at a time, experimenting with different cultures and techniques, reading about blue cheese till I came up with something that was nice."

Nova Scotia has fewer than a dozen licensed cheesemakers, and the number who are federally inspected (meaning they can sell their products in other provinces) is tiny. The quality of local cow's milk is excellent but prices are high — every cheesemaker I spoke to complained about them. Regulations are stringent and can be complex, and the market for artisan cheese is small. It takes a particular kind of tenacity to survive.

Perhaps because of that, Lyndell says cheesemakers tend to be supportive of each other — and it helps that they each seem to have their own unique niche, whether it's making feta, traditional high-end Italian cheeses, spreadable goat cheese, classic Cheddar, Gouda or blue cheese.

At her desk, Lyndell sits surrounded by books with titles including *One-Hour Cheese*, and *Reinventing the Wheel: Milk, Microbes, and the Fight for Real Cheese*.

She launched Blue Harbour with her signature mild Urban Blue cheese, which she describes as "a cheese that people could relate to and is approachable and won't burn your throat out." But — as with any new cheese — getting there involved hours and hours of experimentation.

Lyndell pulls down a catalogue from one of the big manufacturers: page after page of cultures, each explaining what combinations of bacteria it contains and their properties in cheesemaking.

"There's so many different types of cultures for different types of cheeses and they have different characteristics. So when you're trying to figure out which ones to use — some will acidify faster, some slower. Some will create gas within the cheese, which will give you holes that you may or may not want . . . You're looking at the bio-chemical composition of these different cultures and you can go through the catalogue and say these characteristics will give me a creamy cheese, or these will give me a more nutty flavour."

But finding the right culture or combination of cultures is just one step, one component, of what makes a cheese unique. "You can take the same culture and process it in two different ways and get two completely different cheeses," Lyndell says. She recalls her testing days — making dozens of batches of cheese and seeing what changes in the process would bring. "I'm changing the proportions for the quantity of milk, aging them differently, draining them differently. The drier your cheese the longer you can age it." Moister cheeses have a shorter shelf life and risk rotting if they age too long. By comparison, Demmarest Haney says she found a four-year-old hard cheese she had forgotten about in her basement and it was fine. "My son is four and he was like, 'Let's eat it, Mom! Crack it open!' So we're eating this rock cheese, but it was really awesome."

One of the things that seems magical about cheese though is how seemingly minor changes can yield wildly different results. What culture do you use? How thick do you cut the curd? Do you cook the curd? How long do you drain the cheese? Are you going to press the cheese as it ages or not? And do you age it for weeks, months or years?

Cheese is only one of the fermented products you can make with milk, of course. Finland has a fermented milk drink called viili. Koumiss is a slightly alcoholic drink made from fermented mare's milk. And in Sudan, you can get gariss, a drink made from fermented camel's milk. When I met Sandor Katz, he was about to head off to South Asia and told me he was "really

A Simple Homemade Cheese

Cheesemaking can be a complex and involved process. It can also be incredibly easy. It all depends on what kind of cheese you are making.

One of the challenges facing the home cheesemaker is the lack of access to raw milk, which you are not allowed to buy, or to pasteurized milk that has not been homogenized.

Left to its own devices, milk will separate, with the fat globules rising to the top and forming a layer of cream. (Much the same as how oil droplets in a jar of water will rise to the top.)

Homogenization forces the milk under high pressure through tiny openings. This causes the fat globules to become much smaller and denser. As a result, they no longer separate from the rest of the milk and they don't rise to the top. The milk is more stable and has a far longer shelf-life.

Cheeses and yogurt made by Demmarest Haney.

excited to see the diversity of fermented milks in India."

In North America, yogurt is the most common form of fermented milk other than cheese. Where yogurt was once seen as a weird hippie food, today dozens of varieties fill shelf after shelf in supermarket freezers. In its simplest form, yogurt contains just milk and active cultures — the bacteria that allow

The downside? It's not good for making most kinds of cheese.

As David Asher puts it, making cheese with "milk that is homogenized, pasteurized, and one or more weeks old (in other words, most of the milk you'll find in the supermarket) . . . will present challenges."

Why? Because the process of homogenization "results in curds that are weaker and less able to stand up to the rigors of cheesemaking. They fall to pieces, resulting in difficulty handling the cheese, poor cheese yields, and improper cheese evolution."

Only one Nova Scotia producer — Fox Hill — produces non-homogenized cow's milk. They are your best bet if you are in the province and want to make aged cheeses.

But you can make soft cheeses like ricotta or paneer at home with plain old supermarket milk.

Demmarest Haney usually teaches a couple of cheesemaking workshops a year in Cape Breton. She says the one constant is people telling her they had no idea making soft cheeses could be so easy — something I heard too when I went to one of her workshops in Sydney.

"I'm a bit of a cheese pusher, and there's a reason I only do simple cheeses in the workshop. It's because I want people to get that taste of 'I can do this!' before they get drawn into 'Oh my God, it took me two years to make this cheese!' Nobody's going to commit to that until they're hooked . . . All you can do is repeatedly say how easy it is and show them. This is something we can all do and it's not hard."

the milk to set. "I think it's real alchemy that bacteria can turn a liquid into a solid without losing anything," Sandor told a small group gathered in a Halifax restaurant after hours to hear him talk about fermentation.

You can buy freeze-dried cultures for home yogurt making, but all you really need to get started is some plain yogurt containing active cultures. The kind you can pick up at any supermarket or local grocery. (To make your own yogurt, see the recipe on page 264.)

Over time, the cultures you use to make yogurt weaken and need to be refreshed. So after making anywhere from around eight to twelve batches, you'll need to go out and buy yourself some new yogurt to start the whole process again. Sandor says he wondered about this when he first started making yogurt. If he was living in Turkey during the Middle Ages he wouldn't wander off to the corner store to pick up a bit more yogurt when his culture was losing steam.

So what's the difference between older starter cultures and the yogurt cultures available to us now?

The change in yogurt cultures is similar to that with many other yeasts and cultures in the industrial age: they have become isolated and reproducible, in part for the sake of consistency (or quality, if you prefer) but at the cost of diversity. Winemakers might choose to wild-ferment their grape juice, or they can pick a yeast out of a catalogue, looking for specific results. Cheesemakers can choose from an array of freeze-dried mesophilic and thermophilic starter cultures. Brewers might culture their local indigenous yeasts or rely on a very specific strain.

Writing in *The Art of Fermentation*, Sandor Katz explains that the yogurt cultures we use today result from the work of Russian microbiologist Elie Metchnikoff. Metchnikoff, who worked at the famed Pasteur Institute in Paris, believed yogurt might play a role in longevity. (The Parisian press was far more sensational, with one paper urging readers to "taste the delicious Bulgarian curdled milk that the illustrious Professor Metchnikoff has recommended for suppressing the disastrous effects of old age." He isolated some of the bacteria responsible for souring and preserving — fermenting — the milk and transforming it into yogurt.)

Sandor writes that commercially produced yogurt differs from traditional yogurt in that it is made from only the bacteria that have been isolated and reproduced — representing a less complex culture than traditional yogurt. "The cultures and techniques [of making yogurt] probably spread via nomadic herding peoples, and they evolved distinctively in different locations, as does any food that gets spread over a vast territory, especially a fermented one. And besides being regionally varied, traditional yogurt cultures also consisted of more complex communities, involving organisms beyond the two bacteria that the Pasteur Institute identified as the critical ones, and that legally define yogurt in our time. The traditional yogurt cultures were evolved communities, with a certain amount of inherent stability to them."

In other words, more complex cultures are more resilient, if perhaps less predictable. But unless you can find yourself some heirloom yogurt cultures, you'll have to make do with commercial yogurt (which even Sandor admits "render a lovely ferment with a pleasing texture and flavor").

The other milk ferment which seems to have gained an enthusiastic and devoted following locally is kefir.

I knew kefir had gone mainstream when I walked into my local hardware store about three years ago and Shelley, one of the owners, looked up from the cash and told me she'd heard I was interested in fermentation and she wanted a recipe from me. As we talked, she told me about her enthusiasm for making kefir, and I wound up getting some grains from her and starting to make it myself.

There are a few things I love about kefir, and they are not all related to its taste. For one thing, it seems weirdly mysterious. It's a tangy — even sour — and slightly fizzy milk beverage you can drink straight, pour over cereal or flavour with fruit, vanilla or whatever else strikes your fancy.

It's hard to describe kefir in a way that makes it sound appetizing. The starter culture is a gelatinous, curd-like mass of grains made of bacteria and fungi that clump together. (I told you it wasn't going to sound appealing.)

What's in those grains? Well, that's a good question. I'll turn to Sandor Katz and *The Art of Fermentation* once again: "It's a symbiotic entity that self-reproduces," he writes. He refers to the work of biologist Lynn Margulis: "Margulis explains that kefir grains involve a community of 30 different types of microbes, including common food fermentation favorites . . . as well as others more obscure; in fact, according to Margulis, fewer than half the microbes involved are known or named." Isolate some of the components and they won't reproduce and make more kefir. Use the whole gelatinous mass, and you'll be drinking fizzy milk in no time.

Ricotta from Whole Milk

Here is a ricotta recipe inspired by the one Demmarest shared at the workshop. At the end of the session, she said, "Here's our ricotta!" to cheers, followed by everyone in the room trying some.

Materials

- Double-boiler (so you don't scald the milk as you heat it)
- Clean measuring cups and spoons (Demmarest keeps sets dedicated to cheesemaking because "I don't want my cheese to taste like turmeric or any of the things I measure.")
- A deep colander
- Thermometer (Demmarest calls this the most important piece of equipment because "even one- or two-degrees difference will change the texture of your cheese.")
- Cheesecloth or muslin for straining
- Glass or plastic container for storage

Ingredients

- 1 tsp (5 mL) citric acid or 2 tbsp (30 mL) lemon juice
- 1 gallon (4 L) whole milk*
- 1 tsp (5 mL) salt
- 1 to 2 tbsp (15 to 30 mL) heavy cream (optional)
    *If you prefer to use low-fat milk you can, but it will produce a less creamy, thinner-tasting cheese.

Kefir originated in the Caucasus Mountains and became popular in Russia, from where it has spread. Because we don't have much large-scale commercial kefir production in Canada, the best way to ensure a steady supply of kefir is to make it yourself.

I have seen freeze-dried kefir cultures in Nova Scotia stores, but these are not a true kefir culture that will reproduce. You can use them once, and that's it. Kefir grains consistently multiply and increase in size the more you use them. Anyone who makes kefir will have grains to give away. To get started, do as I did and find someone who makes it. I have yet to meet a

Method

If using the citric acid, dissolve it in 1/4 cup cool water, add to the milk and mix.

Heat the milk gently in the double-boiler, stirring often. This step requires a lot of patience. Demmarest says the advantage of the double-boiler is that you're unlikely to scorch your milk. The downside is that it will take quite a while to get up to the temperature you want.

Monitor the temperature of the milk with your thermometer and remove from heat when it reaches 185°F (85°C).

If you did not use the citric acid, stir in the lemon juice.

The milk will separate into curds and whey. The curds are the chunky bits and the whey is the watery liquid.

Line the colander with muslin or cheesecloth and spoon in the curds.

Tie the corners of the cloth and hang the curds up to drain. Make sure to have a bowl or pot underneath. When I'm draining cheese or yogurt (to thicken it more) I usually tie it to a wooden spoon jammed into the handles of my kitchen cupboards and place a bowl underneath.

Let it drain for 30 to 60 minutes. The longer the cheese drains, the firmer it will be.

Place in a glass or plastic container and stir in the salt and cream, if using (Demmarest adds the salt at the end; some other recipes call for adding the salt with the milk). Cover and refrigerate.

Your ricotta will keep for up to two weeks in the fridge.

Make-at-Home Yogurt

Materials

- Saucepan for heating milk
- 1-quart (1 L) Mason jar
- Measuring cup
- Spoon for stirring

Ingredients

- Enough milk to fill a 1-quart (1 L) Mason jar
- Between 1 tsp (5 mL) and 1 tbsp (15 mL) of plain yogurt with active cultures

Method

Heat the milk very gently in a heavy-bottomed pan, stirring frequently. You could also use a double-boiler to reduce the risk of scorching.

Bring the milk to just under boiling. It should start to bubble a bit but not come to boil.

Remove the pot from the heat and let the milk cool to just above body temperature. You can test it by putting a drop on your wrist. It should feel like the temperature of milk you would give a baby, if that's a helpful comparison. If you don't have the time or patience to wait for the milk to cool on its own, you can cool it by putting it in a different container (your pot is hot), placing the bowl or pot of milk in a cooling water bath, or — if it's winter in Nova Scotia — putting it outside for a few minutes. Stir the milk occasionally as it cools.

Once the milk reaches the desired temperature, scoop out about a cupful. Add anywhere from a teaspoon to a tablespoon of yogurt to the cup of warm milk. Stir until it is thoroughly dissolved. Then pour it back into the pot or bowl with the rest of the milk and stir gently.

Pour the milk into your Mason jar, cover and leave in a warm place for eight to twelve hours. Once the yogurt sets up and reaches your desired thickness, refrigerate. It will keep at least a week, and possibly more. (If it has gone bad you will either see mold or it will have an unpleasant smell.) During months when we have the woodstove going, I leave the jar on the mantle overnight. In summer (when it's sometimes not all that warm in Nova Scotia) I might put it in sunny spot and wrap it in a blanket or towel. You could also leave it in the oven with just the light on or sitting on a heating pad.

Make sure to take a spoonful of yogurt out and put it aside to use as starter for your next batch.

If you want to add sweetener or flavouring to your yogurt do it at the end of the process. If you add it with the milk or culture your yogurt probably won't set.

Yield: 1 quart (1 L)

Culture Facts and Fun

When it comes to fermenting, I am generally a fan of experimentation. I find that yogurt lends itself well to this. There are a few things you can do to affect outcomes though, and you can play around with them.

The longer your yogurt sits the tangier it will become. It should also become firmer (up to a point). Avoid the temptation to shake your jar or rotate it. Yogurt likes to be left alone. Paradoxically, using less starter seems to result in a firmer product. If you find your yogurt a bit runny for your tastes, don't add more starter next time. Try making it with a bit less instead.

Perhaps you would like a bit more precision than "just above your body temperature" and prefer to actually measure the temperature of your milk. In that case, the magic number is 115°F (46°C). Stir your culture into the one cup of milk at this temperature or slightly below, then leave your yogurt to ferment.

Over time, you will find that your culture gets tired. If your yogurt is turning out thin, regardless of what you do, it's time to refresh the culture. Buy some yogurt from the grocery store and use a spoonful of it as your starter. You should get anywhere from eight to twelve batches before your culture gets tired.

For your starter culture, buy plain yogurt (no sugar or other flavourings). The package should say something like "active cultures" or "bacterial culture." Sometimes it will list the cultures, e.g., "with active *L. acidophillusbifidus* and *L. casei.*"

TOP: Blue Harbour cheesemaker Catherine Keeler gently stirs curds.
BOTTOM: Blue Harbour assistant cheesemaker Katie Cvitkovitch (left) and cheesemaker Catherine Keeler (right) scoop curds out of the whey at the draining table.

kefir maker who won't share their grains or tips for making the fizzy drink.

I was going to include a recipe for making kefir on a separate page, but it's so simple I'll just include it here. You take your kefir grains, put them in a jar and add milk. (Sandor Katz recommends a tablespoon of grains per litre of milk. You can use a quart-size Mason jar to keep things simple, but don't fill it all the way to the top, because the fermentation process will produce gas.) Now leave the jar in a dark place for the day or overnight — up to twenty-four hours. It will get more sour as it ferments. If you can, give it a little shake every so often.

Once the kefir is done, remove the grains with a spoon, or capture them with a sieve. Store the grains in another jar, covered in fresh milk, and leave them in the fridge until you are ready to make a new batch.

Kefir grains are pretty hardy, but they do need to be used regularly or they will go bad. You don't have to make kefir every day or two, but if you want to keep your grains happy you should get into the habit of making it regularly. If you don't want to be awash in kefir, make a pint jar at a time.

As you will see, the grains will grow — each time you make a batch you should have a few more grains than last time. You can use the larger colony of starter to make larger batches of kefir, or you could give the grains away, find a recipe that uses them or simply put them in your compost.

Back at Blue Harbour, Lyndell Findlay is ready to give me a tour of the cheese plant. "You'll have to kit up," she says. We put on "I'm not a doctor but I play one on TV"-style lab coats, along with hairnets and slippers that are used only in this building. (Another option is paper coverings for footwear.)

In the back room, cheesemaker Catherine Keeler and assistant cheesemaker Katie Cvitkovitch are prepping today's batch of Urban Blue cheese. The room is warm and steamy. When I pull out my camera the lens fogs up immediately. Katie gently stirs the curds, then scoops them out onto a draining table. Whey pours out in rivulets. The more liquid

A Few Cheese Families

With thousands of varieties of cheese in the world, there literally is something for everyone's taste. There are many different ways to categorize cheese. (The graphic memoir *Relish: My Life in the Kitchen* by Lucy Knisley has a very funny page — really! — on cheese classifications.) Cheese can be organized by type of milk, age, region, manufacturing technique and other factors. Flavours for the same kinds of cheese will also vary, of course, depending on who is making it, with what kind of milk and the cows' diet. With that in mind, here is a non-comprehensive listing of families of cheese, including many made in Nova Scotia.

Brine-Aged Cheeses

If you've bought feta cheese, you'll notice that it's usually in a salty brine. The brine helps preserve the cheese and its characteristics (creaminess, for instance) without the need for refrigeration. Brined cheeses developed in warm climates where aging cheese on boards or in caves for months at a time may not have been much of an option. My grandmother, who lived in southern Greece, made cheese this way with milk from her sheep and goats. If you buy brined cheese and store it in the fridge it will last longer. If the cheese starts to get a bit funky you can always replace the brine. Holmestead Cheese, in Aylesford, produces a lovely brined feta made with cow's milk. (They are also one of the longest-running cheese manufacturers in the province.)

Bloomy Rind Cheeses

The most famous cheeses in this family are brie and Camembert. Also called soft surface-ripened cheeses, because they ripen from the outside in. (If you've bought these cheeses, you may have noticed the edges have a tendency to be softer.) Bloomy rind cheeses have a soft, white, fuzzy rind caused by mold. You may want to go "yuck" at the thought of mold — but these fungi are critical to cheesemaking and protect the cheese by preventing the growth of unwanted bacteria.

Washed Rind Cheeses

Washed rind cheeses are full of flavour — or they are stinky, depending on your tastes. As the name implies, the rinds of these cheeses are washed regularly during the first days or weeks after they are formed. Then they are aged. Washing the cheese with a cloth dipped in a brine — which is often whey-based — helps it develop a tasty, tacky, orange-coloured rind. If you want to combine a couple of different fermentation practices you can include beer, wine or hard liquor in the liquid you use to wash the rind. Ciro Comencini, who grew up in Italy and now lives in Hants County, makes a phenomenal Tallegio — a relatively mild but very tasty washed rind cheese. Washed rind cheeses were commonly made in northern European monasteries, where monks milked cows but also made wine, beer and spirits.

Chèvre

Goat's milk can be used to make many different kinds of cheese — from feta to harder Cheddar-style pressed cheeses. But in North America goat's milk is probably best-known for making chèvre — a spreadable, creamy cheese, sometimes flavoured with garlic and/or herbs. In Nova Scotia, Ran-Cher Acres have been in the cheese and milk business for nearly four decades, milking their herd of Saanen dairy goats.

Semi-Hard Cheeses

This is a broad category that includes many different cheeses — not as hard as cheeses like Gruyère or Parmesan, but not as soft as surface-ripened cheeses. Cheddar, Gouda and Havarti all fall into this category. One unique technique for Cheddar making is called (not surprisingly) cheddaring. It involves stacking and pressing the curds. Both Fox Hill and Knoydart Farm make very good (and very different) Cheddars.

Blue Cheese

When it comes to blue cheese, mold is the key. The blue veins in the cheese come from fungal cultures in the same family as penicillin. *Penicilliumroqueforti,* one of the best-known blue cultures, originates from caves in the French Pyrenees mountains, and gives Roquefort cheese its distinctive flavour. Blue cheesemakers need to be careful, because the spores that turn cheese blue and give flavour can easily spread all over a room — and to any other cheese in the vicinity. Willem van den Hoek says the bloomy rind cheese he is experimenting with is starting to show blue on its rind because of the Dragon's Breath Blue made in the same cheese plant. Blue cheeses can be made from any kind of milk. Blue Harbour makes one from cow's milk and one from sheep's milk.

Alpine-Style Cheeses

Originating in the mountains of France, Italy and Switzerland, these cheeses are usually made in large wheels. After being separated from the whey, the curds are cooked, which removes even more moisture. The cheeses are designed for a long aging process and ripen from the inside out (the opposite of bloomy rind cheeses). Making true alpine cheeses at home is a challenge, if not an impossibility, because of the large amounts of milk required. A proper wheel of Parmesan takes 500 litres of milk.

In the cheese aging chamber at Blue Harbour.

Cheese draining before it is aged at Blue Harbour.

Pasta Filata

Pasta filata means "spun paste" and refers to the process through which the curd is stretched and pulled, allowing it to be formed into a variety of shapes. Fresh mozzarella — which is nothing like pizza mozzarella — is one of the cheeses in this family. (I have made my own mozzarella, with limited success, but the stretching and pulling part is a lot of fun.) The famous Italian mozzarella di bufalais made with milk from water buffaloes. Surprisingly, this is something you can find in Nova Scotia thanks to former Montrealers Desiree Gordon and Stefan Kirkpatrick, who moved to tiny West Dublin on the South Shore, where they make a traditional mozzarella with milk from their small herd of water buffalo.

that drains out the less moisture in the cheese. It can take a couple of days for all the whey to drain out, and Lyndell doesn't always like to wait. "I'm always trying to hurry it up — not stir it quite as long, not rest it quite as long." She nods toward Catherine and Katie. "They're much more patient than I am."

Once much of the whey has drained, Catherine and Katie hoop the cheese, placing it in molds where it can drain further. They'll clean up from the morning's work, have lunch, then flip the cheeses every hour or so over the course of the afternoon so that they drain evenly.

If you look closely at the finished blue cheeses you can see little holes in the rind. "People think we inject the [blue] mold into the cheese," Lyndell says, "But we add it right with the milk." The needles introduce air and create pathways for the mold to spread in veins through the cheese, giving it the characteristic blue cheese look.

As she hoops the cheese, Catherine chats with me about other local cheeses and the ones she particularly loves.

Nobody gets into the cheese business in Nova Scotia looking to get rich. Willem van den Hoek told me he's been comfortable for a few years now — but it took decades to get to that point. Cheese plants can cost hundreds of thousands of dollars to set up. The market is small, and getting federally inspected so you can sell your cheese elsewhere is complicated and expensive. And local cheesemakers can only dream about getting the kind of provincial government support — financial or otherwise — given to the wine industry.

I ask Ron Muise if Nova Scotia cheese is where wine was a decade ago, and he says, "Possibly . . . We are doing a lot more than just producing cheese or wine. It's cultural food production. We're looking for ways to increase business, to get us into more marketplaces, to be branding and promoting Nova Scotia products. At the same time, any day you're not selling or making cheese you're losing money. And if you have animals and you're both milking and making cheese you're tired. When I was milking sixty animals here I

Rows of cheese in the aging room at Blue Harbour.

would start at 4 a.m. and finish at 2 p.m. if I was making cheese that day."

The words "labour of love" are a cliché, but they do seem to apply here. Just before I leave the cheese plant, Catherine looks up from hooping and says, "I just love being around the cheese all day! As they age, the mold grows and creates these beautiful blue cheeses. It's never the same mold growth on the cheese. And then we send them out into the world! I love it. I love it. It's just very satisfying."

9
Science, Safety
and What's Going on in Your Gut

In the course of writing this book, I've had countless variations on the same two conversations about fermentation. The first is about safety. It usually starts with something like, "I really want to make kombucha but I'm worried I'll kill someone." The second is about health and runs along the lines of, "Oh, fermented foods — I really need to start eating them for the probiotics."

My interested in fermented foods and drinks is rooted in their flavours, the joy and satisfaction that comes with making them, and the fact that people have been making many of them for hundreds, if not thousands of years.

That's me. But I also know that many people come to these foods because they have heard about their health benefits. In this chapter, we'll learn about the microbiology of our guts, look at the health benefits of fermented foods (and debunk some overblown claims) and I'll try to set you at ease about how safe it is to try fermenting at home.

Remember the hand sanitizer and anti-bacterial craze? When countless stories advised us to keep a bottle of sanitizer on our desks and use it multiple times a day? When supermarkets provided wipes so we could make sure our shopping carts were germ-free? When you were largely out of luck if you wanted to find liquid hand-soap that wasn't infused with anti-bacterial agents?

It turns out this "kills bugs dead" approach to microbes doesn't just kill bugs. It's also bad for us.

We've known for ages that we are teeming with yeasts and bacteria — in our guts, on our skin — but we still tend to get squirmy at the thought of all those critters crawling over us and inhabiting our insides. (Some fermentation super-enthusiasts have tried using these yeasts — like the craft brewer who made a batch of beer with yeast from his beard.)

But over the last few years, researchers having been learning more about the importance of our microbiome — the set of micro-organisms living in and on the human body that varies from one person to another.

In his book *The Mind-Gut Connection*, gastroenterologist Emeran Mayer invites us to "take a moment to ponder the wonders of your gut microbiota. This collection of some one thousand species of microbes comprises 1,000 times more cells than exist in your brain and spinal cord, and ten times more than the number of human cells in your entire body . . .

"The vast majority of gut microbes are not only harmless, but are in fact beneficial for our health and well-being."

If our gut bacteria are critical to our health, it would seem to make sense that we support them by strategies including eating probiotic-rich fermented foods.

Biologists have known for decades that our guts are teeming with bacteria. But they took a very different approach. Many thought the key to health was getting rid of them. Nobel-prize-winning Russian biologist Elie Metchnikoff(1845–1916) believed that bacteria in the large intestine and colon led to senility and early death. In her book *10% Human: How Your Body's Microbes Hold the Key to Health and Happiness*, science writer and evolutionary biologist Alanna Collen says Metchnikoff and others believed "the rotting remains of food . . . create[ed] toxins that brought about not only diarrhoea and constipation, but fatigue, depression, and neurotic behaviour." The solutions to this problem ranged from the horrifying — surgical removal of the colon — to eating food with live cultures. (You may remember Metchnikoff from Chapter 8; he's the one who extolled the virtues of eating yogurt as a key to longevity.)

Soon, there was a craze for eating foods with *Lactobacillus* bacteria as a way to cure all kinds of mental and physical ailments.

What is a Probiotic Anyway?

The word "probiotic" gets tossed around a lot when we talk about fermented foods.

But what exactly is a probiotic?

The word is often misused to mean any kind of beneficial bacteria. And sometimes it's misused to mean any bacteria at all. Asked about probiotics, I heard a doctor on a radio talk show say if you left a burrito out on the sidewalk for a few days it would be full of probiotics. Well, no. It would be full of bacteria. But you wouldn't want to eat it.

The World Health Organization's definition of a probiotic is "live microorganisms which when administered in adequate amounts confer a health benefit on the host."

So probiotics are by definition microorganisms that are proven to be good for us, if we consume enough of them.

Do fermented foods contain probiotics? Probably. But don't expect the kimchi seller at your local farmers' market to be able to tell you exactly what strains of probiotics their product contains, and how you can expect them to benefit your health.

Many people still seek out fermented foods and some drinks for their probiotics. But probiotics can seem overwhelming.

On a trip to the local supermarket, I pull my cart up in one of the pharmacy aisles and look at a row of bottles taking up prime real estate on the shelf directly across from the pharmacist's counter. I see bottles promising pills with five billion, six billion, 10 billion, 30 billion and even 50 billion active cells. Do I need these? And is there an easier way to get them?

"Sauerkraut is the original probiotic superfood."

"Kombucha helps to lower triglyceride levels, as well as regulate cholesterol naturally."

"Studies suggest that [kefir] boosts your immune system, aids in digestive problems, improves bone health and may even combat cancer."

You've probably seen or heard claims like this before. But you should treat them with some skepticism. Or maybe a lot of skepticism. Sure, foods like kimchi and yogurt are full of beneficial microbes, but let's not get carried away in what we think they can do for us.

Registered dietitian Edie Shaw-Ewald lives in suburban Halifax and consults for Atlantic Superstore. She was introduced to fermented foods while hosting an international student from Southeast Asia in the early 2000s. He ate kimchi every day because his mother told him that would support his immune system while he was away. "At that time, I didn't even know what it was," Edie says. "Fermentation was just starting to become something people did in households again."

Now, she recommends eating a variety of fermented foods as part of a varied diet. She says, "I always recommended some type of yogurt, but now I mention to people that they might want to explore other fermented foods too. You know, sauerkraut is very traditional in Nova Scotia, especially down on the South Shore — so I suggest sauerkraut as a condiment, along with drinks like kombucha or kefir. A variety of fermented foods can provide a range of probiotic bacteria."

Across the country, in Calgary, Andrea Hardy, a registered dietitian with a specialty in gastrointestinal disorders and gut microbiome, takes a similar approach. But she warns against seeing any kind of food as a magic health bullet.

She says, "When you introduce bacteria to the gut, those bacteria are going to go to work breaking down other food components. And when they break those down, they produce bacterial metabolites or metabolic by-products that help to maintain our gut integrity. So they can play a role in how our cells prevent harmful substances from getting through, and making sure our immune system functions properly."

We met Mercedes Brian of Wolfville a few chapters ago. She makes and sells kombucha and fermented veggie products like sauerkraut and pickles. Like many people, she became interested in fermented foods after struggling with candida. Frustrated, she threw caution to the wind and gave up her restrictive diet in favour of a wide range of ferments: "I ate blue cheese and sourdough bread and Tancook sauerkraut — a lot of it. Kefir, water kefir, kombucha. And I thought, at worst I'll be in for ten days of hell. Instead my digestion, which had been in an uproar for years, just started humming."

Andrea Hardy says she has seen similar results in some of her clients. After people with gut issues start eating more fermented foods, they frequently report feeling less pain and seeing improvements in their digestion. "I say anybody who has experienced pain as a symptom of their GI disorder, or discomfort, or bloating would likely see an improvement from including fermented and probiotic foods."

There seems to also be evidence connecting gut health to mental health, with the bugs in our guts affecting the release of serotonin.

Even though Andrea finds fermented foods helpful, she cautions against seeing them as super-foods that will solve all your health problems.

And, of course, even if you love your ferments, don't consume them to excess.

"There is a case report of somebody drinking so much kombucha they gave themselves gastroenteritis," Andrea says. "Yeah, you can overdo it."

Dr. Emma Allen-Vercoe is apologizing to me. Emma is a professor in the department of molecular and cellular biology at the University of Guelph, and we're talking about her specialty, the gut. (Her faculty profile page at the university lists her motto as "My microbes told me to do it" — and her emails end with the line "We are the spaceships for our microbes.")

I ask her why she is sorry, and Emma says it's because she thinks she's going to disappoint me by not fully embracing fermented foods as an important contribution to gut health. The reality is a lot more complicated than most people realize.

Emma was part of the Human Microbiome Project, launched by the National Institutes of Health in the United States, in an effort to better understand what's going on in our guts. One of the findings that emerged is that the answer is incredibly complicated, and that results vary wildly from one person to another. Still, she can point to a few signs of a healthy gut.

"The diversity of species seems to be important. If you have more types of bacteria in your gut than other people, you are more likely to have a healthy gut. That's not an absolute hard and fast rule, but it follows ecological theory. If you think about it, if you've got a rainforest and it's full of tons and tons of species you're less likely to see any damage to that ecosystem unless you really try hard by clearcutting it or something. Whereas if you've got an ecosystem that's balancing on the brink of oblivion and has only three or four species in it, you can see how wiping out one of those species might be a bit more problematic."

I get to the key question when it comes to fermented foods and probiotics: Are they good for our guts?

The answer is . . . maybe.

"I see an awful lot of hype. An awful lot of hype," Emma says. "There are people who believe you can cure all manner of ailments by taking a probiotic capsule or eating kimchi for a week or something. And I think this reflects a general lack of knowledge from the general public on how microbes work in terms of ecosystems."

She says even the probiotic-packed food or pill — with billions and billions of microbes — represents a drop in the ocean compared to what's in the gut, and that most probiotics we swallow are headed into a hostile environment resistant to their charms. If they haven't died by the time they arrive in the gut, they're probably "dying or really unhappy" by the time they get there.

But that doesn't mean introducing probiotics has no effect at all.

She explains:

> We have these happy pictures of these microbes nestling into our gut and making themselves at home. But that's just not how microbes work. What I think is going on, is as they are passing through — the ones that are actually alive and able to do so — even if they're not colonizing, they are having an effect on the other microbes that are there. They're having conversations with them. And when I say conversations, I don't mean they are talking. Microbes use a chemical language. A lot of these microbes are responding to each other in terms of the chemicals they are secreting, and that chemical language might actually have beneficial effects on the microbiome. The problem is that everyone is different. So, predicting whether or not the probiotic is going to have any effect on your gut is impossible at this point. Nobody really knows how to do that.

In other words, treat those claims of "total intestinal health" with some skepticism.

That doesn't mean there's no benefit to drinking your kombucha or eating yogurt. As Emma points out, "we've been eating them for generations." It's just that "you have to be very careful about generalizing when we're talking about the microbiome because we know it's so unique to an individual and everyone is going to have a different reaction — even to fermented foods."

Emma speculates that the benefits of fermented foods may come less from the microbes they contain, and more from some of the products of fermentation.

Here's how it works.

As part of the fermentation process, microbes take in food from their surrounding environment and excrete the waste products they don't need. Those waste products cause effects such as making our bread rise and our grape juice alcoholic. They can also produce organic acids, which are able to survive in the harsh environment of the gut and can interact with our bodies in helpful ways.

Not all fermented foods will be the same when it comes to the levels of helpful substances they contain. For instance, most alcoholic drinks don't contain live cultures, because yeasts have been killed either by the level of alcohol rising higher than their tolerance, or by, say, winemakers stopping the fermentation themselves.

In *The Mind-Gut Connection*, Emeran Mayer strongly suggests eating fermented foods and probiotics: "People have been eating naturally fermented, unpasteurized foods for thousands of years, and you might want to include some of them in your regular diet."

And, despite her skepticism, Emma Allen-Vercoe says she regularly enjoys fermented foods too (she's partial to yogurt, sauerkraut and some flavours of kombucha), but "I don't think it is going to magically restore my health. I just think it's a healthy option."

Regardless of what the health benefits may be, fermented foods have a long tradition. And they can be delicious. Those are good enough reasons to eat them, and if they contribute to our gut biodiversity and health — well, so much the better. I just wouldn't take that as the primary reason to start chowing down on sauerkraut.

10

Getting Geared Up

What You'll Need to Start Fermenting at Home

When I began writing this book, I was working out of a shared office space in Bridgewater. The regulars would chat and keep each other up to date on their projects. On one of my first mornings, I mentioned I was doing a book on fermentation. Sky Blu (his legal name), an iOS app developer with a house nearby on the South Shore, told me he liked fermenting vegetables, and that pickled beets were one of his favourites. About this book he said, "So, what . . . you put vegetables into a jar, add salt and water and put on a lid. And, of course, you need to know the water/salt ratio. Is there much more to say?"

Is there more to say? Well, yes, of course there is. But on the other hand . . .

Sky Blu may have been joking, but he's also half-right. Fermenting most foods and some beverages — at least at the home kitchen level — is not all that complicated and takes very little specialized equipment.

Each of the chapters in this book celebrates fermented foods and drinks

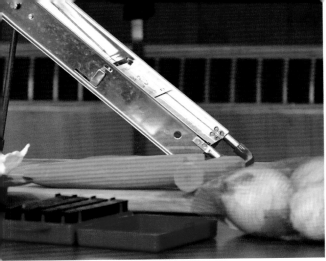

TOP: Mandoline and vegetables.
RIGHT: Ginger, garlic and onions add additional flavour to fermented foods.

of Nova Scotia, their history and the people who make them, along with recipes to try at home.

If you want to start fermenting at home, either with the recipes in this book, or others you want to try, the rest of this chapter will tell you what you'll need to get started.

If you have no interest in making your own sauerkraut, kombucha or other ferments, feel free to skip this chapter. You can always refer to it later if you change your mind and decide you want to try your hand at making some of these tasty and intriguing foods and drinks in your own kitchen.

Let's dive in.

We'll start with what you'll need to ferment vegetables: sauerkraut, kimchi, kosher dill pickles, mixed vegetables, that sort of thing.

The three essentials, as Sky Blu noted, are containers, lids and salt. We will look at a few other helpful items too.

Making kimchi. Note the gloves, to protect from hot chilies.

Jars

The type of container you decide to use depends on what you are making and how much of it you want.

Fermented vegetables need to stay submerged in brine. For most vegetable ferments, Mason jars are an excellent choice. For one thing, they are relatively inexpensive and easy to find. I tend to prefer regular, narrow-mouth jars over the wide-mouth variety. Wide-mouth jars are easy to pack, which makes for an easier and less messy operation, but they don't have the shoulders you'll find on regular jars, which slope inward and taper toward the opening. Those shoulders are very helpful when it comes to weighting down the veggies in our jars to keep them submerged in brine.

Another advantage of Mason jars is they come in many different sizes. Kimchi is a staple condiment in our house, and I make large batches of it, some stored in one-quart jars in the fridge. Quart jars are also good for foods that you will eat over a longer period, and for foods that would be impractical to ferment in a smaller container. Try stuffing whole pickling cukes into a pint jar and you will quickly get frustrated.

Mason jars filled with kimchi.

On the other hand, small jars are great for spicy pickles or other foods eaten in smaller quantities, or those that keep less well. A large batch of sauerkraut is still tasty after a year. Brined green beans, on the other hand? Not so much. Put them in a smaller jar and snack away while they are crisp and crunchy.

If you are starting out with fermentation, make small batches. They allow you to be flexible and experiment with variables like larger or smaller amounts of salt, and to play around with spices and other ingredients to find combinations you like. And if something goes wrong and you need to throw out a whole batch, at least it will be small. There is also the question of taste. Trying out a new recipe? Not sure if fermented stinging nettle is going to be a hit? Better to have made a pint and not a gallon.

For larger batches, I like to use plastic one-gallon feta cheese buckets. Many shops sell gallon tubs of feta. Eat the cheese, use the bucket.

These buckets are practical and much less expensive than many other fermentation vessels. You can pack a lot of whatever you are fermenting into

A jar of Laura Rutherford's fermented yellow beans.

them, they are easy to clean when you are done and because they have a relatively large diameter, you can use a small dinner plate to keep your veggies submerged in brine. They also offer you easy access for tasting your ferments to see when they are done. If you have many of them, they are also easily stackable.

Some people prefer to avoid the use of plastic, and while I try to minimize it, I do find these plastic buckets very handy. They can also be re-used many, many times. If you ferment in plastic, do make sure that it is marked food grade, or food safe.

If you prefer to avoid plastic, you do have other options available for fermenting large batches. One option is one-gallon (or larger) glass jars. The challenge with these, I find, is that it's harder to find a weight that fits well and keeps the vegetables submerged. Look for these jars online (though shipping can be pricey) or at vintage and specialty housewares shops. If you don't mind spending more money, look for ceramic fermentation crocks. Some potters specialize in crocks that are both beautiful and practical. German-style crocks have an ingenious design with a moat around the circumference that creates a water seal — ensuring your veggies stay submerged.

If you are tempted to use a wonderful old crock from a vintage shop or a flea-market, exercise caution. The United States Food and Drug Administration warns that in ceramics made with lead glazing (as much old pottery was), "this lead can leach into food and drink that is prepared, stored, or served in the dishes." It also notes that "no amount of washing, boiling, or other process can remove lead from pottery." Got an old crock you really, really want to use? Go online and buy a lead test kit first to make sure it's safe.

I have a lovely old crock in my basement that I used for precisely one batch of sauerkraut before I learned about the possibility it might be leaching lead.

Lids and Weights

Vegetables are typically fermented in a brine that contains quite a bit of salt. The salt can quickly rust Mason jar lids. At best, this is unsightly, while at worst it can cause your lids to seize up. Look for plastic lids. They can often be found at grocery and hardware stores. The only problem I've had with these lids is that they are not leak-proof. So if you have a very packed fridge (as I often do) and things inside it get pushed to the back or tipped over, you could find yourself cleaning up salty, and maybe garlicky brine from your shelves. And that's no fun at all. If you are storing them in the fridge, keep them on the door to be safe.

If you can't find (or don't like) plastic lids, you could also place a barrier between jar and lid. A piece of plastic wrap or wax paper will help prevent rusting. Be sure to crack the lid open regularly though, because sometimes the plastic wrap will disintegrate, or the rust will make its way through the wax paper.

Over the years that I have been fermenting, I have never used anything but simple lids for Mason jars. I make sure to open the lids regularly to release any gas that builds up during the fermentation process. While this system works well for me, it does require fairly regular attention.

Fortunately, with the rise in popularity of home fermentation, it has become much easier to find specialty products like jar lids designed specifically for the fermenter. If you want a more hands-off experience and don't want to have to worry about cracking jar lids, pick up some lids with a built-in airlock. They fit standard and wide-mouth Mason jars and include a one-way valve similar to the airlocks on wine jugs. The valve keeps flies and micro-organisms out while letting air escape from the jar.

Vegetables ferment in an anaerobic environment that encourages the growth of lactic acid bacteria. So we want to keep our vegetables submerged. Check daily and push down any that may have risen to the surface. Generally, you will need to place a weight in your jar, crock or bucket to ensure that whatever you are fermenting stays under the surface of the brine. Mold can grow at the surface, if the vegetables are in contact with the air. Keep them covered completely by the brine and you'll avoid mold problems.

Again, I tend to favour simple, inexpensive, low-tech solutions. A plate (I look for them at thrift shops) that fits snugly inside a bucket can keep whatever you are fermenting nicely submerged. Just check it regularly to make sure it remains covered in brine and that nothing has risen to the surface. Sometimes I will place a weight on the plate to keep it down. The simplest way to do this is to use a rock. Boil it for several minutes to kill any pathogens, then place it on top of the dish in the bucket. We have a few decorative rocks we keep around the house that occasionally do double-duty as fermentation weights.

If you are fermenting in a Mason jar, a plate and rock clearly won't be practical. But don't worry. Plenty of other solutions are available. The simplest is to use your fingers. Wash your hands, then unscrew the lid and make sure all your sauerkraut, carrot slices or whatever else you are fermenting are submerged. If any of them have broken the surface, push them down, seal up the jar, and check it again the next day.

If your vegetables are not tightly packed into the jar, you may find them rising consistently to the surface. Or they may come up and stay at the top as the fermentation process progresses. If this happens, you'll need something more than just your fingers.

A couple of years ago, fermentation experts Sébastien Bureau and David Côté shared a trick with me that I thought was brilliant — and one I've seen catch on since then: Tear off one of the outer leaves of a green cabbage (not a thinner, less robust cabbage like savoy or nappa) and jam it into your Mason jar to keep your fermenting veggies submerged. The leaf should have enough mass to keep your ferments happy in their brine. This trick works particularly well if you're fermenting something on the counter for a short time (up to a week) before refrigerating it. Any longer, and you risk having the leaf itself start to break down. If you want a more hands-off approach, buy specially designed weights that fit inside a Mason jar. I was given a set of fermentation weights as a gift a couple of years ago, and they certainly are practical.

Now that home fermentation has become popular, all kinds of retailers and manufacturers have stepped in with products that can help make the process easier. These fermentation kits can make the process more accessible, especially for people new to fermenting. They range from simple to elaborate, including any combination of lids, airlocks, weights, pumps to suck out oxygen, date trackers to help you remember what you started fermenting and when and tampers so you can press down your ferments. If a kit will help you feel more confident about fermenting, or demystify the process and make it easier, by all means buy one. But they are certainly not essential — and if you plan to ferment several different foods at the same time, the cost of these types of specialty products can add up.

Salt

Salt is a near-essential element of most fermented foods (as opposed to beverages). Humans have been pickling with salt for millennia. In his book *Salt: A World History*, Mark Kurlansky points to many examples from the ancient world of how salt was used to ferment foods including fish, vegetables and legumes. "The Romans preserved many vegetables in brine, sometimes with the addition of vinegar, including fennel, asparagus, and cabbage," he writes. Kurlansky shares a 2,200-year-old recipe from ancient Rome, recorded by Cato, on using salt brine to preserve olives. (The process sounds similar to the one my grandmother, who lived in Greece, used millennia later.)

Meanwhile, in China, salting food directly was a rarity. Instead, Kurlansky notes, saltiness came from condiments — often fermented fish, vegetables or legumes (in the form of soy sauce).

But . . . what kind of salt should you use?

Among people who are passionate about fermentation, this simple question can lead to strong opinions. Should you use sea salt? Standard-issue supermarket table salt? Does it even matter? Some fermenters swear by traditionally evaporated sea salt with no added iodine. Others like Himalayan rock salt. A few will tell you it doesn't really matter.

Nova Scotia salt maker Colin Duggan says highly refined table salt is "likely 99 per cent or higher" sodium chloride. Less refined salt, whether from land or sea, can include many other compounds, such as Epsom salts, calcium carbonate, and — in the case of some darker grey and brown salt — trace amounts of dirt.

"Uniformity was a remarkable innovation in its day, but it was so successful that today consumers seem excited by any salt that is different," Kurlansky writes. "Grey salts, black salts, salts with any visible impurities are sought out and marketed for their colors, even though the tint usually means the presence of dirt." So put him down on team table salt.

Sandor Katz takes the opposite view. In an article for the newsletter *A Grain of Salt*, he writes, "Of course, not all salts are the same. Definitely avoid the standard American table salt, which is highly refined sodium chloride with added iodine and chemical anti-caking agents. In general, the whiter the salt, the more refined it is. More natural forms of salt . . . [contain] a broad range of nutritionally important minerals together as they are found in nature."

Mercedes Brian, who makes sauerkraut and various other pickled vegetable products, is a fan of French grey sea salt, "because it has lots of extra little minerals in it . . . If you have to have salt, why not make it taste amazing?"

In my kitchen, I have inexpensive Greek sea salt from a warehouse store, standard-issue table salt mined in Ontario, large-crystal Italian sea salt and salt painstakingly evaporated from Nova Scotia seawater. I have produced delicious pickles, sauerkraut and kimchi using plain old iodized table salt. I've also used more expensive salt with excellent results. Maybe my palate is not refined enough to taste a difference, but yours may be. As with so much related to fermentation, I encourage you to try different kinds of salt and see what works best for you.

The Salt Maker

Colin Duggan is a former caterer and social worker with a political science degree. He knows what it's like to have a high-stress job. And now he wants no part of it.

Now, he makes salt.

"It's super-boring to make salt," he tells me. "It takes a particular kind of person. I find it very calming."

Duggan's business, called Tidal Salt, has what he calls a three-step business plan: "Scoop ocean, boil ocean, succeed." On the day I speak to him, he says he is "going to boil water for the next sixteen hours . . . I'm standing in front of my pot of saltwater, making salt from Eastern Passage."

Duggan got into the salt business more or less by accident. He remembers being at Lawrencetown Beach, east of Halifax, one day and thinking about salt in food. (His wife is a chef.) He wondered how hard it could be to make salt. All he'd have to do is, well, boil water.

His early experiments were not successful. He tried making salt from water collected at Cow Bay: "Terrible sea salt. Terrible." But water from nearby Rainbow Haven and Lawrencetown yielded far better results. Why? Duggan is not sure.

He says, "If the heat is too high, the crystals form too quickly and are too small. If you go too slowly, your business plan is going to go to hell because of all the energy you'll use." The trick is to find the right combination of heat and time to create attractive crystals.

Wine and Beer

Fermented drinks require a whole other set of tools and equipment — but again, you can easily get started without having to spend a whole lot of money or buy complex, specialized gear.

Let's start with wine.

I enjoy making what are known as country wines: wines using fruit and flowers. Over the years, I've made wine from dandelions, ginger, elderflowers, apples, crabapples, pears and various combinations of these ingredients.

Soon, he refined his technique: Collecting seawater, carefully filtering it, boiling it at a rate that will produce nice-looking crystals and then drying them.

"We collect our water right before high tide. It's incoming from the ocean, so it's cleaner and has less runoff from the local water table. The higher the tide, the higher the salinity."

He also baffled regulators, because they don't usually get requests from people making artisanal salt. "If I take a bucket of water from the ocean, do I need a permit? Does it have to be tested?"

Some table salt, Duggan says, is "almost metallic — it stings." Good sea salt, on the other hand, "should make you salivate a bit. It should draw moisture, and you get a smooth texture across the back of your tongue."

Duggan says local salt is an extension of the interest in local food generally, and that you can taste differences in salt, depending on where it is harvested and how it is dried. "We have at least three distinctive coastlines here. Sea salt from Eastern Passage and Tatamagouche have slightly different tastes. If you ran them through a spectrometer, you would see the differences."

Salt has been a constant in the history of Nova Scotia — whether for curing meats and fish, packing fish for export or putting up vegetables for the winter. Standing on his back deck in Dartmouth, watching seawater evaporate, Duggan gets philosophical thinking about that history. "We make wine here, we make beer here — we make all sorts of things — but those are all things we brought to this area. The saltwater is already here."

Occasionally, I'll use the grapes that grow in our backyard. As I write this, a gallon of white currant wine in the early stages of fermentation is actively bubbling in a corner of the dining room. Some of these wines have turned out just lovely (the crabapple was surprisingly refreshing) and some . . . well, let's just say I didn't need to buy any cooking wine for awhile.

All these wines were produced with minimal financial outlay, and if you know anyone who makes their own wine you can always ask to borrow their gear. Here is what you need to get started:

Jug/Pail/Bottle

The first step in winemaking involves covering your fruit (or other plants) with water. If you are making a very small batch, say a gallon, the feta cheese pails or one-gallon glass jars I mention above work well. If you are making a bigger batch, winemaking shops will sell you a large food-grade plastic bucket. When I don't have any batches of wine on the go, I use my bucket for storing the rest of my winemaking equipment.

Fermentation bottle

After a few days, your wine will need to go into a bottle with a narrow neck. These are often known as carboys, and are available in glass or plastic. I have one-gallon and five-gallon sizes.

Airlock

A simple device that lets air bubble up and out during the fermentation process, but doesn't let any bugs or dust in. Costs next to nothing.

Siphon

At some point (and possibly more than once) you will need to rack your wine. Racking involves getting your wine out of the bottle and leaving the sediment that has sunk to the bottom behind. I use a length of food-grade plastic tubing I bought at minimal cost from a local hardware store.

Half-filled jug of freshly squeezed raw sweet cider.

Bottles, corks and corker

You can buy bottles, or just hang onto empty bottles from wine you have bought. Corks are cheap, and the corker, which lets you force the cork into the bottle is inexpensive too. Remember to use special, extra-thick champagne bottles if you are making a sparkling wine.

Hydrometer

Another simple, inexpensive item. This one is a device that will allow you to calculate the alcohol content of your wine, so you can stop the fermentation when it reaches the level you want. (I confess that I only use this sometimes; I enjoy the wine I make without having much of an idea of what its alcohol content is.) Sometimes the wine packs a bit more of a punch than I expect though. Measuring the alcohol level is a good idea.

I am not a home beer maker, but many of the supplies you will need for beer are the same as those for simple homemade wines. Most shops for home brewers sell starter kits that provide everything you need to experiment with small batches: plastic fermentation buckets, mesh bags for your grain and hops (if you are making your own mash), a carboy with airlock, thermometer and hydrometer, tubing to siphon out the beer, a handy bottling bucket with a spigot to cut down on the mess and a bottle capper with caps to seal your beer until you are ready to drink it.

As with wine, beer making can become as complex and involved as you want it to. Look at any beer supply website, and you'll find equipment ranging from simple plastic buckets to mills for your grain, oxygenators and even fully robotic brewing systems.

You can start with beer ingredient kits that have everything pre-measured for you, or you can grind and mash your own grains — or even grow your own hops.

Your Fermentation Station

You've got your bottles and jars, your buckets or pails. Where do you set them up to ferment your foods or drinks?

The process of fermentation works best, especially in the early stages, at room temperature. You want a space that is warm enough for the microbiological processes we are encouraging to take place, but not so hot that you risk spoilage. In *Salt*, Kurlansky says the optimal temperature for lactic acid fermentation is 64–71°F degrees (18–22°C degrees), "which, in most of the world, is an easily achieved environment."

When I was growing up, we had a yogurt maker. My mother would prepare milk and culture, then place the liquid in small serving-size pots which fit into the yogurt machine. It gently warmed the individual pots, causing the yogurt to coagulate overnight and be ready to eat in the morning. Yogurt makers are fine, and there is something to be said for the uniformity of temperature they provide, but they are also unnecessary. You can make yogurt perfectly well in a jar on your counter, covered in a blanket, on the hearth above the woodstove, near a hot air vent or in the residual heat from an oven.

As with yogurt making, for the most part you don't need to build or create special spaces in your home in order to ferment. A corner in your kitchen could be all you need. A friend in Toronto told me she wanted to get started with fermentation, but with the caveat that she and her partner lived in an apartment with very little counter-space. I gave her a small-batch kimchi recipe she could make in a jar on her tiny counter, and then put in the fridge after a week or so.

Having your ferments in the kitchen or elsewhere (I'm told my paternal grandfather usually had wine working off behind an armchair in the living room) also allows you to easily keep an eye on them, which can be practical. I made pickles in brine during a particularly hot and humid summer. Because I fermented them in my kitchen, I could see that powdery white yeast was forming in the jar, and that if I just left the pickles they would soon spoil. The high temperature accelerated fermentation, so I dumped out the brine, replaced it with a fresh, less yeasty brine and refrigerated the pickles faster than I would have otherwise.

I can think of a couple of reasons you may want to consider fermenting in a spot other than your kitchen though. First, of course, is the very practical consideration of space. If you don't have a lot of room, you'll have to limit how many things you can ferment at a time. Then there is the question of smell. Yogurt setting up on the counter isn't going to bother anyone. But the garlicky smell of kosher dills may not be everyone's favourite aroma first thing in the morning — let alone other, even more pungent foods. One of my sisters-in-law recoils at the smell of kimchi, because when she was in university her sister would often have a batch fermenting on the counter. And when she came into the kitchen for coffee in the morning, she'd be greeted by the smell of garlic and fermenting cabbage.

I do most of my active fermenting in the kitchen and in an unfinished basement. In summer, the basement is warm enough to provide a comfortable temperature for microbial action. In winter, it is cool enough to serve as a good storage place for large batches of foods like sauerkraut. It is also cool enough to act as a nice spot for aging homemade cheese.

Once your fermented foods or drinks have developed the tastes and textures you want, then you need a cool place to store them. In cooler environments (like your fridge) fermentation will slow right down. As I write this, I have four pounds of pickles fermenting in my kitchen, beside the coffee grinder. Every few days, I pull one out and taste it. The pickles are crunchy and salty, with a pleasant, but not fully developed flavour. In a few days, once the flavour has deepened, I'll move them into smaller jars, give some away and refrigerate the rest. If I make a batch later in the fall, I could move the large jar to the basement instead.

If you have a root cellar or other cool room, go ahead and use that. I also know of cheesemakers who modify the thermostats on beer fridges or other small refrigerators to provide the ideal temperature for aging cheese. This "close enough" approach is fine for most ferments, but please note that if you are making cured meats, proper temperature control is essential. You will need a more precise system for ensuring your meat maintains the ideal temperatures and humidity for aging. Do not take a laissez-faire approach to curing meat.

My approach to fermenting involves a lot of experimentation. I enjoy modifying recipes, trying out new ingredients (what happens if I make that elderflower wine recipe with white currants instead?) and experiencing new flavours. For me, the element of the unexpected — not being sure exactly how the batch of whatever I'm making will taste — is part of the fun of fermenting.

Some batches turn out better than others. Some seem to resist being replicated. No matter how well we control our processes, we are dealing with live cultures and complex microbiological processes. Sometimes things go wrong.

I try to make the best of these situations, and to see if I can repurpose the food that didn't work out. For instance, a hard, flat loaf of bread may make great croutons. I also try to determine what went wrong, so I don't make the same mistake again. If my pickles turn slimy, either the temperature was too high, I didn't use enough salt or I didn't check in on them often enough to see how they were doing — or all three.

If you want to ensure uniform results, take notes as you go. Temperature is an important component to note, as are salt levels (for foods) and pH. If you're making wine, what type of yeast did you use, and how much sugar? Make notes on flavours too. Tracking your results and comparing batches can be fun and is part of the learning experience.

Conclusion

The fermentation revival that has hit Nova Scotia — like much of the rest of North America — doesn't look like it's going to slow down any time soon. On my travels across Nova Scotia, I have had countless conversations with new acquaintances keen to share their enthusiasm and curiosity about the techniques, flavours and health benefits of fermented foods and drinks. Sure, individual foods may come and go in popularity, and new ones will be introduced, but so many people are either making or buying fermented products now, that I don't think this is a trend that will just vanish. In part, that's because this resurgence of interest builds on the centuries of practice underlying so many of these foods and drinks. Cider dates back to the very earliest settlers of New France. Sauerkraut is a deeply established Nova Scotia tradition. Mead is experiencing renewed interest. These are the foods and beverages that have sustained people for centuries or millennia.

One of the beautiful things about fermentation — whether you are making

cider, beer, bread, pickles or any of a number of different foods or drinks —
is that you can get very good results by following simple procedures, but
you can also spend a lifetime tweaking and refining. Experimenting. Many
of the people I interviewed have science or engineering degrees. They are
comfortable in a lab and do complex testing in the course of developing and
assessing their products. But they like to tinker too. Bruce Ewert of L'Acadie
Vineyards is a detail-oriented engineer who controls complex processes in
making his wines — but he also enjoys making a very simple, hands-off
carboy wine for his own use. Alexandra Beaulieu Boivin studied pharmaco-
economics and loves the science of wine- and cider-making, but also gets
jazzed about seeing what comes out of a cider made from a mix of apples
dropped off at the cidery. And people who may make wine or beer for a
living might also play around at home with kombucha and sourdough bread.

I like the metaphor for shepherding that a couple of people in the book used.
We don't fully control the processes carried out by the microscopic organisms
fermenting our foods. But we shepherd them. There really is something
seemingly magical about the process. When I mix up some flour and water and
leave it overnight, I'm always thrilled when I come down in the morning to
find a wonderfully sour, bubbly bowlful of starter waiting for me.

Fermenting encourages a spirit of adventure, both in terms of taste and
food preparation. Some fermented foods require a bit of effort from us.
If you've ever had natto — stinky, slimy Japanese fermented soybeans —
you'll know what I mean. Even though you may not love everything you
try, it's worth it to keep an open mind and expand your repertoire beyond
what your tastebuds are used to. Mercedes Brian says sometimes people tell
her they couldn't stand fermented veggies when they first tried them, and
now they want them with every meal.

As with any adventure, things can go wrong when you are in the kitchen.
But unless they go catastrophically wrong, it's all part of the fun — and the
learning process. I hope you are inspired by this book to seek out more
fermented foods and drinks and to embark on your own adventures.

Suggested Bibliography

This list includes books I relied on for my research on fermentation in general, on Nova-Scotian cooking and on specific foods and drinks.

General Books

The Art of Fermentation, by Sandor Ellix Katz. Chelsea Green Publishing, 2012.

A Cook's Tour of Nova Scotia, by Emily Walker. Nimbus, 1987.

Fermentation Revolution: 70 Easy Recipes for Sauerkraut, Kombucha, Kimchi and More, by Sébastien Bureau and David Côté, Robert Rose Publishing, 2018.

Out of Old Nova Scotia Kitchens, by Marie Nightingale. Petheric Press, 1970.

Pantry and Palate: Remembering and Rediscovering Acadian Food, by Simon Thibault. Nimbus, 2017.

The Rooster Crows at Dawn: My Eighty Years in the Nova Scotia Village of Blandford, by Lee Zinck. Lancelot Press, 1987.

Sauerkraut, Codfish and Apples, by Earle K Hawkesworth. Self-published, 1994.

Wild Fermentation: The Flavor Nutrition, and Craft of Live-Culture Foods, 2nd edition, by Sandor Ellix Katz. Chelsea Green Publishing, 2016.

1 Sauerkraut: The Classic Nova Scotia Ferment

Facing the Open Sea: The People of Big Tancook Island, by George Bellerose. Nimbus Publishing, 1995.

The Tancook Schooner: An Island and Its Boats, by Wayne O'Leary. McGill-Queen's University Press, 1994.

2 Fermenting the Harvest: Enjoy Vegetables Year-round

The Canadian Cook Book, by Nellie Lyle Pattinson, revised edition. Ryerson Press, 1961.

A Taste of Acadie, by Marielle Cormier-Boudreau and Melvin Gallant, Goose Lane Editions, 1991.

Waste Not Want Not, A Booke of Cookery: Some Interesting Recipes of Old Acadia, by Ted Eaton. Omega Publishing, 1978.

3 Preserving Meat: Searching for a Cure

1809 recipe for pork pickled in brine and recipe for sausage flavoured with lemon thyme, sage, and parsley: https://novascotia.ca/archives/cooking/archives.asp?ID=67.

4 Sudsy Stuff: Beer and Other Brews

The Big Book of Kombucha, by Hannah Crum and Alex LaGory. Storey Publishing, 2016.

Brewed in Canada: The Untold Story of Canada's 350-Year-Old Brewing Industry, by Allen Winn Sneath. The Dundurn Group, 2001.

East Coast Crafted: The Essential Guide to the Beers, Breweries, and Brewpubs of Atlantic Canada, by Christopher Reynolds and Whitney Moran. Nimbus, 2017.

Last Canadian Beer: The Moosehead Story, by Harvey Sawler. Nimbus, 2009.

What's Brewing: Oland, 1867–97, a history, by G. Brenton Haliburton. Four East Publications, 1994.

5 Apple Cider: Cheerfulness and Contentment

Comfort Me With Apples: The Nova Scotia Fruit Growers' Association, 1863–2013, by Julian Gwyn. Lupin Press, 2014.

Heritage Apples: A New Sensation, by Susan Lundy. TouchWood Editions, 2013.

The New Cider Maker's Handbook, by Claude Jolicoeur. Chelsea Green, 2013.

Old Trout Funnies: The Comic Origins of the Cape Breton Liberation Army, by Ian Brodie (comics by Paul MacKinnon). Cape Breton University Press, 2015.

Valley Gold: The Story of the Apple Industry in Nova Scotia, by Anne Hutten. Petheric Press, 1981.

6 Wine: Finally Bearing Fruit

First Steps in Winemaking, by C.J.J. Berry. Originally published in 1960, by *Berry's Amateur Winemaker* magazine, it has been updated several times.

The Wine Atlas of Canada, by Tony Aspler. Random House, 2006.

The Wine Lover's Guide to Atlantic Canada, by Moira Peters and Craig Pinhey, Nimbus, 2016.

Wineries & Wine Country of Nova Scotia, by Sean P. Wood, Nimbus, 2006.

7 Bread: No Such Thing as a Perfect Loaf

The Blessings of Bread, by Adrian Bailey. Paddington Press, Ltd, 1975.

La Cuisine de Chéticamp, Recipes collected by Ginette Aucoin. Printed by Imprimerie Nordet, 1980.

Granny Picked Blueberries While the House Burned . . . Traditional Recipes and Remedies. North Queens Heritage Society. The edition I consulted at the Halifax Central Library was a reprint from 2000, but gave no original publication date. However, the illustration on the cover is dated 1980.

Home Baking: The Artful Mix of Flour and Traditions from Around the World, by Naomi Duguid and Jeffrey Alford. Artisan, 2003.

The Laurel's Kitchen Bread Book: A Guide to Whole-Grain Breadmaking, by Laurel Robertson, Carol Flinders and Bronwen Godfrey. Random House, 1984.

8 The Dairy Best: Cheese and other Fermented Milk Products

The Art of Natural Cheesemaking, by David Asher. Chelsea Green, 2015.

Cheese and Culture: A History of Cheese and Its Place in Western Civilization, by Paul Kindstedt. Chelsea Green, 2012.

9 Science, Safety, and What's Going on in Your Gut

10% Human: How Your Body's Microbes Hold the Key to Health and Happiness, by Alanna Collen. HarperCollins, 2015.

The Mind-Gut Connection, by Dr. Emeran Mayer. Harper Wave, 2016.

10 Getting Geared Up: What you'll need to start fermenting at home

Salt: A World History, by Mark Kurlansky. Penguin Books, 2003.

Contacts and Addresses

Chapter 1: Sauerkraut

Big Tancook Island
- Ferry – 902-275-7885
- www.tancookcommunitynews.com

Ross Farm
- 4568 Highway # 12, New Ross, NS B0J 2M0
- 902-689-2210 or toll free 1-877-689-2210, rossfarm@novascotia.ca
- rossfarm.novascotia.ca

Krispi Kraut Sauerkraut
- RR # 3, Lunenburg, NS B0J 2C0
- 902-634-3711, mrkrispi@bwr.eastlink.ca
- No website

M.A. Hatt (makers of Tancook Brand Sauerkraut)
- 405 Northwest Rd, Lunenburg, NS B0J 2C0
- 902-634-8407, mahattandson@eastlink.ca
- tancooksauerkraut.wordpress.com

Chapter 4: Sudsy Stuff

Ashdale (Meander River)
- 906 Woodville Rd, Newport, NS B0N 2A0
- 902-757-3484, info@meanderriverfarm.ca
- www.meanderriverfarm.ca

Shelburne (Boxing Rock)
- 78 Ohio Rd, Shelburne, NS B0T 1W0
- 902-494-9233, no email
- boxingrock.ca

Halifax (Oland)
- 3055 Agricola St, Halifax, NS B3K 4G2
- 902-453-1867
- olandbrewery.ca

Micou's Island, St. Margaret's Bay
- Sunset Dr, French Village, NS
- www.heartofthebay.ca/mucous-island

Chapter 5: Apple Cider

Newcombville (Brian Braganza)
- brianbraganza14@gmail.com
- www.brianbraganza.ca

Bulwark (near New Ross)
- Muwin Estate Wines Ltd. (owners) 7153 Hwy 12, New Ross, NS, B0J 2M0
- 902-681-1545, info@muwinestate.com
- bulwarkcider.com

Chain Yard Urban Cidery
- 2606 Agricola St, Halifax, NS B3K 4C8
- 902-407-2244, info@chainyardcider.com
- chainyardcider.com

Chapter 6: Wine

Petite Rivière Winery
- 1300 Italy Cross Rd, Crousetown, NS B4V 6R2
- 902-693-3033, info@PetiteRiviereVineyards.ca
- www.petiterivierevineyards.ca

Lightfoot & Wolfville
- 11143 Evangeline Trail, Wolfville, NS B4P 2R1
- 902-542-7774, info@lightfootandwolfvillewines.com
- lightfootandwolfville.com

L'Acadie Vineyards /Gaspereau Valley
- 310 Slayter Rd, Gaspereau, RR1, Wolfville, NS B4P 2R1
- 902-542-8463, info@lacadievineyards.ca
- www.lacadievineyards.ca

Chapter 7: Bread

Balmoral Grist Mill Museum (Balmoral Mills)
- 544 Peter Macdonald Road, Tatamagouche, NS B0K 1V0
- balmoralgristmill.novascotia.ca

Birdie's Bread Co. (Dartmouth)
- 380 Pleasant St, Dartmouth, NS B2Y 3S5
- 902-407-0939, no email
- www.birdiesbreadco.com

Lequille, near the site of Port Royal
Lequille, Nova Scotia B0S 1A0. Lequille is located in Annapolis County. It is on Nova Scotia Trunk 8 at the foot of the South Mountain, midway between Annapolis Royal to the northwest and Highway 101 to the south.

Chapter 8: The Dairy Best

That Dutchman's Cheese Farm (Upper Economy)
- 132 Brown Rd, Economy, NS B0M 1J0 (note: If using a GPS please use 4595 Hwy #2, Upper Economy to avoid a back road route during the warm months)
- 902-647-2751, wmvandenhoek@hotmail.com
- www.thatdutchmansfarm.com

Blue Harbour Cheese (Dartmouth)
- Plant Address:
  6 Primrose St, Unit 130
  Dartmouth NS B3A 4C5
- Mailing address:
  PO Box 23020 Dartmouth PO
  Dartmouth NS B3A 4S9
- 902-240-0305, info@blueharbourcheese.com
- blueharbourcheese.com

Chapter 10: Getting Geared Up

Tidal Salt (Dartmouth)
- 902-404-5146, info@tidalsalt.ca
- tidalsalt.ca

Index